THE NEW
STRATEGIC
THINKING

THE NEW STRATEGIC THINKING

Pure & Simple

Michel Robert

McGraw-Hill

New York   Chicago   San Francisco   Lisbon   London
Madrid   Mexico City   Milan   New Delhi
San Juan   Seoul   Singapore
Sydney   Toronto

The **McGraw·Hill** Companies

4 5 6 7 8 9 0   DOC/DOC   0 9 8 7

ISBN 0-07-146224-4

This publication is designed to provide accurate and authoritative information in regard to the subject matter covered. It is sold with the understanding that the publisher is not engaged in rendering legal, accounting, or other professional service. If legal advice or other expert assistance is required, the services of a competent professional person should be sought.

*—From a declaration of principles jointly adopted by a committee of the
American Bar Association and a committee of publishers.*

McGraw-Hill books are available at special quantity discounts to use as premiums and sales promotions, or for use in corporate training programs. For more information, please write to the Director of Special Sales, McGraw-Hill Professional, Two Penn Plaza, New York, NY 10121-2298. Or contact your local bookstore.

 This book is printed on recycled, acid-free paper containing a minimum of 50% recycled, de-inked fiber.

CONTENTS

PREFACE

$\mathbf{M}$any books have been written about companies that have failed. In most of these, the author attempts to explain the reasons for their failure. There are two major flaws in this approach.

First, I am of the opinion that one learns more by gaining an understanding of what creates *success* rather than what causes failure. There is no doubt that one may learn from one's mistakes. This is what is called "experience." And when one has made many mistakes, experience becomes known as "wisdom." Just as parents have the tendency to concentrate on their children's lowest scores in school, these authors dwell on *"failings."* The experts with behavioral "wisdom," however, will tell you that you can achieve better results by concentrating on optimizing a child's *better* scores. Better results come from understanding a person's strengths, in my view, and leveraging these results into "positive wisdom" rather than focusing on the "negative wisdom" that comes from analyzing the cause of failure.

Second, I have found over the years that most of these books are written by authors who have had no personal contact with the CEOs of any of the firms about which they write. As a result, their conclusions can, in the most generous case, simply be "guesses."

The concepts and Critical Thinking Processes discussed in this book, on the other hand, stem from 25 years of working directly with the CEOs and management teams of almost 500 companies around the globe. Through our firm, Decision Processes International, I and my DPI colleagues facilitate these processes, eliminating the need for armies of consultants and endless "strategy projects." Nearly all of these companies have used our processes repeatedly from their first use until today. The reason is simple. Our processes produce *results*. Caterpillar and 3M, for example, have been clients since the mid-1980s. While our concepts are not the sole cause of the prosperity of these perennial winners, the management of these companies has clearly acknowledged the crucial role that our process of Strategic Thinking has played in their ongoing success.

Our concepts of strategy have stood the test of time because we were present in the "war rooms" of these corporations when these CEOs were wrestling with some of the most important decisions of their careers. They ask us back again and again because they are comfortable with our approach, which has helped them to better understand those decisions and their *long-term* implications. That is because our process is a reflection of how *they* think.

And, as the title of the book implies, the concepts of Strategic Thinking work, not just in solving short-term problems, but in creating a continuum of success over the *long term*. It is not about writing a strategic plan and instructing the troops to "make it happen." It is about a fundamental shift in the way senior management, and the people they rely upon, look at the company and its environment. It is about gaining a common understanding of the ingredients for *success* for that company, in its competitive "sandbox." It is about *building* on that understanding and success, achieving results that even the creators of these strategies—the company's management—often would not have thought possible.

The real beauty of this unique approach is that once that common understanding of the company's strategic direction is reached and inculcated throughout the company over time, results are not only sustained but *multiply*, sometimes exponentially. This is because, instead of one CEO thinking strategically for the whole company, there are dozens, or even hundreds of strategically tuned individuals, with their eyes, ears, and minds targeted to the same goal—supremacy over competitors.

Our view is that the goal of strategy is not "adequacy," or attempting to keep up with one's competitors. Rather, the goal of strategy is *supremacy* over one's competitors. Secretariat's goal was not to look sideways to see which horse might be a nose ahead of the pack but to look back and see his closest competitor *31 lengths behind!*

The ultimate goal of strategy is to widen the gap between you and your competitors, not by outmuscling them in the marketplace, but rather by *outthinking* them in the planning rooms. As General Eisenhower once said:

Wars are won in the planning room, not on the battlefield.

In our view, however, one must achieve *supremacy of thinking* before one can achieve *supremacy of strategy.* This is what this book is all about.

One well-known case in point is the world-renowned company Caterpillar, which used Strategic Thinking to prevent its own demise in the late 1980s when it was under attack by a Japanese competitor.

During Komatsu's 30-year assault, Caterpillar's reaction was denial. They simply ignored Komatsu and pretended they didn't exist. In spite of their diminishing market share, in the early 1980s, Caterpillar's management at the time decided to invest a few hundred million dollars to build a "temple." Instead of bolstering its product line, Cat put their money into building a new headquarters, a massive new distribution center, and an avant-garde sales and service center for the training of their dealers' personnel and customers.

In the middle of these projects, George Schaefer was appointed CEO. Within nine months of taking over his new post I received a call from him.

"How can I help you?" I asked.

"We've got a problem," he replied, "but I read your book and I like what I see. I think you might be able to help."

"What caught your attention in the book?" I asked.

"We've been involved with the so-called 'best' strategy consulting firm in the world and, after more than 15 months, we're no further ahead today than we were the first morning of the first day. Besides we've been invaded by an army of 25-year-old MBAs who are telling us to do things to this company that we all know are just plain wrong. I like your approach better. It taps into the knowledge and experience base of our key executives and allows them to formulate their own strategy" he replied.

"How much has it cost you to find this out? I inquired.

"Three million dollars" was his reply.

"I can save you a lot of money and get you some concrete results very quickly," I stated.

Two days later I was giving an overview of our Strategic Thinking Process to the Executive Committee. We were hired on the spot, and you will find out more about what happened next in the following section of this book, in which three consecutive Caterpillar CEOs tell this remarkable tale from their point of view—in the driver's seat. The point of the story is that, using their own knowledge and *thinking* with the DPI process, Caterpillar not only repulsed their attacker, but went on to reestablish their competitive supremacy over the next 15 years. We are proud to have played a small role, and that, as Don Fites states, our Strategic Thinking Process was the "catalyst" that got Caterpillar management to stop Komatsu's assault and reassert Caterpillar's supremacy in their "sandbox."

At this point you may be thinking, "Okay that's great. But what does Caterpillar's story, as compelling as it may be, have to do with my company?"

The answer is that this is just one of several hundred companies that have achieved the same kinds of results in their own respective sandboxes. Interviews with the heads of many of these DPI client companies appear later in this book, all of them validating the results achieved over the long term, which is the litmus test of any successful strategy.

We have learned, through more than 25 years of work with nearly 500 companies, that our Strategic Thinking Concepts work for *any company*, of *any size*, in *any industry* and *in any country*. This is because they are basic common sense, and thrive, not on the "industry knowledge" of consultants, but on the knowledge and experience of those who run the company. We have developed a reliable process by which all of that wisdom can be channeled into a strategy that makes sense to those who will implement it. It worked for Caterpillar and hundreds of other companies. It will also work for you, whatever your business.

Good reading!

Michel (Mike) Robert

THE NEW STRATEGIC THINKING

PART ONE

The Caterpillar Story: How Three Successive CEOs Used Strategic Thinking to Regain Supremacy

"For 60 years Cat was a rocket. This company could do no wrong. Then in the early eighties, our business underwent profound change. We had 60 years, all very successful, in which we built what we said the customers wanted and needed. Then the whole ballgame had changed," said George Schaefer, CEO of Caterpillar (Cat) from 1986 to 1990. Recognizing that his company was in grave danger, he set in motion one of the most remarkable turnarounds in history.

Boosted by a worldwide infrastructure building boom for most of the twentieth century, Caterpillar had been a seemingly invincible juggernaut. Anchored by a vast network of Caterpillar dealers in all of the growth areas of the world, Cat had the products, distribution, and service to dominate the global market for earth-moving equipment and spare parts. Cat also had been able to support that network with the right components—knowledgeable and dedicated people, extensive global manufacturing, a huge field population of machines and engines, and service facilities within easy reach of customers literally everywhere.

But like the Big Three automakers in Detroit, Caterpillar was caught by surprise in the early 1980s when new offshore competitors began to arrive on the scene with high-quality products and disruptive marketing and sales approaches. The biggest threat among Caterpillar's new rivals was a Japanese company called Komatsu. "Eat the Cat" had been Komatsu's war cry since its inception in the years after World War II. Komatsu's plan, which it methodically implemented, was to circumvent Caterpillar's service advantage by making machines that "don't break down," thus rendering the leader's key strategic capability irrelevant.

By 1986, the little-known Komatsu was succeeding in their plan. Working tirelessly to undermine the strategic strength of Cat's dealers, they made significant inroads in convincing heavy equipment owners that Komatsu's new equipment did not break down as often and needed far less service than Caterpillar's—and was therefore less dependent on a local dealer to keep operations running. Their strategy had effectively changed the rules of play in a market Cat had ruled as long as anyone could remember. Further crippled by a widespread building recession that had taken place in the early eighties, Cat was in trouble.

But as impressive as Komatsu's feat may seem, the fact is that they had not really done anything particularly brilliant. The Komatsu attack was actually made possible by previous Caterpillar executives in the 1970s as they lost sight of the strategy that had made Caterpillar successful for so many decades. Throughout its first 60 years, Caterpillar had been practicing what we at DPI call a "Product-driven strategy." The bottom line for a company whose strategy is focused around a single product (heavy earth-moving machinery, in Cat's case) is very simple: the best product wins. As such, resources need to be continually reinvested so a company can ensure that its products are always the best.

In Caterpillar's case, the leaders had forgotten what had put them out in front all those years. And as Cat was generating more cash than the company needed in the 1970s, management became distracted by this development and began looking for a "big acquisition." They found one in a company called Towmotor. Caterpillar management rationalized that "moving material"—Towmotor's business—was very similar to their own business of "moving dirt."

That assumption proved to be very wrong and very costly over the next decade. The strategies of Caterpillar and Towmotor were incompatible, a mismatch that undermined both businesses, leading to huge losses and depleting Cat's strategic advantage.

THE CAT AWAKENS

Fast-forward 10 years, and the impact of the Towmotor acquisition combined with the attack by Komatsu had taken its toll. "This was in the late eighties," said Don Fites, Cat's CEO from 1990 to 1999, who was president at the time. "We'd experienced a decade without really any shareholder value being created . . . we were very concerned about our Japanese competitors. When I joined this company, all of our competitors had been American companies—and most of them were put out of business by the Japanese and Europeans, who are fierce competitors. *Survival* was a word that we were talking about around here."

As U.S. competitors such as International Harvester succumbed one by one to this new environment, Cat management could find no clear path to regaining its growth of the past. Not that they didn't try.

"A lot of people had written us off, as they had many American 'Rust Belt' companies," says Caterpillar CEO Glen Barton (2000–2004), who at that time was running the Solar Turbines division. "We went through a period of time in which we closed a lot of factories and tried to become a low-cost source, not necessarily to compete on price, but to make a profit on the prices at which we were already selling our products. We still wanted to concentrate on selling value, and we still do that today. We believed, and still do, that our products have more value than our competitors' offerings, with the combination of performance, reliability, resale value of the product, and the ultimate life of the product. We have that distinct advantage today. But, in order to compete, then we had to sell our products at a price where we couldn't make any margin, and obviously, we couldn't do that forever.

"Komatsu had been making inroads outside the United States, not much inside the United States," Barton recalls. "When they started taking us on in the home market, we bit the bullet and decided that we had to maintain our market position regardless of circumstances, until we could get our own house in order, which we then embarked upon doing."

Cat's management went about the task of seeking the best advice on strategy it could find among America's top business minds. As Barton remembers, "We went through a number of different consultants who worked with us. Among several others, we had the top strategy consultant at the time, Michael Porter, and Noel Tichy, who was a facilitator that had worked with General Electric on their breakout process. At the same time we were in the process of visiting other corporations to see what they had done and what guidance they could provide us."

None of these efforts yielded useful answers, as red ink continued to mount. As George Schaefer put it: "We were floundering despite help from the top consultants available. We had too much good advice."

Recalls Barton: "Somewhere or other we came across Michel Robert's book that talked about the Strategic Thinking Process. We were all impressed by the simplicity of his approach. Rather than spending two or three years getting the background material, as a traditional strategy consultant like Michael Porter might have wanted to do before he was ready to move forward, we felt that the DPI process was a much more straightforward approach. It was one we believed we'd feel comfortable working with and get faster results, which at that time was important."

Schaefer's team believed the Strategic Thinking Process might be the tool they needed to mine the hundreds of worker-years of experience residing right there in the heads of their people in Peoria. They reasoned that creating their own strategy based on that knowledge would lead to a better strategy than one based on studies done by outsiders. But more than anything else, Schaefer, as CEO, was determined to find a way to gain consensus and commitment to a strategy that would revive the struggling Cat.

STRATEGIC THINKING COMES TO PEORIA

So a call came into DPI's offices from Caterpillar asking me to go to Peoria and make a presentation to the executive committee. Of course I accepted, and during the presentation I asked them to tell me Caterpillar's "bumper-sticker" strategy statement. One of them replied that it used to be "earth-moving machines" but that it had been changed to "earth-moving and material-handling machines." I then asked them if the addition of the words *material-handling* had been made *before* or *after* the acquisition of Towmotor. There was a dead silence in the room and I thought that surely the question had just cost me an opportunity to work with Caterpillar. But they were wiser men than I was giving them credit for. They understood the meaning of the question and the implications of their tacit answer, and decided to proceed with our process.

Says Glen Barton of that first session: "I will always remember a comment Mike Robert made to us at the meeting, that 90 percent of what we needed to know to restructure our business was already in the heads of the people in that room. And I think if we contrasted that with Porter's approach, he would have said that less than 5 percent of what we needed to know was in the heads of the people in our company. Mike's point hit home with us.

"The idea of going out and doing a lot of surveys of individual market segments and collecting a lot of information about customer groupings and logical fits of customer groupings didn't appeal to us at all. We'd already done some of that, and it didn't work all that well," says Barton. "Some of these projects never end, they just keep rolling along and become bigger and bigger, and longer and longer, and more involved. I think we all welcomed and still appreciate the fact that there's a finite course that you go through with DPI. In the last 10 years, we have used the Strategic Thinking Process many times and when we undertake it we know that there's an end. When we get to the end, there are decisions we're going to make and directions we're going to take and move on from that."

A MEETING OF THE MINDS

Caterpillar assembled an exceptionally strong team of senior managers to go through the process, among them the three men who would be Cat CEOs through the next 15 years—George Schaefer, Don Fites, and Glen Barton.

Very quickly, during the initial Strategic Thinking session, it became clear what had gone wrong in the business. Cat, they realized, had gradually grown complacent over the years, neglecting to nurture the fundamentals of its Product-driven strategy. And the acquisition of Towmotor had dragged the whole company off its course.

Through the logic of the process, Caterpillar executives quickly discovered that "moving dirt" was generally a *horizontal* operation, while "handling material" was generally a *vertical* operation. It also became apparent that the skills required for each business were completely different and most were not transferable from one business to the other. Just about everything about the two strategies was different:

- Manufacturing processes
- Customers
- Distribution methods
- Selling methods
- Service requirements
- Design factors
- IT requirements
- Suppliers
- Competitors

The clash of the two fundamentally different strategies was dragging both parts of the business down into the mud. Enormous amounts of cash were diverted to make up for the losses in the material-handling division. Product quality lagged, and service had lost touch with the real needs of its customers. Even worse, as part of an attempt to pay for Towmotor and cover the losses that began to occur immediately after the acquisition, Caterpillar management made a nearly fatal decision. They reduced the Product

Development budget from a high of 7.8 percent of sales to about 1 percent of sales. This gutting of R&D crippled Caterpillar's ability to continue making the "best product," giving Komatsu the opening it needed to close the gap between the performance of their machines and Caterpillar's. The good news was that it also quickly became obvious what they needed to do to reestablish their product-driven dominance.

Said Schaefer: "Mike and his process helped us sort everything out. We knew that we were moving in a more orderly and focused fashion. We saw it all: businesses entered without commensurate expertise, misunderstood market share, and so on. It was priceless. Noses got bent out of shape . . . but when noses get bent out of shape, you generally get better decisions."

Recalls Barton: "One thing that impressed us as we moved through DPI's process was the fact that, first off, it was excellent to have such a skilled facilitator. With all the people who had worked with us before, we would come up against a touchy issue and we'd get stuck. I think that one of the things we learned was that having a strong facilitator is very good for moving the meetings forward and keeping us talking, even though we would come up against a roadblock from time to time. These were sometimes very sensitive issues to a lot of people, and the directions that the group might decide to go were maybe disappointing to certain individuals within the group. But Mike drove the process, drove us through considerations of what kind of company we wanted to be, whether we were Product-driven or a Market-driven company, or a Technology or a Production Capability–driven company. We logically arrived, through the process, at what we thought we were and what we still think we are today, which is a Product-driven company. That helped us a lot as we moved forward in trying to strategize how we could better organize this Product-driven company to serve the needs of the marketplace."

Schaefer saw the recognition of Caterpillar's Driving Force as the turning point in Cat's strategic awakening. "It helped us to understand our options and alternatives," he said. "This was critically important to helping us understand our strengths and weaknesses, and to delineate the Critical Issues for the next decade. The discipline of the approach gave us the confidence that we were right on track."

DIFFICULT AND COURAGEOUS DECISIONS

During that work session, Cat's management team made a number of what have proven to be historic decisions for the company. By recognizing their

Driving Force and the related Areas of Excellence, concepts we will talk more about later, Cat's senior management team had no trouble deciding on the following actions:

- To divest themselves of Towmotor and take a loss of nearly $300 million
- To remain a U.S.-based manufacturing company due to the fact that moving their 14 Illinois plants abroad would have been a major blow to the economy of that state
- To invest $2.5 billion in a program named PWAF (Plant With A Future), which was intended to significantly reduce costs by a factor of 10, converting their batch-oriented plants into fully automated ones
- To restore the Product Development budget to the previous level of nearly 8 percent of sales and rededicate themselves to making and selling the "best product"
- To refuse to accept a labor contract "patterned" for the automobile industry and not to Caterpillar's distinctive needs, and to accept a union strike if need be
- To be profitable at the "bottom of the trough." Caterpillar, historically, had suffered wild swings in its profit results, with the price of its shares following suit—reaching record highs during good economic times and record lows during economic downturns. During that first work session, they decided they needed to be profitable all the time.

All of these decisions, Cat's Critical Issues, were implemented between 1987 and 1990, and their impact on Caterpillar and its shareholders was "nothing short of spectacular," as Don Fites said at the time.

Fites, who took the CEO reins in 1996, recalls: "The first sessions were an honest, hard look at who we were, how we were organized, and how we were going about doing business. It's a difficult process. It's easier to have somebody else tell you what you are and what needs to be done. In our case, though, I think this process was exactly the right approach to take, because ours is a company where most of the people spend their lifetime.

"We're very attached to the business and the equipment. We know the market and the customers. We know the business very well, and it's not a business that is easy to grasp. I mean, there aren't a whole lot of companies—there aren't really *any* companies—in the world like Caterpillar. We don't have any models to follow. Forcing us to do that assessment was exactly the right thing, because only we, in the end, could have made that assessment, arrived at the conclusions, and taken the path that we eventually did.

"I think that the idea of someone from the outside telling people who have spent their whole life in a company that something will or won't work is not really a good idea. They don't have the insight into what really makes the company tick. I think the thing that this process does very well, and I've seen it done over and over again in different circumstances, is it forces you to come up with the good news and the bad news. And you find the answers to these issues yourselves."

CAT FIGHTS BACK

Immediately after the first work session, Fites had an inspiration: Could the 20 people at Caterpillar with the greatest knowledge of Komatsu use DPI's Strategic Thinking Process to determine Komatsu's strategy and develop an anti-Komatsu plan?

With a bit of reverse engineering of the process, the new team went to work. Caterpillar learned more about Komatsu in the first few minutes of that session than they had in the previous 30 years. The guts of the discussion revolved around the concept of Driving Force. By looking at the scope of Komatsu's products, including those that do not compete with Caterpillar, such as robots, elevators, and machine tools, it was decided that Komatsu's Driving Force was technology—namely hydraulic technology. In other words, Komatsu was in Caterpillar's "sandbox" simply because it was another place to exploit their hydraulic expertise.

That discovery led Caterpillar to develop and/or acquire a host of other technologies to reduce the importance of hydraulics in their machines. By going at the very essence of Komatsu's strategy and neutralizing it, Caterpillar regained its advantage, and it went on to reestablish its supremacy in the earth-moving sandbox.

BUILDING THE NEW CATERPILLAR

One of the most significant moves resulting from Cat's new strategy, in Glen Barton's view, was a major restructuring of the company. The need was clear, but the implementation plan took a bit more discussion.

Two new units were created immediately, but it took a firm shove from an influential board member, who, seeing the wisdom of the conclusions reached in the DPI process, pushed them to compress their timeframe for a complete reorganization.

Barton remembers how it happened: "We were creating the divisions. After a lot of debate we got eight or nine people to pretty well agree on what we thought the different divisions of the company should be. We got the executive office at that time to buy into that. Lou Gerstner (the ex–IBM CEO) was on our board. At that point he was still with American Express. We had created the first two divisions, and Lou asked the question at a board meeting, 'When do you intend to go forward with the reorganization of the rest of the company?' And, frankly, within the company at that point in time, within the executive offices, there was a three/three split in terms of whether we should go forward with the whole reorganization of the company at once or whether we ought to wait until we had some experience with the first two divisions before we proceeded with the balance. So Lou spoke up again, as only Lou can do, and said, 'Look guys, my biggest concern is that you're going to reorganize this company over a two- to three-year period of time and find yourselves organized differently but operating in the same manner that you're operating today. The only thing I can say to you is that if you're going to cause people to change the way they do things, you've got to follow through on this plan you've made and reorganize the whole company at the same time.' We moved forward and we never looked back.

"I think the reorganization is the most significant thing that has happened as a direct result of the DPI process and I think we had a total turnaround in our company in recent years as a result of it," Barton states.

Said Fites: "We completely restructured our company from what was essentially a functionally organized company into profit-center divisions and service divisions. Originally there were 18, and then 23. We completely distributed accountability and responsibility down into the organization from what had been a structure where virtually all important decisions were made by a few people at the top. We drove the accountability and responsibility broadly into these divisions, held them accountable for their own plans."

Caterpillar's sheer mass would mean, though, that the transition would not be an easy task. At the end of the decade of the 1980s when the implementation of the new strategy began, Caterpillar was doing business in more than 200 countries, with 32 plants in 12 countries, employing more than 60,000 people. In addition, its network of some 190 dealers was spread throughout the globe. Turning around a company of that enormous size is akin to turning around an ocean liner. It takes time, planning, and the coordinated efforts of a lot of committed people to change the inertia. By driving the strategy and related decision making more broadly and deeply in the organization, the transformation would be less top-down and would happen much more quickly.

During the strategy sessions with DPI, a set of 13 Critical Issues was created, with individual executives taking ownership of each, to assure steady, determined progress. To make sure that each of the newly created units had a plan it could execute in sync with the corporate strategy, each SBU went through the Strategic Thinking Process.

"Once we got ourselves organized corporately, a lot of the people who are running these divisions had been involved in the first sessions or were aware of the work that had been done. They immediately began using the Strategic Thinking Process to flatten their own organizations and also to do a self-assessment on a more micro basis of what they were and what they were trying to do." The goal was to cascade the strategy concepts down through every level of the organization so it could eventually move forward as one.

As the years rolled on, those plans created in the corporate unit strategy sessions and, subsequently, the business unit strategy sessions became realities, restarting the engines of long-term growth. The days of facing extinction became a distant, though chastening, memory in Peoria. The results in the years immediately following Cat's strategic rebirth were nothing short of phenomenal. In fact, in 1997 the *Wall Street Journal* ranked Caterpillar number three of all the companies it tracked in five-year average shareholder return—at 29.8 percent.

As Fites described the turnaround at that time: "As far as the shareholders are concerned, the creation of shareholder value has been rather spectacular. But also from a customer standpoint, the acceptance of our products from around the world is at an all-time high. Our product development process is working better than ever. And now, instead of having seven people at the top of the organization trying to come up with all of these ideas on how we're going to grow, how we're going to be successful, we have thousands of people in the organization coming up with all sorts of ideas. Our job now at the top of the company has changed—we're put in the position of choosing and picking the best ideas. We've got more growth opportunities identified than we really want to try to implement.

"I think it is one of the truly remarkable success stories of the 1990s. The track record is there in terms of financial results, market shares . . . percentage of sales . . . the whole nine yards."

By 1996, with competitors such as Komatsu and Hitachi still there and battling tenaciously, Cat's sales had risen to a historical high of $16.52 billion from about $8 billion in 1989, and its record profit reached $1.36 billion. Exports were the highest in company history, at $5.5 billion. Cat had, after a brush with extinction, landed squarely on its feet. But the job wasn't complete. When they undertook the Strategic Thinking Process, they were as much interested in long-term supremacy as they were in resolving their immediate crisis.

OPENING A NEW MARKET BY CHANGING THE RULES

More than a decade after its initial recognition of its Product-driven strategy, Caterpillar continued to refine the concept and their product mix. One of the product lines they introduced was small machines for the rental market. These products, and some rule-changing marketing, opened a lucrative new opportunity in a market in which Caterpillar had not been a player. Not only did it increase sales but it did so in such a way that it allowed the company to use its vast dealer network as a strategic advantage once again.

As Barton explains: "The entrance that we made into the compact construction equipment business for the rental market was driven in large part by us changing the rules of the game. Rentals of small construction equipment are an industry that had been growing very rapidly. Most of that growth had occurred through the consolidation of independent rental dealerships into larger companies who wanted the purchasing leverage to buy their equipment manufacturer-direct. If we would participate under their rules, we would have had to bypass our dealer organization, which we refused to do. So we changed the rules of the game a bit and decided to get our dealers into the rental services business."

Caterpillar designed and built a line of small construction machines specifically for the rental market.

"A key part of the plan was having the right equipment for the rental services business," he says. "And that's how the investment we made on our compact construction equipment line paid off. This type of equipment is the staple of the rental services fleets. It's much smaller than the equipment that we would typically produce. They rent it on a different basis; the small machines are what people like you and I would use if we decide on a Saturday to go and dig up our backyard. The new products we introduced now were designed specifically for that type of use."

The program was rolled out in North America and in selected markets outside the United States.

"We created a competitor for this new rental services opportunity and did it with a marketplace that we already had access to because our dealers buy our equipment. So we used the strategic advantage of our dealer network to change the rules in our favor."

KEEPING THE GLOBAL STRATEGY ALIVE AND FLEXIBLE

Of course, for a company as large as Caterpillar to achieve consistently outstanding results, the biggest challenge would be to keep all of its global businesses focused on the strategy yet flexible enough to change with conditions. The company put in place a management accountability structure that has assured ongoing implementation and aggressive progress on Critical Issues. The basis of it was, and still is today, the common understanding and consensus on the underlying strategy developed in 1989 and 1990 through the Strategic Thinking Process, with regular reviews to adjust for changing conditions.

"We have a process and we stick to it. It's all been very well documented. Our mission. Our vision," Fites explained in 1997. "And where it's really well documented is in what we call our Critical Issues. We have an ongoing strategy committee whose work it is from time to time to look at all those documents drawn from people at various levels in the organization . . . take a look at our mission, vision, and particularly at the Critical Issues. Our mission and vision are in place. But Critical Issues can change as the world changes, as competitors change. We make sure that those are kept up-to-date.

"Our people are motivated personally, they're motivated financially to stay on strategy and to demonstrate that the strategy is not something that's just been pulled out of the air. It's something they're going to implement . . . in fact are implementing. And there's a timeline for that implementation."

The role of top management is to monitor progress, set ambitious goals, and manage the strategic processes. Cat's formal review process has continued to assure ongoing reevaluation and implementation.

As Don Fites laid it out: "We have what we call EORs, which are our Executive Office Reviews, through which each division meets with the executive office anywhere from a half day to a day. We do these generally in the February–March time period, and this is a detailed explanation by the division of what their strategy and plans are, which the executive officer approves. We're essentially looking at a three-year plan. And we measure that against what we were told three years ago, or two years and one year ago. And if we like what we see, and they're meeting the benchmarks that we have jointly established, then the division is further funded or further encouraged or given the green light to proceed. If they're not meeting the long-term benchmarks that we think are required by the enterprise, then we chart some other plan for that division.

"And then to further enhance that process so that knowledge just doesn't rest with the five members of the executive office, we then meet once a year with all of the divisions as a group and for a week each division explains to the rest of the organization, i.e., to their peers, what their strategy is, what their performance has been against their plans, and what it looks like three years out. At that point we also take a look out as far as six years ahead as to what might happen.

"That meeting encompasses about a hundred people—our top people from around the world. And I think those reviews are even tougher for the divisions than the reviews with the executive office, because they're a committee of your peers, who are judging your plans and your performance against how it will interface, whether it will have synergy with what they are doing.

"And that's how I think we keep driving the vertical integration throughout the company, which is very important to us. But also I think it's important to how each division strives to maximize performance. And particularly peers tend to be tougher, I think, on each other than we are."

Because of the remarkable resurrection at Cat, Fites became a firm believer in the use of the Strategic Thinking Process to face the tough issues and find real answers. But with a cautionary note he adds, "It's not a process you dare to take lightly. It's not a process where somebody's going to give you the answer. If you're concerned about your long-term success, it's very worthwhile doing this because it drives you to make the best decision you can make, because it uses the best knowledge available and that's the knowledge within you and the people you're surrounded with—who really are your best and brightest. It uses their knowledge to identify and correct those things that can be corrected and also weds the organization to that new plan and that new organization. It makes you very determined to implement and make it work.

"This is not a process for wimps," he states emphatically. "It is not a process where somebody is going to tell you how to save or maybe even improve your organization. But it is a process that if you go into it recognizing that you've got to change, that you've got to do better—if you want to maintain your leadership or even survive—this process, better than any I've seen, will get the job done.

"Nobody likes change. But it helps you reach the right conclusion. If you implement with candor and with determination and with honesty in terms of telling the organization where you're going, what your goals are, 90 percent of the people are going to buy in and they're going to try and make it work. There are always going to be a few people who don't, but that's part of the process. If you reach the right conclusion, your organization is smart enough to understand it. They realize the tremendous upside—a brighter future than they ever thought about."

To this day, Fites credits the Strategic Thinking Process with being the catalyst that enabled all those forces to work together toward a common goal. Looking back, Fites concludes: "Had we come up with a workable strategy, we would have been just as successful. But I'm not sure that we would have. We worked with several very well-known consulting organizations . . . we never could come to a conclusion. In fact the conclusions that we semireached, a lot of us never really bought into. And I think it was because we didn't feel the ownership of those conclusions. So I'm not sure we ever would have gotten to that point. Or if we had, it would have taken too long. Perhaps we would have gotten there at some point, but that would have been too late . . . too late for the company or certainly too late for some of us charged with running the company."

SUSTAINING ADVANTAGE IN THE TWENTY-FIRST CENTURY

Caterpillar management has revisited its corporate strategy periodically over the past 10 years. Like many companies that have used the Strategic Thinking Process, they find that it is a dynamic process that allows them to change with the times.

Says CEO Barton about one of these strategy sessions: "It was time for us to look at our strategy again. We had a new chairman and had this reorganization in place for almost nine years. It was time for us to go back and revisit our original vision, our mission, our Critical Issues, and reexamine where we're trying to take the business, the kind of business we think we want to be, look at where the growth is within our businesses and how we can better plan for the next decade. We picked up the debate at a higher level than what we did the last time around and went back to reevaluate our strengths and weaknesses, which changed some during that period of time, and evaluate some of the opportunities or threats.

"As we look at the world today, it's changing much more rapidly than it's ever changed before, with the influence of new information technology and so on. And the way we do business today versus how we may be doing business 20 years from now, it's hard to imagine that it's going to be the same. That has some tremendous implications for companies such as ours. As a result, I think it just says you have to continue to do this over and over and over. Once you've gone through the Strategic Thinking Process and put your strategic plan in place, don't wait too long before you get another group started looking at it yet again to see if there's yet another need to do something differently because the world is really changing fast."

Since 1990, Caterpillar has been profitable every year, without exception, despite the economic roller coaster everyone rode during that tumultuous decade. Recently, the company announced record sales of $20 billion in 2003—a long way from the $8 billion and falling the company reported in 1987—a formidable achievement in what some would call a "mature market." Glen Barton reaffirmed that the company was on track to make its sales target of $30 billion by 2010, a goal set back in that first Strategic Thinking session in 1987, at a time when the company's demise was being predicted by many "experts." In fact, Caterpillar's strategy is gaining strength. In 2004, sales increased from $22 billion to over $30 billion, an increase of 36 percent. Caterpillar has reached its 2010 goal *six years* ahead of plan and its stock price has reached an all time record high of $98 from its bargain basement low of $8 in 1988.

It is a testament to the courage and wisdom of those Caterpillar executives that even in the face of seemingly overwhelming conditions, they were able to envision a strategy that would assure Caterpillar's longevity and competitive supremacy in its sandbox for perhaps the next hundred years.

CHAPTER 2

LONGEVITY: THE LITMUS TEST OF A SUCCESSFUL STRATEGY

If you feel a need to constantly change your business strategy, in my opinion that's a clear signal that "you ain't got one." A successful strategy doesn't change with every gust of competitive or environmental wind that brushes across your sandbox. A successful strategy works to the benefit of a company over a long period of time. In fact, the litmus test of a successful strategy is its longevity.

One would think, from reading the business publications, that companies come and go according to some preordained law of commerce that dictates that companies rise and fall according to certain events, cycles, or trends. It is easy to understand why one could come to that conclusion. These publications overflow with stories of failed companies. In the last couple of years, these have included Xerox, Polaroid, DEC, Enron, Lucent, MCI WorldCom, and Global Crossing. A proponent of the above thesis would declare that "such is the natural order of things and it's simply Darwinism at work."

In fact, a recent study identified that only 74 of the companies that were on *Fortune*'s original 500 list in 1957 were still on the list in 1997. That same study concluded that the "life span" of the modern corporation is 15 to 25 years, and that that number will recede to 10 to 15 years in the next decade.

Yet, there is still a significant number of companies that have been around a much longer span of years and remain strong and healthy. The following are some of these companies:

The "Seniors" (over 100 years)

Company	Year founded
Chubb	1882
Coca-Cola	1886

Corning	1851
Diebold	1859
Dow Chemical	1897
Exxon	1882
General Electric	1892
Johnson & Johnson	1886
J.P. Morgan	1838
Pfizer	1849
Phelps Dodge	1849
Shell	1892
Salomon Brothers	1873

The "Adults" (over 50 years)

Company	Year founded
3M	1902
Boeing	1916
Caterpillar	1925
Disney	1923
IBM	1911
Medtronic	1949
Merck	1930
Morgan Stanley	1933
Newmont Mining	1921
Nordstrom	1901
Philip Morris	1902

The "Teenagers" (over 30 years)

Company	Year founded
FedEx	1971
Intel	1968
Microsoft	1975
Schwab	1971
Southwest	1971
Wal-Mart	1962

What's going on here? Why is it that these companies can outlast their competitors? Is Darwinism really at work? We at DPI think not.

With over 25 years of work in the area of business strategy with the CEOs and executive teams of over 400 companies in 30 countries, we have come to a different conclusion. In our view, the difference between companies that succeed over the long term and those that fail and disappear is a process we call Strategic Thinking. In other words, long-term successful companies have CEOs and senior executives who are better strategic thinkers than companies that fail. Failure, in our humble opinion, is a self-inflicted wound.

Companies that are successful over long periods of time simply outperform their competitors by outthinking them in the boardroom and not by outmuscling them in the marketplace. As Dwight Eisenhower once said, "Wars are won in the planning room, not on the battlefield."

The single most important element common to companies that attain long-term success as opposed to those that fail is this: They have a clear, coherent strategy that they pursue with singularity of purpose; they have total dedication to it and no deviation from it. Simply put, they have a better strategy that strives for supremacy in their sandbox. However, in our view, one must have supremacy of thinking before one can achieve supremacy of strategy.

> Supremacy, not adequacy, is the sole objective of a long-term strategy.

What do Intel, Wal-Mart, Home Depot, Microsoft, Dell, Apple, Oracle, Schwab, E*TRADE, Amazon.com, FedEx, Caterpillar, IBM, General Electric, Nokia, Progressive Insurance, Canon, Sony, Disney, and Southwest Airlines have in common? Let's try to answer this question through a process of elimination by first looking at what is different about them:

- They are in different industries.
- They have different products.
- They serve different customers and markets.
- They have different modus operandi.
- They are headquartered in different countries.
- They cultivate different corporate cultures.
- They were conceived in different eras.

The list could go on ad infinitum. For example, another factor in the way they differ is that they have different CEOs. However, these different companies have, or had at one point, CEOs who had one trait in common: a grasp of the concepts of strategy, strategic thinking, and competitive supremacy. In other words, their goal was not to have a strategy that allowed their companies to compete *adequately* but rather a strategy that aimed at *supremacy* over their competitors. Supremacy, not adequacy, is the ultimate goal of strategy.

These companies were all influenced at some point in time—usually during their infancy—by a CEO who conceived a clear strategy, with its intent being long-term supremacy in its chosen sandbox. The following are some examples:

- Chubb's intent to dominate the "insurance needs of the well-to-do"
- Boeing's intent to "be the world's preeminent aerospace company"
- Coca-Cola's intent to be the "foremost global beverage company"
- Diebold's intent to dominate the "financial transaction device" market
- Schwab's intent to be the "sole financial advisor to the independent investor"
- Microsoft's intent to be the "primary provider of software in the world"
- Southwest Airlines' intent to be the world's best airline, with its strategy of "One mission: Low fares."

On the other hand, several companies that ran into serious trouble and disappeared, or are today in poor health, have failed due to poor strategic decisions made by a previous CEO many years ago. The following are some examples, among many:

- Xerox's decision in the 1970s to enter the insurance business diverted resources and management attention from their real business—copiers—and gave Canon a 10- to 15-year window to penetrate and eventually terminate Xerox's supremacy.
- Polaroid's refusal to accept the fact that Sony's introduction of the Mavica digital camera in 1984 was a death threat to Edwin Land's strategy of "instant photography."
- Exxon's foray in the 1980s into the foreign world of office equipment almost led to its downfall. Fortunately, Exxon was smart enough to recognize its mistake and made the right decision to exit that business a few years later.
- Daimler-Benz's attempt to become the "world's best managed company" by acquiring a host of "basket-case" companies, none if which were related to cars, almost put that company out of business.

Another threat to long-term supremacy comes from a totally different source, from left field. This is the advent of a competitor that isn't even on your radar screen.

THE STEALTH COMPETITOR: SUPREMACY IN JEOPARDY

A few years ago, the CEOs of the two dominant book retailers in the United States—Barnes & Noble and Borders—were sitting in their respective offices, listening to the business news on CNN's *Moneyline*, contemplating ways and means of taking away some of each other's business. During the newscast, there was a short interview with a gentleman named Jeff Bezos, who declared that he had formed a company named Amazon.com, which, effective immediately, would start selling books online through the Internet. Furthermore, he stated that Amazon.com would carry over one million titles—a hundred times that of the average bookstore, that the price would be 30 to 50 percent less than in a bookstore, and that users could make a purchase in a couple of minutes from the comfort of their homes by simply using a PC.

A few weeks later, the CEO of Merrill Lynch, watching the same TV program, was thinking about ways and means to compete with Smith Barney. Another young entrepreneur announced the launch of an online brokerage company called E*TRADE, which would allow individuals to trade stocks from their home PCs at a fraction of the cost of dealing through a broker.

While the CEOs of American Airlines, United Airlines, Delta, and US Airways were brainstorming ways of eating away at one another's customer base, a new Internet-based company called Priceline.com ran full-page ads in all the major newspapers. They announced the introduction of a new booking service that would provide lower fares than the lowest offered by any airline. Within a few weeks, Priceline.com was booking flights for over 200,000 travelers per week.

"Ama . . . who? E . . . who? Price . . . who? Doing . . . what?" must have been the reaction of these CEOs on the day of these announcements. All were caught completely off guard, and, since then, despite the dot-com crash, many of these new companies have become each CEO's biggest nightmare.

The day that Amazon.com went online, Barnes & Nobles' and Borders' business models were put into jeopardy. The day that E*TRADE went online, Merrill Lynch's business model of selling stocks through thousands of highly commissioned salespeople was put into jeopardy. Priceline.com simply took control of the airlines' pricing policy.

SURPRISE! SURPRISE! SURPRISE!

Why were Ford, General Motors, and Chrysler caught by surprise and unable to see that smaller, high-quality automobiles from Japan would drastically erode their market shares? After all, the Big Three were the dominant players in the U.S. auto game and had the resources to employ hundreds of futurists who could have looked ahead a few years and seen trouble coming.

Why was Singer, which had invented the sewing machine and had put one in just about every home in the developed world, caught in the same trap? Why was IBM, the powerhouse of the computer industry, also taken by surprise by Apple's introduction of the first PC? Why was Wang, which invented the word processor, caught in a similar trap when PCs emerged that could handle word processing as well as just about any computing task the business world would need?

Why were RCA and Zenith also caught completely off guard by Sony's introduction of a VCR linked to a TV set? After all, they were the largest, strongest, and richest in their industry and should have foreseen Sony's entrance into their sandbox.

Why were Polaroid and Kodak surprised by Sony's introduction of the Mavica digital camera in 1984, an event that has completely disrupted their lives and to which neither company has found an adequate response more than 25 years later? In fact, in our view, Canon and Sony have achieved long-term competitive supremacy by changing the game of imaging and also being "stealth" entrants at the same time—a double competitive jolt for Kodak and Polaroid. These companies are practicing a DPI concept that says that winning occurs by "changing how customers buy and how companies compete."

Changing the game . . . stealth competitors . . . competitive supremacy. Who are these guys? In other words, where do these concepts come from? The answer is simple: DPI—the company I founded in 1980 that now consists of over 50 professionals located in 16 countries. And the sources of these concepts, and others you will be introduced to in this book, were our clients—CEOs and their management teams who served as "laboratories" for us. In other words, DPI's Strategic Thinking concepts were developed and validated by being present, not in academia, but in the "corporate war rooms" of over 400 major corporations around the world. Furthermore, the concepts have withstood the test of time, as most of our clients remain long-term clients. An example is Caterpillar, which has been a client since 1986. And there are many more.

Companies that practice these concepts of Strategic Thinking have consistently become leaders in their industries, in many cases achieving long-term strategic supremacy—companies like Caterpillar, FedEx Custom Critical, LandAmerica, Pulte Homes, and many others. As I have said before, this does not occur by chance. In our experience it is achieved by a deliberate process of assessing your landscape and creating corporate strategies that continually take your competitors by surprise, and offer your customers something they can't get anywhere else. That deliberate process is called the Strategic Thinking Process, and it can be practiced by the management teams of any type of company in any industry, including yours, every day.

CHAPTER 3

10 Deadly Sins That Lead to Strategic Malaise

"It's easy to develop a strategy; it's the implementation that's difficult." This is a statement we have frequently heard over the years. Our own experience proves the exact opposite to be true. If a CEO thinks that he or she has a solid strategy, and yet it's not being implemented, only one of two things can be happening:

1. The management team doesn't know or understand the strategy. (It's very difficult to implement a secret strategy.)

2. If the strategy is understood but still not being implemented, it's because some members of the management team don't agree with it and may, in fact, be trying to sabotage it.

In our view, there are 10 deadly sins that an organization can commit that will inevitably lead to these two conditions—and eventually to corporate extinction.

SIN 1: STRATEGY BY OSMOSIS

In too many organizations, the strategy of the company is *implicit* and resides solely in the head of the chief executive. Most CEOs have some kind of strategy. However, they often have great difficulty articulating it to the people around them in words that allow these people to make consistent and intelligent decisions on behalf of the company. A senior executive of a Fortune 500 company once said to us, "The reason I have difficulty implementing my CEO's strategy is that I don't know what it is!"

Because many CEOs have difficulty verbalizing their strategies, most people are placed in the position of having to "guess" what the strategy is, and they may guess wrong as often as they guess right. Or else they learn what the strategy is over time by the nature of the decisions they recommend that are either accepted or rejected. Gradually, a subordinate learns where the line of demarcation is between the things that are permitted by the strategy and those that are not. This is called "strategy by groping." This results when the strategy becomes clear or explicit only over a long period of time, during which people may have spent too much time pursuing and implementing activities that did not fit, while neglecting opportunities that represented a better strategic fit. Worse than that, the strategy may never become clear, or it may be badly misinterpreted by people making an earnest effort to figure it out.

As one of our CEO clients once told us after our initial session: "I was astonished that our senior management group had no concept of our strategy and disagreed with it once they learned of it."

Lesson 1: People can't implement a strategy that has not been revealed to them.

SIN 2: STRATEGY IN ISOLATION

A second reason the strategy may not be implemented properly is that the CEO developed it in isolation. This is a natural enough tendency, since a CEO's job is strategy. Furthermore, most subordinates have no experience thinking strategically, so there is no inclination, or framework, to involve others.

Many CEOs have a strategy, but their key people are not involved in the process of developing it and therefore they have no ownership. In such a case, subordinates usually do not understand the rationale behind the strategy and will spend more time questioning it, or trying to figure out where they fit, than implementing it. The CEO becomes more and more impatient as subordinates question his or her logic more and more often. The CEO, on the other hand, can't comprehend why his people are not executing what, to him or her, is a simple strategy.

Some CEOs might involve one or two people in the formulation of the strategy. This is better than doing it alone, but it is still not good enough. The entire management team must be involved in order to achieve accurate understanding and proper execution. This cannot be accomplished simply by "going offsite" with this group to discuss the strategy. A methodology, or process, is needed to guide the discussion and keep it "strategic," not operational. This is the basis of DPI's Strategic Thinking Process, which we will unfold for you later in this book. Involvement by senior managers in the basic strategic decisions is the most effective way to create a strategy that not only looks good on paper but also actually gets implemented.

As John Davis, president of American Saw and Manufacturing Company, and a DPI client, put it: "I think that, too often, strategies are made in a vacuum. The management is given a copy of the plan and asked to implement it. I'm not sure they buy into that kind of plan. But, by going through the Strategic Thinking Process, there's a lot of debate, and everyone sees the reasons why certain Critical Issues surface and things get done much more quickly."

Lesson 2: People don't implement what they don't understand.

SIN 3: OUTSOURCING THE STRATEGY TO AN OUTSIDE CONSULTANT

The worst of all strategic crimes and the "kiss of death" for any strategy—even a good one—is to have an outside consultant develop your strategy. No outside consultant has the right to set the direction of your organization or knows as much as your own people about the business and the environment it is facing. Most strategies developed by outside consultants end up in the wastepaper basket for two reasons:

1. Everyone can quickly tear the conclusions apart because they are not based on an intimate knowledge of the company, the business, or the industry.

2. There is no commitment to that strategy by senior management because it is not their strategy.

Experience has shown that almost any strategy will work to some degree, unless it is completely invalidated by negative environmental factors. Experience has also shown, however, that no strategy will work as well as it should if a couple or a few members of senior management are not committed to that strategy. In effect, if total commitment is not present, those uncommitted to the strategy will at best implement it halfheartedly and, at worst, on a day-to-day basis, do everything in their power to prove it wrong.

As another client, Kurt Weidenhaupt, CEO of American Precision Industries, said:

> I have been exposed to McKinsey, Boston Consulting Group, and Bain. They are all very capable and I'm sure their approach is very sound. The only problem is that their product is not of the people, by the people, through the people. It's not owned by the people who later have to live with it. When the strategy is developed by an outside third party, it is an alien product no matter how well it relates to the company.

In order to obtain commitment, key managers must be involved at each step of the process so that their views are heard and discussed. Participation, although it may seem time consuming, builds commitment and, in our experience, saves exponentially more time on the deployment end of the equation. Key managers buy into the strategy because they helped construct it. It is as much their strategy as the CEO's.

Many CEOs have used our process knowing the outcome in advance. They did so anyway, using it as a tool to tap the advice and knowledge of their people and to obtain commitment to the conclusions, so that implementation of the strategy can then proceed expeditiously. Still others, thinking they knew what the outcome would be, discovered new ideas, or flaws in their assumptions that would have caused difficulties down the road. By gathering the collective knowledge of key people, such ideas can be evaluated and problems can be flushed out and dealt with before they happen.

Three other of our CEO clients expressed it this way:

> I think the process increases management's understanding. I could probably have relayed that kind of thinking to that same group by other means, but not as successfully or in that same condensed timeframe. My belief is that the best strategy is the one that people believe in, because then they are driven to achieve it. You can have the best strategy on paper, but if nobody is driven to achieve it, you don't succeed. I believe that to be successful, your key people must be part of the process. The DPI process brings you to consensus on the Critical Issues that need to be addressed. In a very short timeframe, you can get the whole management team there.

Lesson 3: Don't outsource your thinking to an outside consultant.

SIN 4: OPERATIONAL MANAGERS ARE NOT TRAINED AS STRATEGIC THINKERS

Because most people spend their entire careers with an organization dealing exclusively with operational issues, they are not good strategic thinkers, as noted earlier. With few exceptions, we have found that only the CEO or the general manager sees the "big picture" and views the business and its environment in strategic terms. There usually is only one strategist in any organization, and that is the CEO. Most managers are so engrossed in operational activity that they have not developed the skill of thinking strategically. Therefore, they have difficulty coping with strategic issues, especially if these are sprung on them out of the blue at a "retreat."

"The problem," says Milton Lauenstein (a planning guru) in an article in the *Journal of Business Strategy*, "is that many executives have only the fuzziest notion of the functions of strategy formulation." This is why a process that guides the management team through these strategic issues is essential. Expecting your operational people to suddenly become strategists without such a tool will create more problems than it solves. On the flip side, given such a process, most senior managers will surprise you with their ability to think strategically and creatively once they have the framework, permission, and opportunity to do it.

Lesson 4: The CEO may be wise to encourage the participation of key subordinates in the strategy creation process for strictly educational value.

SIN 5: PLANNING NUMBEROSIS

People will implement a strategy more effectively if they understand the difference between a strategic process and either long-range or operational planning. They also need to be able to distinguish between strategic and operational issues. Participation in a clearly strategic process is an eye-opener for most managers. Most have never participated in a strategy session, or if they have, most find that they have primarily dealt with operational issues, and so never learn the difference. Again, Milton Lauenstein concurs:

> Management should understand that planning encompasses two distinct functions: long-range operational planning and strategy formulation. Confusing these two activities has contributed to

the sorry record of strategic planning. They are better performed separately.

The process needed to determine the future direction of an organization is not strategic planning but rather strategic thinking. Strategic thinking is a process that enables the management team to sit together and think through the qualitative aspects of the business and its environment. The team can then decide on a common and shared vision for the future of that company.

Although most companies have very sophisticated operational planning systems, they do not have a formal process of strategic thinking. As a result, even when they do want to spend some time at the "mountaintop retreat" to think through "where we are going as a company," they usually do not have a process to "think strategically" and quickly revert back to what they do best—operational issues!

Some companies have attempted to stitch together some strategic and some operational concepts into a "process," making the exercise laborious and confusing. Our suggestion is that the processes are different and must be separated. The factors and elements studied and evaluated in the Strategic Thinking Process are not the same as those in the operational planning system. For this reason, different time slots should be allocated to each process.

Lesson 5: Planning does not a strategy make.

SIN 6: MEANINGLESS MISSION STATEMENTS

In the last few years we have noticed a substantial increase in the number of corporations that have attempted to construct mission or vision statements that try to articulate the business's raison d'être. Unfortunately, these efforts are usually fruitless because they lack a structured process that could help them in their discussions. As a result, they end up with statements that are so "motherhood" in tone that everyone can agree with them, but useless as guides to help people make intelligent decisions on behalf of the group. Over time, the statement is quietly discarded. We will talk more about this in Chapter 7.

Lesson 6: A strategy statement must serve as a filter for decisions.

SIN 7: NO CRISIS, NO STRATEGY

Good times are another obstacle that impedes strategic thinking. When the numbers are good and all the charts are pointing upward, who needs to think about where they are going? The need to think about strategy and direction usually surfaces after a crisis. Our view is that strategic thinking should occur during good times as well as bad times because, if you wait until the bad times, it obviously becomes more difficult to do.

Bill Gates, one of the country's foremost strategic thinkers, is of this opinion as well:

> My success in business has largely been the result of my ability to focus on long-term goals and ignore short-term distractions. Taking a long-term view does not require brilliance but it does require dedication. When your business is healthy, it is difficult to behave as if you are in a crisis. That is why one of the toughest parts of managing, especially in a high-tech business, is to recognize the need for change and make it while you still have a chance.

Lesson 7: Strategizing should occur during good times as well as bad.

SIN 8: THE CRITICAL ISSUES ARE NOT IDENTIFIED

One aspect of strategy is its formulation. Another is thinking through its implications. Most strategic planning systems we have seen used in organizations don't encourage people to think through the implications of their strategy. As a result, they end up reacting to events as they are encountered and many people start losing faith in the strategy.

Every strategy, especially if it represents a change of direction, has implications. A good strategic process should help management identify, anticipate, and effectively manage the strategy's implications on the company's products, markets, customers, organization structure, systems, processes, personnel, and culture.

Lesson 8: Thinking through a strategy's implications is key to its success.

SIN 9: NOT UNDERSTANDING THE DIFFERENCE BETWEEN PROCESS AND CONTENT

In every strategy session that we facilitate, there are always two dynamics at work, namely process and content. Content is information or knowledge that is company or industry specific. Telephone company executives know a lot about cables, switch gears, PBXs, analog or digital devices, transmission, and so on. They know all this "content" because they were "brought up" in the industry and that is the content that is specific to that industry. It is part and parcel of their lexicon.

Executives at 3M or Caterpillar, however, know nothing about analog or digital devices or switch gears but they do know a lot about their own content. Caterpillar executives can mesmerize you for hours talking about metallurgy, welding, payloads, diesel horsepower, and their ability to "cut iron" better than anyone else. This is their content—and their comfort zone.

At 3M, all executives at the top have degrees in chemistry or chemical engineering and, as a result, can talk for hours about polymer chemistry and its use in coating and abrasive applications. Such is their world.

In order to climb up the ladder in most companies one needs to be a "content expert." This is necessary in order to be able to manage your way through the day-to-day "content-laden" operational issues. Most executives get to the top of their respective silos because of their content expertise, and rightly so.

At the strategic level, which is above the silos, content expertise alone is not sufficient. In fact, too much content knowledge may be a major impediment to good strategic thinking. This is because strategic thinking is process based rather than content based. Operational management requires the skill of analysis while strategic management requires the skill of synthesis.

Analaysis is the ability to study content and put it into logical *quantitative* pieces. *Synthesis* is the ability to make rational decisions based on highly subjective, sometimes ambiguous or incomplete, pieces of data. *Synthesis* is highly *qualitative* in nature. Strategic thinking falls into this category. It is the ability to take subjective data and opinions and bring these into an objective forum where rational decisions about the future of the enterprise can be made. In order to achieve this outcome, a CEO must have a "process of strategic thinking" that enables the CEO and the management team to assemble all available information, put it into perspective, separate pertinent from nonpertinent information, and draw out rational conclusions.

This approach works especially well for groups of decision makers in that it organizes information, separates fact from myth, and enables groups to reach consensus decisions objectively. Strategic thinking is, essentially, applied common sense, and is easy for anyone to understand once the methodology is available.

Lesson 9: Good strategic thinkers separate process from content.

SIN 10: USING A CONTENT CONSULTANT

A CEO who elects to seek outside assistance to help decide the future direction of the company is faced with having to choose between two very different types of consultants.

One is the "content" consultant. This is the traditional type of firm such as McKinsey, Bain, Boston Consulting Group, and Monitor. These consultants' claim to fame is that they have "industry experts" who know their industry better than the client does. Their objective is to formulate a strategy for you since your people are not as knowledgeable as their "experts." In other words, they do it for you, or to you.

In our view, this form of consulting may be appropriate in regards to operational issues, but it is not appropriate to strategy and strategic direction. These firms are "content" consultants and they are selling content.

Unfortunately, they sell the same content to all their clients in that industry. The best result is a me-too strategy that does not set you apart from your competitors and will never bring supremacy over them. You are, in our humble opinion, outsourcing your thinking.

A better service to a CEO and the management team, in our view, is to bring them a critical thinking process and guide them through that process. It is their content going into the process and it is their content coming out. When the strategy has been constructed by the people who have the best content to offer and who also have a vital stake in the outcome, such a strategy gets implemented much more quickly and much more successfully than one that is imposed on them by an outside third party.

Laurie Dippenaar, CEO of FirstRand, one of South Africa's largest financial services firms, agreed after the company used our process:

> What's affected us more than anything else is the fact that it systematically extracts the thinking and ideas from the executives'

heads, rather than imposing the consultant's thinking. I think it almost forces it out of their heads. That obviously leads to the strategy being owned by the company, rather than by the consultant. I'm not just repeating what DPI says, it actually works that way.

Lesson 10: Process assistance speeds up strategy implementation.

CHAPTER 4

STRATEGIZE FOR THE FUTURE, NOT THE PRESENT

More and more CEOs with whom we work tell us that it is not possible to predict the future, and it is therefore impossible to create a strategy for that future because changes are occurring faster and faster. Computer and biomedical technology, and political and economic conditions, to name a few factors, are changing faster and in more unexpected ways than ever before. As a result, many claim, no one can keep up with—much less predict—what else will happen in the future. To some extent, they are right.

Although this claim is partly true, the notion that change happens too quickly to be anticipated is somewhat of a myth. Our experience leads us to a different hypothesis.

In our view, there are two modes to deal with changes: proactively or reactively. Many executives deal with most changes in a reactive mode. Their skill is corrective in nature rather than being proactive or anticipatory. Proof of this is in the pudding. If their key skill was anticipatory, why were the CEOs and senior executives of thousands of corporations around the world caught by surprise by the advent of the Internet? We believe they just weren't looking. The Internet had been around for years.

We also contend that by using the following methodology, not only can you predict the future in your competitive landscape, you *must* predict it or your company will inevitably become a dinosaur.

ENVISION THE FUTURE

"How can anyone anticipate what the future will look like? The future is a big place, and no one has a crystal ball." This is usually the statement we hear immediately after we offer the above hypothesis. In fact, this reaction is understandable, yet our premise has a very simple and rational explanation. It has been shown that many things that look big and complex at first glance turn out to be an assembly of a limited number of smaller elements with a limited range of variables when scrutinized more closely. In reality, the future business arena (or "sandbox," as we at DPI refer to it) in which any company will compete down the road consists of 12 discrete compartments from which disruptive trends, or indications of the future, might emerge:

- Economic/Monetary trends
- Political/Regulatory trends
- Social/Demographic trends
- Market Conditions/Trends
- Customer Attributes/Habits
- Competitor Profiles/Mix
- Technology Evolution
- Manufacturing Capabilities/Processes
- Product Design/Content
- Sales/Marketing Methods
- Distribution Methods/Systems
- Resources—Natural/Human/Financial

Once the complexity of the Future Business Arena has been deciphered into these 12 "building blocks," one can begin to anticipate what the future will look like. By placing yourself, and your key executives, in a "time machine" and moving yourself ahead x years and describing the characteristics you believe each compartment will have at that time, you will have a very good "picture" of the future.

Then comes the next objection: "We don't have any futurists in our company. How can we foresee changes that will occur in the future?" The good news is that you don't need a guru to predict the future. Our contention is that most changes that will impact your business 10 years from now are in place in some form today. Most changes that will affect a company announce themselves well in advance of the time they will strike.

DECODING THE FUTURE TODAY

Naturally, one cannot be 100 percent right about the future, and totally unexpected events do show up. But, if one knows where to look, one can decode the future today. Our thesis says that the future is not one place, but a collection of five places where you can get a glimpse of the future that lies ahead.

Your future lies hidden in these five "futures":

1. The future ahead

2. The future beyond

3. The future behind

4. The future around

5. The future beside

The Future Ahead

This "future ahead" is a future that has already started but not yet arrived. Like a train, it has already left the station but has not yet arrived at its final destination. However, because it is moving along a set of rails whose direction is preestablished, one can determine its eventual destination.

This future ahead comes with a predetermined set of "rails" that allows one to foresee the eventual outcome. In fact, the future ahead comes on two sets of predictable "rails":

- The future that can be projected by extrapolating current phenomena
- The future that is branching along two or more sets of paths or "rails"

Let's look at them one at a time. The first is the future ahead that can be projected, or predicted reasonably accurately, because it is an extrapolation of current and predictable phenomenon. An example is demographics. It is a fact today that by the year 2010, in the United States, 50 percent of the population will be over 50 years old, 30 percent over 60, and 250,000 people over 100 years old. That future has already left the station. It has not yet arrived at its ultimate destination, but it will arrive. This future started after World War II and has been progressing through the U.S. population and building momentum each year since then. That trend, which will reach its peak in 2010, could have been projected for the last two or three decades because it is a trend that is traveling along an irreversible, preestablished "track."

However, there is an interesting dichotomy happening with these demographics. Most of the remainder of the world is going in the opposite direction! The majority of the population of Mexico is under 25 years of age, as is most of that of Asia. This dichotomy will have an enormous impact on the design of many products and marketing plans. An example might be exercise equipment, which one of our clients designs and makes. Until recently, this company had been designing exercise equipment on the concept that "one size fits all." In other words, every machine was believed to serve a uniform, worldwide need.

However, sales in the company's home market, the United States, were beginning to drop and management couldn't determine why. Using our Strategic Thinking Process, they concluded that the possible cause might be the aging U.S. population. Some further research proved this hypothesis to be correct. Older people have "stretching" and "flexibility" needs, while younger people have "strength" and "endurance" needs. Our client's machines were clearly designed to satisfy "strength and endurance" needs, because they had not looked into the future to see the impact of this change that had been predetermined decades ago. As a result of having recognized this "future ahead," the company is now marketing a brand-new-to-the-market machine specifically designed to satisfy the "stretch and flexibility" needs of the above-50-year-old market. This machine is only marketed in the United States and Canada, where the "future" demographics give them a new opportunity that their competitors have not yet recognized.

The second type of future ahead is the one that has started but is branching along two or more "sets of rails" or paths. As a result, its eventual destination, or outcome, is projectable but not totally predictable because the path that will eventually win out is not yet known. However, being able to project two possible outcomes is better than projecting 20 or no outcomes. An example of the "branching" future came with the introduction of the videocassette recorder, or VCR. When that event occurred, two standards emerged in the United States—Betamax and VHS—and the eventual winner was not clearly identifiable until both standards were in the market for several years. Right from the beginning, however, the advantages of VHS were clear, and anyone could have projected that it would probably be the winning standard.

Another example that has not yet played itself out might be the electric/gasoline hybrid car versus the hydrogen fuel-cell car versus the gasoline-powered car. The political and environmental problems associated with burning hydrocarbons and the need for alternatives are obvious. But what branch will the future ahead follow—and how might that and other related changes affect your business?

The Future Beyond

The future beyond the future ahead is one that is projectable because it comes with some predictable boundaries. In other words, this event or trend comes with some known constraints that will make its eventual outcome almost predictable.

A current example is Airbus's announcement that it will construct a Super Jumbo airplane. Without much effort, Boeing can quite accurately project the size of that aircraft and the number of passengers it will carry. The laws of physics have already determined that data. The laws of physics have determined that if the aircraft travels at higher than Mach 1 speed, the windows will shatter. Therefore, it will have to travel at slightly less than Mach 1 speed. At that speed, the optimum fuel-to-weight ratio will limit the size of the aircraft to approximately 800 passengers. Without any "guessing," this future beyond can be quite accurately projected since it comes with known constraints, or boundaries.

The Future Behind

What can one learn about the future by looking at the "future behind"? The answer is simple: History repeats itself. The future behind is one that happened in the past, yet it provides a template for the interpretation of current events that will have future implications. By looking at the future behind, one can learn about the behavior of past events or trends. As Andrew Grove, ex-CEO of Intel, once said: "If you want to know what will happen in the technology in the next 10 years, simply look at what has happened in the last 10 years."

One repeating phenomenon we can learn from is that of "disruptive technologies" that gather so much inertia that a temporary crash will not stop their momentum. Eventually, after an initial frenzy of speculation and a "bubble burst," they come roaring back. The following paragraphs give some examples.

In the mid-1700s there was a canal mania in Europe, with hundreds of companies building canals all over Europe. Then, suddenly the bubble burst and many declared it a commercial disaster. Yet, 10 years later there were almost five times as many canals as there were before the crash. Canals became the backbone of commerce in Europe, and that inertia made the canal phenomenon unstoppable until years later when the railroads came along.

In the mid-1800s in the United Kingdom, a rail mania took place. Hundreds of companies were laying down hundreds of miles of rails across the country. Huge and, it turns out, highly speculative investments were made. Again, the bubble burst and fortunes were lost, yet 10 years later there were thousands of miles more rail in use than there were before the crash. Like the canals before them, rails eventually became the backbone of the industrial revolution, and their inertia made that trend unstoppable until the advent of cars and trucks.

At the beginning of this century in the United States there were over 100 manufacturers producing a few thousand cars. Then suddenly the industry crashed and most of the early producers went out of business. Yet, some 15 years later, there were half a dozen companies producing over a million cars per year. The introduction of the automobile was an event that came with so much inertia that it was unstoppable.

What recent innovation, which has recently had a setback, will coming roaring back? Right. The Internet! The Internet is a technology with so much inertia that it will eventually change the modus operandi of every company in the world. In fact, it's happening right now, and its impact will gradually increase for the foreseeable future, just like the canal, the railroad, and the automobile did in the past.

Looking at the future behind can give us great insights about the future ahead. What changes or trends that are happening in your sandbox today might have blueprints in the past to help you to see where they might be going?

The Future Around

The "future around" is one that is already present in your sandbox but is not yet fully deployed. These are events or trends that are in your sandbox and will amplify over time. If you have not taken stock of these events, they will catch you by surprise and bite you badly. An example is the work going on in the area of human genomes. No pharmaceutical company in the world can afford to ignore the developments occurring in this area of their sandbox, as they will dramatically change the nature of their future products. Another similar area of development is bioelectronics—the convergence of biological and electronic and even mechanical technologies. Might the exercise equipment company mentioned earlier be interested in that?

The Future Beside

The fifth type of future you will encounter consists of events or trends already in place in adjacent sandboxes that will eventually migrate into yours—the "future beside." Unfortunately, these sandboxes are probably not on your current radar screen and if you haven't spotted them, they will catch you by surprise when they arrive. Two examples follow in the next paragraphs.

If I were in the liquor business, I would pay close attention to what happened in the tobacco sandbox. There is a good chance that the litigation that hit that sandbox will eventually migrate into the "liquor sandbox."

A second example is what recently happened to McDonald's. A man in Vermont who has developed cancer claims that his disease was caused by his daily intake of the fat in that chain's hamburgers. Maybe that's why they have announced lower-fat french fries. If I were KFC, which is in an adjacent "fast-food sandbox," I would start tracking this event, because it will eventually migrate its way into my sandbox.

Recently, PepsiCo's CEO, Steve Reinemund, announced a goal of making at least 50 percent of the company's products "nutritious." Do you think they may have glanced into the McDonald's sandbox?

Exploring adjacent sandboxes for events that are happening there will enable you to quickly assess the ability of these events to migrate into yours and, more importantly, enable you to take actions to manage and/or control these events to your advantage.

Auto companies, for example, have looked at the adjacent sports equipment sandbox and noticed a trend—an explosion in outdoor sports. Look around and you will quickly see that Subaru and several others have designed very successful "lifestyle" vehicles that appeal to those who either participate in, or want to appear to participate in, these exciting activities.

FIVE PLACES TO LOOK FOR THE FUTURE

It is in these five places—the futures ahead, beyond, behind, around, and beside—that the future stalks and may spring into your sandbox and catch you unprepared. Or, if you look, you may discover opportunities that others have not yet recognized. And that brings us to a wise quote from one of our clients:

You cannot predict the future, but you can prepare for and control the future.

CHAPTER 5

VISION AND STRATEGY: TWO INSEPARABLE CONCEPTS

The "vision thing," said George H. Bush shortly after being elected president, "is something I don't understand." Less than four years after mouthing those words, he was ousted from office. "IBM doesn't need a vision or strategy," quipped Lou Gerstner at his first press conference the week after being named CEO. When he returned to his office, he was immediately bombarded by an avalanche of phone calls. But this onslaught of calls didn't come from the press or other outsiders. They came from his own employees who wanted to remind him that Thomas Watson made IBM one of the world's most successful companies through his "vision" of automating data processing with computers that would "substantially increase the productivity of corporations and contribute to raising the standard of living of people all over the world."

THE VISION/STRATEGY RELATIONSHIP

Although the concepts of vision and strategy are frequently used, few executives understand the relationship between them. Let us attempt to demystify these two separate but complementary concepts. Vision, in our view, is the construction of a "mental picture" of what an organization should "look like" sometime in the future. It is the "painting," by management, of a "profile" that the company should grow into over time. Strategy, in our view, is a verbal description of the "business concept" that the enterprise will deploy to realize that "picture" or "vision" of itself in the future. The content of a vision will be discussed in this chapter.

THE POWER OF VISION

A vision serves several purposes in an organization. First and foremost, it captures the organization's "future intent." In other words, it paints a "picture" of what the company intends to become, not what it is today. A vision should stand the test of time and perpetuate the enterprise over long time-frames. A vision can serve several purposes:

- *A vision bonds.* Companies are populated with individuals possessing a diverse set of skills, languages, cultures, personalities, and cultures. A vision can give people a common cause and direct their energies toward a unifying goal.
- *A vision inspires.* Although all corporations measure their progress over time with numbers—growth, profits, or both—numbers generally do not inspire ordinary people to do extraordinary things. But a more "noble" vision and strategy can inspire beyond anyone's expectation.
- *A vision is an anchor.* When times are difficult, a vision gives an organization an "anchor" that will steady the ship and hold everyone together until the storm passes.
- *A vision is a potent competitive tool.* Having a sense of what one wants to become when grown up gives the organization an enormous competitive advantage over those that, as my 11-year-old daughter would say, "haven't got a clue."

REQUIRED ATTRIBUTES
OF A SUCCESSFUL VISION

A vision that will mobilize a large population of people who might not have any other attachment to an organization than that it is their job and source of income, must have certain attributes in order to get ordinary people to do extraordinary things.

- *A vision must be clear.* The vision cannot be ambiguous. Most people in an organization do not want to be leaders—they simply want to be good followers. As such, what they want to know from their leaders is: "Where are you taking me so I can decide whether I want to follow you there?" As a result, the leader must design a clear vision that can quickly and clearly be understood by all employees.

- *A vision must be compelling.* A goal of becoming a billion-dollar company will not motivate ordinary people to do extraordinary things. Numbers usually are not compelling enough to mobilize large groups of people to want to achieve beyond their capabilities. In order to motivate people to overachieve, the vision must "compel" people to want to overachieve voluntarily. Thus the reason for Steve Jobs attracting John Scully to join Apple, even though he gave up a very lucrative job with Pepsi—not with the promise of large financial incentives, but rather with the "opportunity to change the world." What foresight Steve Jobs exhibited back in 1971! That is exactly what the PC industry, led in large part by Jobs and Apple, has done.

- *A vision must be distinctive.* Not many people want to work for an imitator, where every transaction the company engages in turns out to be based strictly on price. That is not a fun world. The best companies have a distinctive vision that does not attempt to imitate their competitors but sets them apart from these competitors. Like the super racehorse Secretariat, their notion of competition is not to run side by side with their competitors but, rather, to lead the next best competitor by 31 lengths, pulling farther and farther ahead with each lap of the business cycle. As Samuel Johnson once said, "No man has achieved greatness by imitating another man."

- *A vision must be consistent.* A vision that is constantly being adjusted is usually not going to impress anyone, particularly your own troops. Visions that are forever changing reflect the lack of any forward thinking and will become the butt of everyone's corporate jokes—the proverbial "vision of the week."

THE STRATEGY/OPERATIONS RELATIONSHIP

Over the last two or three decades hundreds of books have been published on the subject of strategy. Unfortunately, most of these books have confused rather than demystified this subject. The reason, in our view, is that each author uses the word *strategy* with a different meaning. Some authors define strategy as the goal or objective, while others define it as the means or the tactics. Others view strategy as long-term planning versus short-term. After reading most of these books we became as confused as their authors.

WHAT IS STRATEGY?

Our definition is simple. Strategy is *what* and operations is *how*. Strategy determines *what* you want to become as a company, and operations determines *how* you get there. These two types of thinking are distinct and should be conducted separately, since they include distinct concepts that should not be intertwined. Unfortunately, in most organizations, they are intertwined under the catchall phenomenon of "planning," and their distinctiveness and usefulness are vastly diluted.

"Strategy" and "operations" require different processes of thinking and contain different concepts. Our experience has shown that few companies are highly proficient at both. In fact, all organizations can be found in one of four modes of proficiency around these two skills, which are illustrated by the matrix shown in Figure 5-1.

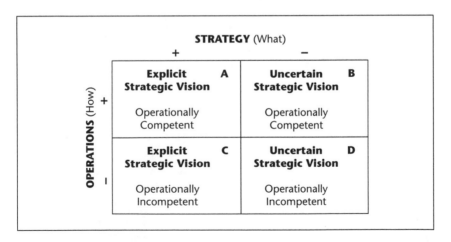

FIGURE 5-1

Some organizations are proficient at both strategy and operations. In other words, they have a clear strategy that is sound and well understood and they are very competent operationally. Such companies include Wal-Mart, Intel, Southwest Airlines, Charles Schwab, Home Depot, and Johnson & Johnson (quadrant A). (See Figure 5-1a.)

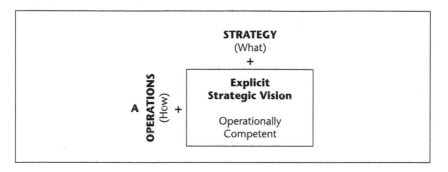

FIGURE 5-1A

Some organizations belong in quadrant C—strategically competent but operationally ineffective. This quadrant would include most of the 140 to 150 personal computer manufacturers of the last two decades whose strategy of being the best "Wintel" clone proved to be short-lived. (See Figure 5-1b.)

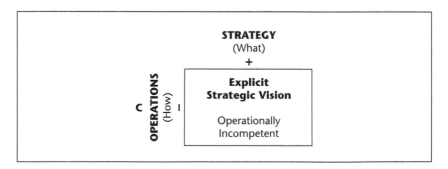

FIGURE 5-1B

In quadrant D we find the worst of both worlds—companies that have shown incompetence at both. This quadrant would recently have included Kmart, Xerox, Polaroid, and Compaq. (See Figure 5-1c.)

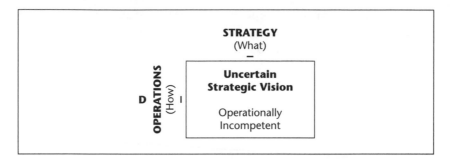

FIGURE 5-1C

The quadrant in which we find most companies however, is B—operationally competent but strategically deficient. (See Figure 5-1d.)

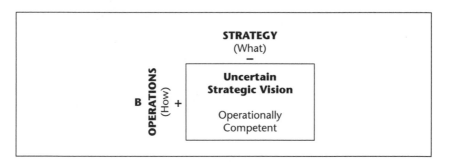

FIGURE 5-1D

These companies belong to the Christopher Columbus School of Management:

- When he left, he did not know where he was going.
- When he got there, he did not know where he was.
- When he got back, he could not tell where he had been.

THE CEO'S VISION: THE CORNERSTONE OF STRATEGY

As stated previously, many CEOs that we work with have a "vision" in their heads as to what they want their company to "look like" at some time in the future. Frequently, that "look" is different from what the company "looks like" today. (See Figure 5-2.)

FIGURE 5-2

WHAT IS STRATEGIC THINKING?

Strategic thinking, to us, is the type of thinking that goes on in the heads of the CEO and the management team, which attempts to transform this conceptual and abstract vision into a working and dynamic tool that we call a *strategic profile*. In fact, strategic thinking is akin to "picture painting," whereby the management of an organization literally "draws" a picture or profile of what they want the business to look like at some point in the future. (See Figures 5-3 and 5-4.)

Why should the management team take time to do this? How will this effort help the organization?

The answer is simple. Such a profile will give the organization's employees a "target" to help them make consistent and logical decisions over time. People can then pursue decisions and plans that fall within the "frame" of the picture and avoid pursuing those that fall *outside* that frame.

FIGURE 5-3

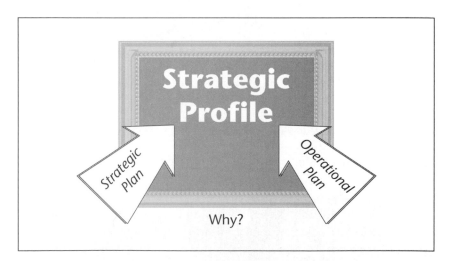

FIGURE 5-4

This leads to the next question: If I wish to draw a "picture" of what the business should look like in the future to help my people make better decisions, what should I draw in that picture? (See Figure 5-5.)

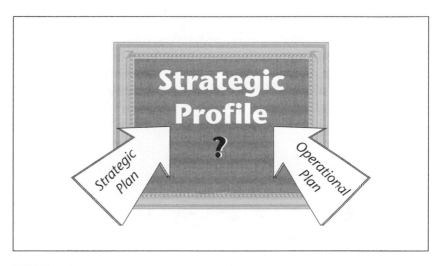

FIGURE 5-5

An organization's profile is found in four basic traits. Just as a person's profile is made up of eyes, ears, nose, and mouth, an organization's profile is found in four areas—its products, customers, industry or market segments, and geographic markets. (See Figure 5-6.)

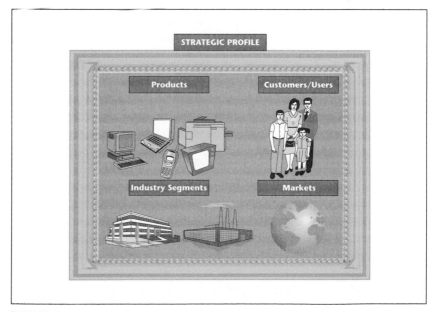

FIGURE 5-6

Everything else that goes on in an organization is either an input to this profile (such as capital, manufacturing processes, and distribution systems) or outputs from this profile (such as margins, profits, and dividends).

However, Strategic Thinking goes one step further: identifying the products, customers, market segments, and geographic markets upon which the company should place more emphasis, as well as those upon which it should place less emphasis. (See Figure 5-7.)

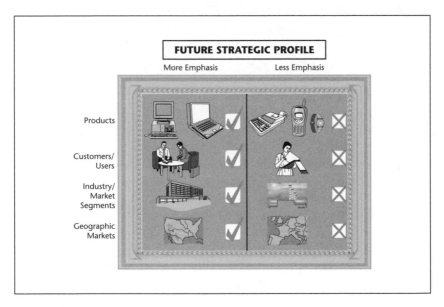

FIGURE 5-7

This Strategic Filter is then used as a tool to *allocate resources* and to *screen opportunities*. These are the two categories of decisions that go to determining the company's future look.

What, then, determines which products, customers, and markets to emphasize more and which ones less? The answer is simple: the organization's Driving Force—a subject we will discuss in the next chapter.

CHAPTER 6

DRIVING FORCE: THE DNA OF STRATEGY

To achieve competitive supremacy, a company needs to have a strategy that establishes a significant and sustainable point of differentiation—one that enables it to add unique value that competitors will have difficulty duplicating. Of course, most companies have a strategy of some sort. Yet few are able to create a clear definition of that single differentiating factor—if there is one—that has enabled the company to be successful in the past. Still fewer have looked down the road to create a scenario, or strategy, that will enable them to be successful in the environment they will face in the future.

We call that defining factor the *Driving Force*. It is the component of the business that is unique to that company and is the key determinant of the choices management makes with regard to future products, future customers, and future markets. Without an understanding of, and agreement upon, that Driving Force, management will have a difficult time creating a strategy for the future that will breed supremacy over its competitors.

WHAT MAKES YOUR STRATEGY TICK?

The best way to determine whether a CEO and the management team have a strategy is to observe them in meetings as they try to decide whether or not to pursue an opportunity. When we have sat in on such meetings, we have noticed that management would put each opportunity through a hierarchy of different filters. The ultimate filter, however, was always whether there was a fit between the products, customers, and markets that the opportunity brought and one key component of the organization. If they found a fit there, they would feel comfortable with that opportunity, and would proceed with it. If they did not find a fit there, they would pass.

Different companies, however, looked for different kinds of fit. Some companies looked for a fit between similar products. Others were less concerned about the similarity of products than about a fit with the customer base. Still others were not interested in the similarity of products or of the customer base but rather a fit with the technology involved, or a fit with its sales and marketing method, or its distribution system. The following paragraph describes some examples.

What fit was Daimler looking for when it bought Chrysler? Obviously, the fit was one between similar products. Johnson & Johnson (J&J), on the other hand, looked for an entirely different kind of fit when it acquired Neutrogena creams from one company and the clinical laboratories of Kodak, each bringing dramatically different products. J&J was looking for a fit between the class of customers served—doctors, nurses, patients, and mothers—the heartbeat of J&J's strategy. 3M looked for still another fit when choosing opportunities. 3M did not care what the products were or who the customers were. What 3M did care about was whether there was a fit between the technology that the opportunity required and the technology—polymer chemistry—that lay at the root of 3M's strategy. If the technology fit, then 3M management felt comfortable in pursuing that opportunity.

10 STRATEGIC AREAS

The next question that came to our minds was: What are the areas of an organization that cause management to decide how to allocate resources or choose opportunities? We discovered that each of the 400-plus companies we had worked with consisted of 10 basic components.

1. Every company offered a *product* or *service* for sale.

2. Every company sold its product(s) or service(s) to a certain *class of customer* or end user.

3. These customers or end users always resided in certain *categories of markets*.

4. Every company employed *technology* in its product or service.

5. Every company had a *production facility* located somewhere that had a certain amount of *capacity* or certain *in-built capabilities* in the making of a product or service.

6. Every company used certain *sales or marketing methods* to acquire customers for its product or service.

7. Every company employed certain *distribution methods* to get a product from its location to a customer's location.

8. Every company made use of *natural resources* to one degree or another.

9. Every company monitored its *size and growth* performance.

10. Every company monitored its *return or profit* performance.

As a result of these observations, two key messages emerged. First, all 10 areas exist in every company. Second, and more importantly, one of the 10 areas tends to dominate the strategy of a company consistently over time. It is to favor or leverage this one area of the business time and again that determines how management allocates resources or chooses opportunities. In other words, one component of the business is the engine of the strategy—that company's so-called DNA, or Driving Force. This Driving Force determines the array of products, customers, industries, and geographic markets that management chooses to emphasize more and emphasize less. (See Figures 6-1 and 6-2.)

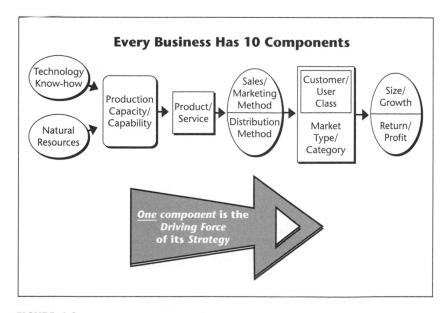

FIGURE 6-1

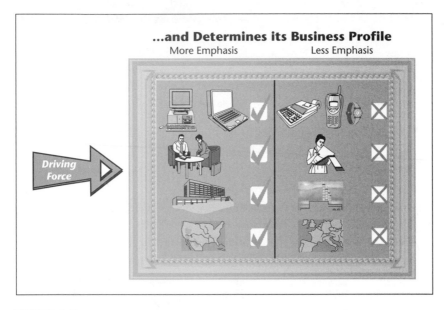

FIGURE 6-2

In order to explain this concept more clearly, one needs to look at an organization as a body in motion. Every organization, on any one day, is an organism that has movement and momentum and is going forward in some direction. Our thesis is that one of the 10 components of a company's operation is the strategic engine behind the decisions that management makes. Some typical examples follow.

A Strategy Driven by a Single Product or Service

A company that is pursuing a Product-driven strategy has deliberately decided to limit its strategy to a single product and its derivatives. Therefore, all future products and the "current" product are linear, genetic extrapolations of the very first product that company ever made. In other words, the look, form, or function of the product stays constant over time. Examples are Coca-Cola (soda), Boeing (airplanes), Michelin (tires), Harley-Davidson (motorcycles), and many of the automobile manufacturers (GM, Toyota, and Volkswagen).

Strategy Driven by a User or Customer Class

A company that is driven by a User or Customer Class has deliberately decided to restrict its strategy to a describable and circumscribable class of end users or customers (people). These end users or customers are the only ones the company serves. The company then identifies a common need of the user or customer class and responds with a wide array of genetically unrelated products. Examples are Johnson & Johnson (doctors, nurses, patients, and mothers), AARP (adults over 50), Playboy ("entertainment for men"), and USAA (military officers).

Strategy Driven by Market Type or Category

A company that is driven by Market Category has deliberately decided to limit its strategy to a describable marketplace or market type. The company identifies a common need among buyers in that market and then responds with a wide variety of genetically unrelated products. Examples are American Hospital Supply (now Allegiance) and Disney's concept of "wholesome entertainment for the family."

Strategy Driven by Technology

A Technology-driven company is rooted in some basic, hard technology, such as chemistry or physics, or some soft technology, such as know-how or expertise. The company then goes looking for applications for its technology or expertise. Once it finds an application, the company develops a product that is infused with its technology for that application and offers the new product to all the customers in that market with a similar application. While growing that business, the company goes around looking for another application to repeat the same process. Examples are DuPont (chemistry), 3M (polymers), and Intel (microprocessor architecture).

Strategy Driven by Production Capability or Capacity

A company driven by Production Capacity has a substantial investment in its production facility. The key phrase heard around the company is "keep it humming"—three shifts per day, seven days per week, 365 days per year. The strategy is to keep the production facility operating at a maximum level of capacity. Examples are steel companies, refineries, and pulp and paper companies.

A company driven by Production Capability has incorporated some distinctive capabilities into its production process that allows it to do things to its products that its competitors have difficulty duplicating. As a result, when the company goes looking for opportunities, it restricts its search to opportunities in which these capabilities can be exploited. Specialty converters in a variety of industries are good examples.

Strategy Driven by Sales or Marketing Method

When a strategy is driven by a Sales or Marketing Method, the company has a unique or distinctive method of selling to its customers. All the opportunities it pursues must utilize that selling method. Examples are companies that sell door to door (Avon, Mary Kay, and Amway), direct-response companies (Dell and K-tel), and catalog companies (L.L. Bean and Land's End). A recent addition is Amazon.com, whose strategy is to use the Internet to sell a wide array of consumer products.

Strategy Driven by Distribution Method

A company driven by a Distribution Method has a unique or distinctive approach of moving tangible or intangible things from one place to another. All the opportunities such a company pursues must optimize that distribution method. Examples are Wal-Mart, FedEx, Home Depot, Staples, and Nextel.

Strategy Driven by Natural Resources

A company whose entire purpose is the pursuit and exploitation of oil, gas, ore, gold, timber, or other resources can be said to be pursuing a Natural Resource–driven strategy. Examples are Exxon, Shell, Newmont Gold, and Anglo-American Mining.

Strategy Driven by Size or Growth

A company driven by Size or Growth is usually a conglomerate of unrelated businesses. Its sole strategic interest is growth and size for their own sake.

Strategy Driven by Return or Profit

A company whose sole strategic focus is a minimum level of Return or Profit is also a conglomerate of unrelated businesses. The best example during the 1970s was ITT under Harold Geneen. His dictum of "an increase in quarterly earnings, every quarter, from every unit, regardless what" led ITT into 276 different businesses. These businesses were deliberately kept separate so that when any one unit missed its profit target for three consecutive quarters, it was gone in the fourth. Other examples are Tyco, AlliedSignal, and General Electric, under former CEO Jack Welch, where his dictum of an 18 percent return on assets (ROA) landed GE into everything from lightbulbs to television networks to financial services to turbines and aircraft engines.

KEY STRATEGIC QUESTIONS

When we take a client through our Strategic Thinking Process, we have the CEO and the management team debate three key questions to enable them to identify the company's current and future Driving Force.

- Question 1: Which component of your business is currently driving your strategy and has made you look as you look today in terms of current products, customers, and markets?

  If there are 10 people in the room, how many answers do you think we get? Ten, and sometimes more. The reason is simple. Each person has a different perception as to which component of the business is the Driving Force behind the company's strategy. These different interpretations lead to different visions of where the organization is headed. The difficulty, while this is going on, is that each member of the team makes decisions that pull the company left and right, so the company zigzags its way forward without establishing supremacy in any one sandbox. The inevitable result is that resources are wrongly employed.

  The methodology we bring to bear at DPI encourages management to look back at the history of decisions they have made and, by doing so, recognize a pattern. Typically, most of their decisions were made to favor one component of the business. Thus, the management team recognizes the current Driving Force behind their current strategy.
- Question 2: Which component of the company should be the Driving Force behind the company's strategy in the future?

  This question is more important, because it indicates that the company's future strategy should not be an extrapolation of the current strategy. Any strategy needs to accommodate the environment the company will encounter in the future, and that environment could be very different from the one encountered in the past. This question is the basis for envisioning "breakaway" strategies that explode the assumptions of the current sandbox to envision a new one that offers significantly greater opportunities to establish supremacy over competitors. Such a strategy enables the company to create, or reposition itself in, a future sandbox in a way that offers it more growth and profitability than competitors, and control of that sandbox.

- Question 3: What impact will this Driving Force have on the choices the company must make regarding future products, future customers, and future markets?

  The Driving Force the company chooses as the engine of its strategy will determine the choices its management makes as to the products, customers, and markets that they will and will not emphasize in the future. These choices will shape the profile of the company, and maybe even the industry, over time. Each Driving Force will cause management to make very different choices that will make the company look very differently than the way it looks today. In other words, just as your personal DNA determines what you look like and why you look different from other people, the same is true for your corporate DNA. The component of the company you select as the DNA of its strategy will determine what that company will eventually look like and why it will look different from its competitors.

FUNDAMENTAL CONCEPT OF STRATEGY

The concept of Driving Force—to us at DPI—is fundamental for any successful CEO to understand. It is the recognition and understanding, by all members of the management team, of that one predominant component of the business—its Driving Force—that will allow the organization to formulate a strategy based on a distinctive and sustainable advantage that can give it long-term supremacy over its competition.

AREAS OF EXCELLENCE: AMPLIFYING THE SUPREMACY GAP

Areas of Excellence are specific skills or capabilities that a company deliberately nurtures to a higher level of proficiency than any other competitor.

Superiority in two or three unique capabilities that give impetus to the Driving Force keeps the organization's strategy strong and healthy and widens the supremacy gap over their competitors.

Some CEOs understand this concept and know exactly which Areas of Excellence give the company its strategic advantage over its competitors.

David Glass, the former CEO of Wal-Mart, said: "Our distribution facilities are the key to our success. If we do anything better than other folks, that's it."

Knowing that, Glass invested over $1 billion during his reign on sophisticated computer systems to maintain and increase that supremacy gap.

Fred Smith, CEO of FedEx, also knows what contributes to its supremacy over its competitors: "The main difference between us and our competitors is that we have more capacity to track, trace, and control items in the system."

DETERMINING THE STRATEGIC CAPABILITIES THAT AMPLIFY SUPREMACY

Product-Driven Strategy

A Product/Service-driven company survives on the quality of its product or service. Witness the automobile wars. Who's winning? The Japanese. Why have Americans been buying Japanese cars and even been willing to pay premium prices for the last 40 years? The answer is simple: The Japanese make better cars. The bottom line for a Product-driven strategy is, the best product wins. Raster Graphics, a small maker of specialized computer printers, and a DPI client, achieved a stunning victory over two much larger competitors—Xerox and a division of Lockheed. It ultimately drove both out of the computer printer business through a simple, unwavering commitment to developing a steady stream of better printers than their competitors'.

One Area of Excellence, therefore, is Product Development. Compared to U.S. cars, Japanese cars of the late 1950s (when cars from Japan came onto the market) were far inferior. But Japanese car manufacturers understood well that "the best car wins," and they strove to improve the product—to make it better and better—to the extent that Japanese cars eventually surpassed the quality of U.S. cars. Ford, traditionally Product-driven, is learning this lesson the hard way. Wandering into ancillary businesses has diverted resources—and the company's attention—away from the constant drive to develop new and better cars. It has cost them their supremacy.

A second Area of Excellence is Service. IBM, which also pursues a Product-driven strategy, is well aware of this requirement. Ask IBM clients what they admire most about IBM, and 99 out of 100 will say they admire its service capability. IBM deliberately invests more resources in its service function than any of its competitors do, and thus it has a considerable edge in response time and infrequency of product failures.

In a Product-driven mode, you amplify your supremacy by cultivating excellence in Product Development and Product Service.

Market Category / User Class–Driven Strategy

An organization that is Market Category / User Class–driven must also cultivate excellence to optimize its strategic supremacy, but in dramatically different areas.

A Market Category / User Class–driven company has placed its destiny in the hands of a market category or a class of users. Therefore, to survive and prosper, it must know its user class or market category better than any competitor. Market or User Research, then, is one Area of Excellence. The company must know everything there is to know about its market or user in order to quickly detect any changes in habits, demographics, likes and dislikes. Procter & Gamble interviews consumers (particularly homemakers) over two million times a year in an attempt to anticipate trends that can be converted into product opportunities.

A second Area of Excellence for a Market Category/User Class–driven company is User Loyalty. Through a variety of means, these companies, over time, build customer loyalty to the company's products or brands. They then trade on this loyalty. Over time, Johnson & Johnson has convinced its customers that its products are "safe." Johnson & Johnson will not let anything undermine the loyalty it has developed because of this guarantee. Whenever a Johnson & Johnson product might prove to be a hazard to a person's health, it is immediately removed from the market.

Production Capacity / Capability–Driven Strategy

When there is a glut of paper on the market, the first thing a paper company does is lower the price. Therefore, to survive during the period of low prices, one has to have the lowest costs among any of the competitors. To achieve this objective, Manufacturing or Plant Efficiency is a required Area of Excellence. This is why paper companies are forever investing their profits in their mills—to make them more and more efficient. An industry that has lost sight of this notion is the U.S. steel industry. By not improving their plants, they have lost business to the Italians and Japanese, who have continually implemented such improvements. One notable exception in the United States is Nucor, which has done very well because it has the lowest costs of any of the steel mills, including the Japanese and Italian ones. As a result, Nucor's revenues and profits have consistently improved.

DPI client Teckwah, a Singapore-based commercial printer, had traditionally been Production Capacity–driven. The company had done all it could to optimize its printing operations, yet it realized that a saturated market allowed little growth. As Managing Director Thomas Chua said: "There's no point to trying to keep up the capacity if you don't have the business."

In going through the Strategic Thinking Process the company decided to focus on a couple of industries and expand its range of services beyond printing. It, therefore, changed its Driving Force to Market-driven and changed its Areas of Excellence to Market Research and User Loyalty. Exceptional growth in both top and bottom lines has resulted.

A second Area of Excellence for the Production Capacity–driven strategy is Substitute Marketing. Capacity-driven companies excel at substituting what comes off their machines for other things. The paper people are trying to substitute paper for plastic; the plastic people are trying to substitute plastic for aluminum; the concrete people are trying to substitute concrete for steel; and so forth. The same is true in the transportation industry, where bus companies are trying to replace trains with buses, train companies are trying to replace airplanes with trains, and so forth. This is why Southwest doesn't consider its competitors to be other airline companies but rather Greyhound Bus, and most of Southwest's customers have come at the expense of Greyhound.

A Production Capability–driven company is one that has built special capabilities into its production process that allow it to make products with features that are difficult for its competitors to duplicate. It then looks for opportunities where these capabilities can be exploited.

Job shops and specialty printers are examples. As a result, these companies are always looking to add to or enhance these distinctive production capabilities, because therein resides their competitive advantage.

Technology/Know-How–Driven Strategy

A company that is Technology-driven uses technology as its edge. Thus, an Area of Excellence required to win under this strategy is Research, either basic or applied. Sony, for example, spends 10 percent of its sales on research, which is 2 or 3 percent more than any competitor. Its motto, "research is the difference," is proof that the company's management recognizes the need to excel in this area.

By pushing the technology further than any competitor, new products and new markets will emerge. Technology-driven companies usually create markets rather than respond to needs, and they usually follow their technology wherever it leads them.

A second Area of Excellence for Technology-driven companies is Applications Marketing. Technology-driven companies seem to have a knack for finding applications for their technology that call for highly differentiated products. For example, 3M has used its knowledge of polymer technology to develop Post-it note pads and some 60,000 other products.

Each Driving Force brings with it a requirement to excel in a very different set of skills. No company can outexcel its competitors across the board. One cannot outmuscle every competitor in the market. Therefore, it becomes important to identify the company's Driving Force and the corresponding Areas of Excellence, which are then given preferential treatment. These areas keep the strategy strong and healthy and build a long-term strategic advantage over competitors.

CHAPTER 7

Meaningless Mission Statement to Effective Strategic Filter

"**F**ollow me," shouted Lawrence of Arabia to his Arab troops as he led his army's charge into battle.

Although the term *leadership* is frequently used, few executives in business today can be considered true leaders. The ultimate test of a leader is whether he or she will be followed, as Lawrence of Arabia was followed by an army of people who were not of his race or religion. For the followers to allow themselves to be led assumes their implicit belief in the leader's ability.

Many books have been written on leadership, but few have been able to describe it in comprehensive terms except to attribute it to a "trait of personality." Nor have they been able to describe the skills of leadership in any detail. John P. Kotter, in his book *The Leadership Factor*, explains that leadership can be defined, analyzed, and learned. He also points out that it is not taught in business schools. Unfortunately, like the others, he did not articulate how leadership can be attained. Jack Welch, the former CEO of General Electric, views it this way:

> A leader is someone who can develop a vision of what he or she wants their business, their unit, their activity to do and be. A leader is somebody who is able to articulate to the entire unit what the unit is, and gain through a sharing of the discussion—listening and talking—an acceptance of that vision. And most importantly, a leader can then relentlessly drive implementation of that vision to a successful conclusion.

This definition of leadership is as good as any definition we could conjure up ourselves. However, we have found that many CEOs have great difficulty articulating their vision to their people. Their strategy, vision, or both, is usually implicit and resides in their heads. Unfortunately, as long as the strategy of an organization is implicit and resides in one or two people's heads, it is very difficult for others around these one or two individuals to implement a strategy that is not clear to them. Followers want to know where they are being led. General Motors' former CEO, Roger Smith, said that the only thing he would do differently if he started his term as CEO over again would be to communicate his vision of GM earlier and more frequently than he did. He cited this failure as the major reason for his inability to turn the company around.

As a result, most CEOs realize that it becomes important to make the strategy, or the business concept, explicit.

MEANINGLESS MISSION STATEMENTS

Over the last few years we at DPI have noticed a substantial increase in the number of corporations that attempt to construct mission or vision statements that articulate the organization's business concept. Unfortunately, their efforts are often fruitless because of the lack of a structured process to help them. As a result, they end up with statements that are so "motherhood" in tone that everyone can agree with them, but that are useless as guides to help people make daily operational decisions. Over time, the statement is quietly ignored.

Here are a few examples:

> We are a successful, growing company dedicated to achieving superior results by assuring that our actions are aligned with shareholder expectations Our primary mission is to create value for our shareholders.

> Our mission is to provide products and services of superior competitive quality and value, to achieve strong growth in sales and income, to realize consistently higher returns on equity and cash required to fuel our growth, and to have people who contribute superior performance at all levels.

> Our primary enterprise objective is to increase the value of shareowners' investment by managing our resources and servicing our customers better and more efficiently than our competitors.

Why do I call these statements meaningless? After all, they were put together by groups of intelligent people who were attempting to gain consensus. They contain words that are nice sounding and to which everyone can agree. However, when used as a filter to make decisions, they fall apart because they allow everything through. Nothing is eliminated.

Increasing shareholder value . . . by doing what? By making what products? By selling to which customers? By concentrating on which market segments? By pursuing which geographic markets?

Without answers to these questions, how can someone be expected to allocate resources properly and choose the appropriate opportunities to pursue?

And then, to make matters worse, along comes the Sybil syndrome! Remember Sybil, the woman who had multiple personalities? Many corporations suffer from the same malady, as the following mission statement will show. They don't know where they are going because they can't decide who they are.

> Ethyl Corporation strives to be a profitable and growing global manufacturer and marketer of value-added chemicals, an innovative supplier of niche life insurance and annuity products, and an increasingly significant force in the pharmaceutical industry.

This company had such difficulty living with itself that it ultimately separated into four independent public corporations.

Even Dilbert has taken a swipe at useless mission statements: "A mission statement is defined as a long, awkward sentence that demonstrates management's inability to think clearly."

No wonder so many of the Fortune 500 companies have lost large chunks of their markets and have had to engage in massive downsizing programs. The above are fairly representative of the kinds of meaningless mission statements in use in hundreds of corporations, which have led to the "hollowing" of America.

THE NEED FOR A CONCISE BUSINESS CONCEPT

To us, the words *strategy, mission, charter, mandate, business purpose*, and *business statement* are all synonymous. If you were to browse through the annals of business history books, you would be told by author after author that on any day of its existence, every corporation is practicing some concept of conducting its business. In other words, there is an underlying concept of business being practiced by the management of any organization although that concept may not be apparent to the members of that organization. Thus, the reason for the term *business concept.*

Says management guru Peter Drucker in his book *Innovation and Entrepreneurship: Practice and Principles*: "Every practice rests on theory, even if the practitioners are unaware of it." Another expert on the subject, Alfred P. Sloan, who was CEO of General Motors in the first half of this century, put it this way in his book, *My Years with General Motors*:

> Every enterprise needs a concept of its industry. There is a logical way of doing business in accordance with the facts and circumstances of an industry, if you can figure it out. If there are different concepts among the enterprises involved, these concepts are likely to express competitive forces in their most vigorous and most decisive forms.

Yet another guru, Henry Mintzberg, has also made a similar observation, as reported in a 1980 article in *Harvard Business Review*:

> Strategy is the organization's conception of how to deal with its environment for a while. If the organization wishes to have a creative, integrated strategy . . . it will rely on one individual to conceptualize its strategy, to synthesize a "vision" of how the organization will respond to its environment. A strategy can be made explicit only when the vision is fully worked out, if it ever is. Often, of course, it is never felt to be fully worked out, hence the strategy is never made explicit and remains the private vision of the chief executive.

Peter Drucker, the guru of all management gurus, calls it the "theory of the business." In a 1994 *Harvard Business Review* article, he outlined his thesis:

> Every organization, whether a business or not, has a theory of the business. Indeed, a valid theory that is clear, consistent, and focused is extraordinarily powerful. These are the assumptions that shape any organization's behavior, dictate its decisions about what to do and what not to do, and define what the organization

considers meaningful results. These assumptions are about markets. They are about identifying customers and competitors, their values and behavior. They are about technology and its dynamics, about a company's strengths and weaknesses. These assumptions are about what a company gets paid for. They are what I call a company's theory of the business.

Our view on the subject of mission statements is simple:

- A good business or strategic concept should not be longer than a paragraph or two. There is no need to have pages and pages describing what the business is about. However, every word, modifier, or qualifier must be carefully thought through, because each moves the line of demarcation between the products, customers, and markets that will receive more emphasis and those that will receive less.
- It is our opinion that the ability of people to execute a CEO's strategy is inversely proportional to the length of the statement.

Therefore, the statement must be precise and concise. The Driving Force concept explained in the previous chapter is a tool that allows management to identify which area of the business is at the root of the company's products, customers, and markets and is strategically more important to that company than any other area. However, it is also a tool that allows management to articulate its concept of doing business in that mode.

HOW TO CONSTRUCT A MEANINGFUL BUSINESS CONCEPT

A business concept that can serve executives of a corporation as a test bed to make consistent and intelligent decisions on behalf of the company must contain the following elements:

- The first sentence must *clearly describe the Driving Force of the organization*. In other words, it must isolate that specific component of the business that gives the company a strategic and distinctive advantage over its competitors. If one is Product-driven, then what is the specific product that drives the business? If one is Technology-driven, then which specific technology is at the root of the business? If one is Production Capability–driven, then which specific production capability drives the business?

- The second part of the statement should contain words—nouns, adjectives, qualifiers, modifiers—that will delineate the line of demarcation between the "nature" of the products, customers, market segments, and geographic markets that the Driving Force lends itself to and those to which it does not.
- The statement should *have a "tone" of growth*, since growth is a given in business. Every business must grow in order to perpetuate itself.
- It must *have a tone of success*, as success is, naturally, implied by a sound strategy.
- Finally, it must *reflect future intent and not present condition*. The statement should give people a feel for what it will be in the future, not what it is today.

Depending on the choice of Driving Force, each business concept will be dramatically different.

EXAMPLES OF STRATEGIC BUSINESS CONCEPTS

The following are examples of business concepts that we have helped our client organizations to construct. For reasons of confidentiality, the names of the companies involved have been omitted. In each instance, the Driving Force and the strategic heartbeat are italicized.

The first two examples are from Product-driven companies, one in the manufacturing sector:

> Our strategy is to market, manufacture, and distribute *saw blade products*, made from strip metal stock, that provide exceptional value.
>
> We will concentrate on high performance, material separation applications where we can leverage our integrated manufacturing capabilities to develop customized, innovative, consumable products with demonstrable advantages that bring premium prices.
>
> We will seek out customer segments and geographic markets where the combination of superior distribution and technical support services will give us an additional competitive advantage.

The second example is from a service industry:

Our strategy is to provide *reinsurance products* to assist organizations in managing life, health, and annuity risks.

We will differentiate ourselves by leveraging our mortality and morbidity risk management expertise.

We will concentrate on market segments where we can establish and maintain a leadership position.

We will concentrate in growth-oriented, "free" geographic areas with reliable databases and predictable risk patterns where we can achieve critical mass and a balanced portfolio.

The next two are User Class–driven concepts:

We proactively seek out the building, repair, and remodeling needs of *professional tradespeople* in the commercial and residential construction industry.

We respond with cost effective, differentiated staple products that enhance the performance or ease the installation of key building materials and are category leaders.

We concentrate in geographic markets with a significant and/or growing construction industry and an adequate distribution infrastructure to reach a critical mass of end users.

Our intent is to be the recognized leader in the products we offer.

Our strategy is to fulfill the complete spectrum of health-care needs of *cancer patients* and their families.

We respond with treatment options that truly make a difference, delivered by the ablest professionals in a seamless and sensitive manner that empowers patients to make coherent decisions.

We will concentrate on geographic markets in which we can develop competitive advantage with all constituencies involved in the continuum of cancer care.

Our intent is to be the recognized leader in providing positive, measurable outcomes.

The following statement is from a Market Category–driven company:

We will proactively seek out the professional information/education needs of the *health science market*.

We will respond with added-value content that maximizes the development of valuable copyright materials through multiple formats, languages, and/or distribution channels to capitalize on profitable customer segments in English-speaking countries.

The following two examples are those of Production Capability–driven companies.

Our strategy is to leverage our cutting edge *integrated specialty textile manufacturing capability* to exploit interior service applications for which we can develop customized, differentiated products.

We will target and strive to dominate market niches that offer above average margins/profit.

We will continue to be the leading international producer and marketer of specialty chemicals and powders that leverage our *metal-based process capabilities* to produce high added-value products.

We will seek high volume, high quality, value-added industrial applications in market segments in which we can have a major presence through our ability to customize and differentiate our products/services to specific customer requirements.

We will do this in geographic markets which have multiple market segments where manufacturing proximity can be an additional competitive advantage.

Then there is a Production Capacity–driven concept:

Our strategy is to market transportation fuels through our own and other value-added distribution systems to *optimize our refining capacity.*

We will stress end-user sales to high-volume customer segments and geographic markets where location provides a competitive advantage.

Our intent is to gain enough critical mass to dominate the niche markets we operate in or enter.

The next two statements are examples of Technology-driven concepts:

Our strategy is to proactively exploit *our proprietary biomedical technologies* (materials/electronics) to satisfy therapeutic and diagnostic extension applications in the fields of cardiovascular and neuromuscular science to alleviate pain, restore health, and extend life.

We will respond with differentiated, ethical medical devices distributed through a highly trained sales force focused on discrete customer segments.

We will concentrate on geographical markets with a critical mass of applications, an established base of medical expertise, and an adequate healthcare infrastructure.

Our strategy is to leverage our know-how in the formulation and manufacturing of polymer-based composites.

We will seek growth opportunities and niche applications in market segments for which we can design differentiated, value-added, consumable products.

We will concentrate in geographic areas with growing demand where we can provide superior technical support.

The following two statements represent Distribution Method–driven concepts:

Our strategy is to provide the most *efficient distribution network* to serve the tire and wheel industry.

We will tailor our products, services, and facilities to satisfy the evolving needs of our customers and suppliers, and respond with a proprietary advantage in the areas of cost, cycle time, or product diversity.

We will be the premier owner/operator of *international wireless networks* that deliver differentiated and value-added products to businesses with mobile workers.

We will concentrate on customer segments that require multiple services customized to various applications which create recurring revenue streams.

We will focus on metro adjoining areas and connector corridors in North America and other countries with emerging infrastructures and above average profit potential.

Exotic? Definitely not. Sexy? Absolutely not. Powerful? You bet! The purpose of a clear business concept is not to arouse people but to provide them with a clear sense of direction and equip them with an easy-to-use tool to make intelligent and consistent decisions on behalf of the organization. In the next section we explain how the business concept is used to screen opportunities.

TURNING THE BUSINESS CONCEPT INTO A STRATEGIC FILTER

The following statement is the business concept of another one of our clients.

> Our strategy is to leverage our *multipurpose, continuous process capability to combine metals and polymers* to produce and market multilayered structures.
>
> We will proactively seek out applications where we can respond with differentiated products that add value, are tailored to the specific needs of customers and end users, and bring cost, performance, and/or quality competitive advantages.
>
> We will concentrate in growth-oriented industry segments in which we can be a leader and in geographic markets where there are multiple applications available to us.

Although this business concept sounds highly technical, here is how it can be transformed into a very effective and simple binary filter to screen opportunities that come to the business. One simply filters an opportunity through a series of questions that demand a yes or no answer (see the Strategic Filter on the next page).

The more "checks" the opportunity receives on the "no" side of the ledger, the larger the red flag should become, because that opportunity is violating major aspects of the strategy of the business.

The more areas of the strategy it violates, the more it will be an "exception to the rule," and exceptions always end up being problem areas.

Strategic Filter

	Yes	No
Does the opportunity . . .		
▶ leverage and/or enhance our multi-purpose, continuous-process capability to combine metals and polymers?	___	___
▶ produce multilayered structures?	___	___
▶ provide an ability to respond with differentiated products that add value?	___	___
▶ provide products tailored to the specific needs of customers?	___	___
▶ bring:		
▶ cost advantages?	___	___
▶ performance advantages?	___	___
▶ quality advantages?	___	___
▶ target a growth-oriented industry sector?	___	___
▶ bring geographic markets with multiple applications?	___	___
▶ allow us to be a leader?	___	___

THE "BUMPER-STICKER" STRATEGY

Even though we advocate a business concept no longer than a paragraph in length, many CEOs still find this information too long and difficult to communicate. So many companies attempt to extract the essence of the statement and condense it down to "bumper-sticker" size.

For example, our Technology-driven client whose statement appears in the section entitled "Examples of Strategic Business Concepts" has captured the essence of its strategy in the phrase "Real-time systems for real-world applications." In fact, this phrase has become the thrust of all of that company's advertising.

One CEO who clearly understands this concept is Steven Reinemund, now CEO of PepsiCo, who once ran Pizza Hut. "We're a distribution system for pizzas," he declared in a *Fortune* article—thus his decision to extend Pizza Hut's stores in airports and malls.

Sometimes, the Driving Force will be found in the name of the company itself—Polaroid, for example—obviously a Technology-driven company whose business concept was founded on the Polaroid instant photography technology.

Even though different companies follow the same Driving Force, they may still have business concepts different enough from one another to be going down separate roads. Let's look at some examples in the automobile industry. Volvo, BMW, Mercedes, Volkswagen, and General Motors can all be said to be Product-driven: automobiles and more automobiles. However, each of these companies has a very different conception of its product. For example:

- Volvo—"safe and durable cars"
- Mercedes—"best-engineered car"
- BMW—"the ultimate driving machine"
- Volkswagen—"people's car"
- General Motors—"a car for each income strata"

As a result, each of these companies goes down a different road and seldom competes with the others even though they all make cars.

The following are other examples of bumper-sticker statements:

- Federal Express's concept of "guaranteed overnight delivery of letters and small parcels"
- Koji Kobayashi's (ex-CEO of NEC) concept of the "convergence of computers and communications," stated 30 years ago
- IBM's Thomas Watson's vision of "processing information," articulated over 50 years ago
- 3M's motto of "innovation working for you"
- Sony's concept of the "ingenious use of electronic technology"
- Southwest's concept says it all: "30 Years. One Mission. Low Fares."

Each of the other categories of Driving Force brings with it a difficult business concept that can be more clearly articulated once the notion of strategic drive is understood.

The business concept influences all aspects of a corporation's activities. It determines the scope of products, customers, and markets; the organization structure; the technologies required; the type of production facilities; the distribution channels; the marketing and selling techniques; and even the type of people employed. Basically, it sets the tone, climate, and behavior of an organization.

WHAT IS THE STRATEGIC QUOTIENT OF YOUR ORGANIZATION?

If you are interested at this point in assessing your organization's strategic position, you may wish to answer the questions below and have your direct reports do the same. If all the answers are similar and each person's business concept is identical, then you are in good shape. The wider the discrepancies in their replies compared to yours, the less clear your strategy is, and you may wish to call DPI for assistance.

1. Do you have a well-articulated, clear statement of strategy?

   Yes _____ 10   No _____ 1

2. Could each member of your management team write a one- or two-sentence statement of that strategy without consulting the others?

   All could _____ 10   Some could _____ 5   None could _____ 1

3. Do you have your strategy in written form?

   Yes _____ 10   No _____ 5

4. Do you and they use this statement as a guide for the choices you make together when deciding which products, customers, and markets your company will pursue?

   Use frequently _____ 10   Use sometimes _____ 5   Never use _____ 1

5. Do you and they use this statement as a guide to decide which products, customers, and markets your company will not pursue?

   Use frequently _____ 10   Use sometimes _____ 5   Never use _____ 1

6. Do you use this statement as a filter to decide how resources are allocated within the company?

Use frequently ___10 Use sometimes ___5 Never use ___ 1

7. Do you use this statement as a filter to choose which opportunities your company will pursue and which ones it won't?

Use frequently ___10 Use sometimes ___5 Never use ___ 1

8. Have you ever sat down as a management team to try to obtain consensus about the future direction of the organization?

Regularly _____ 10   Once in a while _____ 3   Never _____ 1

9. Was a consensus obtained, or are there still different visions of what the organization is trying to become?

One vision _____ 10   Several visions _____ 1   No vision _____ 1

10. Do you have a separate process of strategic thinking to determine what you want to become as opposed to how you will get there?

Formal, codified process _____ 10   No process _____ 1

Total Score _____

If all the answers are similar and each statement is identical, you are in good shape. The wider are the discrepancies in replies between your direct reports' and your's, the less clear your strategy is to them, and you may want to entertain the idea of taking your management team through the process described in the remainder of this book.

SCORING YOUR STRATEGIC IQ

If you wish to get a numerical assessment of your strategic quotient, simply add up the scores next to all the questions to which you responded. The following is our assessment of your score.

Score 100
You're perfect. There is no need for you to read the remainder of this book unless you don't know why you are so good.

Score: 70-99
There is some degree of ambiguity over strategy among the management team, with periodic disagreements over direction, particularly in regard to significant issues. You are on the cusp of great success if this ambiguity can be removed. Your record includes a few more wins than losses, but that record could be substantially improved through the removal of this ambiguity. Exposure to a good strategic process would bring considerable value.

Score 40-69
You are suffering from a severe case of fuzzy vision. There are widely differing views of strategic direction among the management team, which has resulted in erratic operational performance. There are frequent disagreements over strategic issues, and you probably are surprised frequently by competitive tactics. Failure to clear up this ambiguity eventually will lead to even worse operational results. It's time to bring a process into play that will relieve the organization of this ambiguity and stop the bickering.

Score 1-39
A score in this range indicates too much of a focus on operational issues and short-term results. Decisions are made on an event-by-event basis as opposed to being made within a set of strategic parameters. There is little agreement among the management team over direction, with continuous and heated debates. As a result, decisions frequently are arbitrated and dictated by the CEO in order to break the stalemate. The company is in a me-too strategy mode and is frequently surprised by competitive tactics. Most actions are reactions to competitive initiatives. It is time for a rethink.

WHO'S ON FIRST?

Or, as Abbott and Costello might pose the question to today's CEOs, "Who's in control of the sandbox?" In fact, there would be two questions regarding the sandbox.

- Who is in control of the rules in the sandbox?
- Who influences the rules in the sandbox?

DELIMITING THE CURRENT SANDBOX

In order to "change the game," or sandbox, to one's advantage it is important to understand how the game is played currently. Therefore, the following questions need to be answered:

- How is the game played today?
- Who are the participants in this sandbox?
- Which entity is in control of the rules in this sandbox?
- Which entity influences the rules in this sandbox?
- Which companies are at the mercy of those mentioned above?
- What can we do to upset their control or influence?

The following is an example from the garment industry.

In this model, Wal-Mart is king and is in absolute control of the sandbox. Wal-Mart does this by imposing the following rules: It controls both demand and supply. The company aggregates demand to extract better prices from suppliers by doing the following:

- Employing extensive and expensive IT systems to track sales online
- Keeping prices lower than competitors every day
- Replenishing stores each day through a hub-and-spoke system
- Applying price pressure on the entire chain of vendors, giving countries with low labor costs such as China and India an advantage

The "influencers" in this chain are the designer and the garment manufacturer. The designer can influence the type of cloth he wants and the manufacturer can obviously influence the costs. All of the other players merely play by the rules set by those other companies, unless they can figure out a way to change the game.

CHANGING THE GAME

For the last 25 years, we at DPI have been preaching the need to "change the rules" if a company aspires to establishing supremacy over its competitors. However, in the last four to five years, we have come to the conclusion that changing the rules is not enough. In this competitive era, one must now "change the game itself."

TACTICS THAT CHANGE THE GAME

There are four different forms of tactics to "change the game" that we have so far discovered:

- Changing enough rules to make a response by competitors impossible
- Turning a competitor's unique strength into a unique weakness
- Making the competitor's strategy redundant
- Changing how customers buy and companies compete

WAL-MART

Until Wal-Mart came on the scene, the game and the rules for department store retailers were the same for all the players across the country. The game was played this way:

- Stores were located in city centers and in suburban areas nearby.
- The offering consisted of "dry," nonperishable goods.
- Marketing was "pull" oriented.
- Periodic sales on selected items occurred.

Wal-Mart started by changing the rules. Contrary to the other chains that offered lower prices only on certain items each week, Sam Walton introduced the concept of "everyday low prices."

Not satisfied, Walton went even further and changed the game itself when he introduced several additional concepts. First, he avoided large cities and located his stores in midsize rural towns. Second, he clustered 10 to 12 stores around a warehouse that could replenish these stores within 24 hours. Third, he stocked the shelves with both perishable and nonperishable goods. Fourth, he instituted a program to exert severe pressure on suppliers to continuously reduce their costs and prices to Wal-Mart.

The game had never been played in this manner. Sam Walton, by changing so many rules, created a new game that put Wal-Mart on a path to strategic supremacy. To this day, some 40 years later, Kmart, Sears, and J.C. Penney are playing to Wal-Mart's rules and have yet to develop adequate counterstrategies. In fact, all have fallen upon economic hard times as a result. In the meantime, the gap between Wal-Mart and its competitors gets wider and wider.

CANON AND XEROX

In 1980, Xerox had 98 percent of the copier market. Seven short years later, it had 12 percent market share. What happened? Simple: Canon came into the sandbox and completely changed the game. Instead of offering big copiers, Canon introduced small copiers. Instead of selling direct, it sold through distributors and agents. Instead of leasing its machines, it sold the copiers outright. It took Xerox five years to decide to sell through distributors and seven years to wean itself from its leasing revenue stream. Canon turned two of Xerox's unique strengths into unique weaknesses.

SONY AND POLAROID

When Sony introduced the world's first Mavica digital camera in May 1984, Polaroid's days were numbered. The reason is simple. On that day,

Polaroid's concept of "instant photography" was made redundant. It took Polaroid 25 years to accept this reality and file for Chapter 11.

MAGNA INTERNATIONAL

This company, which started as a small auto parts supplier in Toronto, has become the largest supplier of components to the worldwide automotive industry. They have done this by changing how customers buy and companies compete. For example, it was the first company in that business to sell "systems" instead of "components." And it has done it again. In Europe, Magna not only is a supplier of components and systems, but it has recently started to assemble cars for Volvo and BMW in its factories. This is the ultimate form of outsourcing. This initiative by Magna will totally change the game in the automotive market worldwide. By the way, Magna makes money doing business exclusively with automotive companies, in spite of all the CEOs who are exiting this industry because "we can't make any money with these guys."

DON'T CHANGE
THE RULES, CHANGE
THE GAME ITSELF!

"Supremacy" is not an absolute numeric advantage over competitors but rather the *degree of control* a company has of its competitors over a long period of time. Temporary control of a sandbox is not an indicator of the staying power of a strategy. The real test of a successful strategy has to be its ability to breed supremacy over competitors throughout an extended time frame. In other words, it needs to stand the test of time. The thesis that we propose in this book is that the ability to control the sandbox over a long period of time demands a distinctive strategy that not only changes the rules of play but changes the game itself. Any strategy that doesn't change the game will probably only provide a temporary advantage.

There is a fine, but extremely important, difference between the two concepts. The following examples are meant to illustrate that distinction.

AMAZON.COM

In book selling, the game has always been played in a well-known manner. In order to play the game, one built a chain of stores, stocked them with as many books as could be squeezed into each store's space, and then waited for the customer to come in, browse, and, one hoped, buy a book or two. Two chains, Borders and Barnes & Noble, attempted to change these rules by building stores several times larger than had been seen before, and they carried over 100,000 book selections compared to 10,000 in the traditional bookstore. Furthermore, they encouraged you to browse by giving you coffee and a reading area. The new rules worked in their favor extremely well, as they took more and more market share away from the operators of smaller stores.

These new rules, however, were still designed for the familiar gameboard of "bricks and mortar." Then along comes the Internet, and Amazon.com creates a brand-new game. Amazon.com shuns the traditional concept of company stores—bricks and mortar—and, instead, enables you to buy books right off the Internet, offering a selection of over one million titles at significant discounts. Furthermore, it allows you to do this from your home with your PC. Your order is confirmed while you are online and the book arrives at your door within 24 to 36 hours, all without the need to go anywhere near a bookstore. New game, no bricks and mortar, new gameboard—the Internet—and totally new rules set by Amazon.com. To this day, Borders and Barnes & Noble have yet to come up with a counterstrategy while they watch Amazon.com gradually establishing its supremacy over the industry.

HOME DEPOT

For the last 50 years or so, if you were doing some repairs to your home and needed some lumber or a few two-inch screws, you would walk over to your neighborhood lumberyard and pick up a few two-by-fours and then mosey over to Joe's Hardware Store to pick up the screws. Every community had its mom-and-pop lumberyard and hardware store, and the game was played that way across America . . . until Arthur Blank and Bernie Marcus arrived on the scene and decided to radically change the nature of the game.

Instead of the 10,000-square-foot mom-and-pop store, Blank and Marcus built massive, 100,000-square-foot monsters that stored both lumber and hardware in quantities and varieties unseen before. To appeal to the amateur handyperson, they staffed each section with a craftsperson licensed in that trade, which reassured buyers that they were being served by a knowledgeable professional. Furthermore, they built hundreds of stores around the country so quickly that they established their supremacy over the mom-and-pop operators and other home centers before any of them realized what hit them. When was the last time you saw the names Channel, Pergament, or Builder's Square? The game was changed for good.

ROBERTS EXPRESS (NOW CALLED FEDEX CUSTOM CRITICAL)

There was a time in the trucking industry when the rules were the same for all the players. The basic rules were as follows:

- Buy a fleet of trucks.
- Determine whether to concentrate on short hauls or long hauls.
- Hunt down customers.
- Always try to get a return load from wherever you go so that you minimize empty legs.
- Beat down your competitors on price, which leads to razor-thin margins and volatile periods of profit and losses.

When the industry was deregulated in the late 1970s, most trucking companies saw that event as an opportunity to extend their routes into other companies' territories. However, they continued to play the game as they did before, which only led to more intense competition and even greater amounts of red ink.

The management of one company, Roberts Express, looked at the same event and saw an opportunity to change the game itself. Let's assume that you run a car assembly plant in Detroit, and you are on a Just-in-Time (JIT) basis with your suppliers. Engines, for example, are delivered one shift prior to the time they are used. One day, your engine supplier has problems of his own and the engines don't show up. You are now faced with the possibility of having to shut down the plant and send 5,000 employees home.

That is when the Roberts Express strategy kicks in. Roberts has a network of 2,000 independent truck owners who identify themselves under the company's brand name located across the country waiting for your call. While you are on the phone with the Roberts dispatcher, he or she is locating, through their proprietary satellite system, the truck nearest to your engine supplier's plant. Within seconds you have a guarantee that the engines will be picked up within plus or minus 15 minutes of a specific hour and delivered to your plant within the same window, also at a specific hour. This is a radically different game.

On top of this, Roberts has built-in cost and flexibility advantages. Roberts doesn't own any of the trucks, thus saving a large capital expenditure that weighs down other trucking companies. The drivers, who buy their own trucks, are all independent contractors, which means that Roberts has none of the administrative responsibilities that come with having those employees. But the real beauty of that strategy is that Roberts gets premium prices in an industry that is renowned for cutthroat pricing.

In fact, Roberts's strategy resulted in such a large "supremacy gap" over the industry that its success attracted the eye of another company that believes in strategic supremacy—FedEx. It is now a member of that family.

SOUTHWEST AIRLINES

Since the airline industry was deregulated in the early 1970s, all players have played the game in the same manner. All have a "hub-and-spoke" system; all use aircraft of different sizes and configurations manufactured by different companies; all have invested billions of dollars in sophisticated reservation systems; and all continuously complain about how stupid an industry they are in, with stupid competitors and even stupid customers.

All . . . that is, except Southwest Airlines, which has made a profit every day since its inception in 1971. Why? Southwest has created its own game. Instead of operating through hubs, it operates on a point-to-point basis. It floods these two locations with up to a dozen flights per day at "everyday low—and only one—price," thus drawing a multitude of first-time passengers who would normally travel by bus. Instead of using multiple aircraft, it employs a single aircraft—the Boeing 737—and as far as a sophisticated, costly reservation system . . . it has none.

Whose strategy is quickly ascending toward supremacy over the industry? You're right. Southwest. The strategy is so far superior to those of the other airlines that Boeing custom-built a "stretch" version of its 737 model only for Southwest. Furthermore, all of Southwest's growth has been organic, whereas most other airlines' growth has been through acquisitions. For 30 years, none of the other airlines have been able to put together a viable response to this strategy, and Southwest has grown year after year at their expense.

DELL COMPUTER

Michael Dell is another individual who has built a powerhouse, multibillion-dollar company in a few short years by first changing the rules and then by changing the game itself. Instead of marketing computers through retail stores, as the industry rules dictated back then, he decided to market PCs through direct-response marketing methods. This was an attempt to change the rules, which enjoyed early success. But the company's products were the same as its competitors'. A few years after the company's creation, Dell decided to change the game itself. He married the concept of direct marketing with that of on-demand, made-to-order computers.

The result? A multibillion dollar company that has the highest revenue per employee, the lowest inventory per employee, the highest return on capital, and a stock price that has outperformed the market by a factor of a large-scale earthquake despite the volatility of the PC market.

In 1997, Dell decided to change the game again by converting its direct marketing method from catalogs to the Internet. Only a few months after it extended this mechanism around the world, Dell was booking over $10 million in orders per day. Dell has caused other computer companies, such as Compaq, to rethink their own strategies and try to do things Dell's way. Unfortunately, they have found themselves on Dell's gameboard, and those rules are controlled by Dell. Most of its competitors have recognized the supremacy of Dell's strategy and have since given up.

Starting from zero, Dell was a $30 billion company by 2002. Overall, Michael Dell's strategy is relatively simple: commoditization of differentiated products. Dell likes to take innovative products, such as PCs, and turn them into commodities that can be assembled quickly from prestocked components and tailored to each customer's individual needs. Since the entire PC market has been commoditized, Dell is the sole player with a market advantage. This strategy anticipated this condition years ago and planned for it. With 14 percent of the global PC market, Dell could be considered to have achieved supremacy already, but its strategic intent says that supremacy will come when the company has 40 percent of the worldwide *computer* market—not only the PC market. Dell's strategy is being extended to include servers, switches, modems, storage, and any other piece of hardware that is related to PCs for both the business and home markets. And supremacy, not adequacy, is the goal. Watch out IBM, Cisco, Gateway, and anyone else. Your sandbox is about to be disrupted in a major way.

BOEING'S STRATEGIC COUP

For most of this century, Boeing had established its supremacy in the aircraft design and construction sandbox. Its supremacy was so pronounced that almost all other competitors gave up and Boeing had the sandbox pretty much to itself.

That was so until a consortium of European governments decided, as an attempt to blunt Boeing's supremacy, to form a company to build commercial aircraft, which they named Airbus. Airbus's strategy was very simple: copycat Boeing. In other words, whatever size aircraft Boeing made, Airbus decided to duplicate it. And because Boeing was not accustomed to intense competition, Airbus eventually took 40 percent of the market away from Boeing.

For a while, Boeing did not know how to respond, and it engaged in a battle with Airbus whereby each company attempted to outdo the other by making bigger and bigger planes. Both companies were now pursuing an "imitation" strategy, basically cloning each other. For Boeing, this was not a winning proposition. Boeing had to rethink its strategy. Finally, at the Bourget Air Show in 1999, Boeing went public with its new strategy and announced that it would build a mega-jetliner that would carry over 800 people. It would do this by "stretching" its 747 model rather than building a brand-new aircraft.

A mega-plane had been part of Airbus's thinking as well. But Airbus had been reluctant to pursue such a gigantic aircraft because of its enormous development costs. However, in light of Boeing's announcement, Airbus had no other choice than to aggressively explore this path. In an attempt to try to finally separate and differentiate from Boeing's shadow, Airbus announced that its mega-plane would not be an extension of a current model but, instead, would be a brand-new design. In March 2000, Airbus introduced this new model with great fanfare. In an attempt to outdo Boeing, Airbus designed an aircraft that would be "double-decker," like the buses in London. Airbus got press around the world and many pundits started predicting the end of Boeing's supremacy and possibly the beginning of the end.

Exactly two weeks later, Boeing held its own press conference and no one expected to hear what they heard. Boeing announced to the world that, instead of imitating Airbus, Boeing was going to reinvent the game. The company told the world's press that it had decided to scrap its plans to extend the 747. Instead, it would build a new midsize, super-fuel-efficient aircraft that would reduce travel time by 40 percent, with the same operating costs as the jet-propelled airplane. All the experts agreed immediately. This was a much better strategy than Airbus's, since everyone knows that frequent fliers are not interested in traveling with more people, they simply want to get there more quickly.

Boeing has decided to change the game in an attempt to regain its supremacy. Now, for the key question: Do you really think that Boeing ever intended to build a "stretched" 747? My answer is: "Never in a million years!"

That announcement made back in 1999 was, in my view, simply a ploy to entice Airbus into action and commit itself to a strategy that Boeing knew they could make obsolete very quickly. Airbus is now in the difficult position of having to retract its "mega-plane" strategy and switch to a super-fuel-efficient platform, about which they have very little knowledge, putting them three to four years behind Boeing. So far, so good! In the first quarter of 2005 both companies rolled out their first working models. And guess what? For the first time in five years Boeing's new 777 is outselling Airbus's new jumbo.

One of the other concepts that we have been promoting for over 20 years is that a good strategy allows you to manage your competitor's strategy to your advantage as well as your own. However, this can only be achieved by attaining supremacy of thinking, which then leads to supremacy of strategy.

CHARLES SCHWAB: STRATEGIST "PAR EXCELLENCE"

Some individuals have such an innate understanding of the concept of attaining strategic supremacy by changing the game, rather than just the rules, that they have done it several times. Charles Schwab is such an individual. Schwab has an uncanny ability to anticipate future trends before his competitors do and then create a new game.

Schwab founded Charles Schwab & Company in 1971 by first changing the rules of the stock brokerage business, starting with the most cherished rule in the industry. He set transaction fees at half the industry norm. Furthermore, unlike his competitors, Schwab offered no research, one of the most costly services a broker extends. With these rule changes, Schwab spawned the discount brokerage business. Unfortunately, many imitators sprang up.

In 1995, however, Schwab decided to change the game itself. Schwab saw the growing dissatisfaction with ever-increasing, and sometimes exorbitant, management fees that mutual funds imposed on their investors. The company introduced a program named ONE SOURCE, which permitted investors to purchase a mix of mutual funds from a single source—Charles Schwab, naturally—rather than from each mutual fund company individually. The ONE SOURCE program allowed each investor to choose from a portfolio of over 700 funds without paying any commission whatsoever, and to switch from one fund to another without any penalty charge. The concept completely revolutionized the marketing of mutual funds and found the industry leader, Fidelity, asleep at the switch.

In 1997, Schwab decided to create yet another game. He introduced a program that allowed investors to trade stocks online. Within a matter of weeks, Schwab was trading over $4 billion per week, which represented over 50 percent of its revenues. It has since climbed to over 90 percent of its revenues. This time, Schwab caught Merrill Lynch asleep at the switch. Until Schwab introduced this program, stocks were traded over the phone through an army of highly paid salespeople backed by expensive research. This new game has put that model in jeopardy and has forced all the brokerage houses to rethink their strategies and explore how they might respond. Unfortunately for them, the existing rule of selling through highly paid salespeople makes it extremely difficult to change but, more importantly, they would be playing on Schwab's gameboard and according to Schwab's rules.

Still not satisfied, Schwab decided to change the game yet again. In June 2000, the company announced the purchase of U.S. Trust Corporation, a money manager and financial adviser to the carriage trade, where customers are not considered customers until they have been so for generations—not days, weeks, or months. What the heck is Schwab doing in such an environment? Charles Schwab, being a very astute strategist, has glanced into the future and detected that there is a significant shift happening in the demographics of the United States. It is a fact that sometime between the years 2010 and 2015, 50 percent of the U.S. population will be over 55 years old. Many of them will have inherited large sums of money and will now be faced with complex issues in an attempt to manage this wealth and preserve it for their children. Over $13 *trillion* will be transferred from one generation to the next during this period. Many of the recipients of this wealth are probably current Schwab customers. Most will require personalized advice to help them optimize their returns. Do you get the connection? Is Charles Schwab about to create another new game?

On May 16, 2002, Charles Schwab changed the game again. In the past decade or so, there has emerged an army of so-called financial planning consultants, who advise individuals on how to manage and invest their money. Thousands of independent, one-person shops have sprung up all over the country, many of which have questionable, if any, credentials. Putting up a shingle and claiming to be a financial planner is their only qualification to enter this thriving industry. Many people, including myself, have been reluctant to use their services because of their lack of known qualifications.

Enter Charles Schwab with a totally new game. Schwab has announced the creation of a "network of independent financial planners certified by Charles Schwab & Company." Independent financial planners will be invited to apply to become members of this network. But only those who pass a series of rigorous standards and abide by a stringent code of ethics will be accepted.

The Schwab reputation will be the backbone of the network and is bound to increase the credibility of those that can claim to have the Charles Schwab seal of approval. Obviously, these members will be expected to conduct their transactions through Schwab.

What new game will Charles Schwab invent next? Stay tuned!

PROGRESSIVE INSURANCE

From a zero-based start in the 1970s, Progressive Insurance has become the nation's fourth-largest auto insurer, with revenues of over $6 billion. It did so initially by changing the rules of play.

In the car insurance industry, there is a "golden" rule: Don't insure drivers who are prone to accidents. That is an industry rule that no insurance company would ever violate. That is, until Progressive entered the game and changed the rules. Progressive did the exact opposite and only insured individuals who had had accidents . . . and at a premium.

Until Progressive came along, all insurers calculated their risk exposure with a particular driver based on that driver's age and an accident-free past. In other words, only insure those individuals who have not had an accident. As a result, one can calculate the probability of risk quite accurately. The difficulty with this approach is that every other insurer is doing the same and everybody ends up with a me-too strategy that might match, but never gain supremacy over, those competitors.

Progressive's strategy was designed to do the exact opposite. Somewhere along the way, Progressive noticed that people who have had one accident are less likely to have any more. Progressive's actuaries got to work and confirmed that the probability of someone having a second accident was lower than that of having their first. Thus, the growth of Progressive to this day.

Now, Progressive may be about to change the game itself. Anticipating a future where most people will be at ease with all the gadgets of the digital age, Progressive has conducted a pilot program in Texas that could revolutionize the auto insurance industry and make Progressive the focal point of that new game. The company installed devices in several cars that measure the amount of time that the car is in use, who is driving, and, through a link-up to a global positioning satellite (GPS), where the car went. All this data is captured online and transmitted back to Progressive, which then uses it to calculate that driver's premium. In other words, insurance by the mile. Like a meter in a parking lot, you only pay for the time used. Sounds like Progressive may have another homerun on its hands, especially since giant competitor Allstate complains that such an approach "would require a massive restructuring of a well-functioning underwriting system."

FEDEX: DAVID CHANGES THE GAME ON GOLIATH

There was a time not so long ago when all letters and small packages were delivered exclusively by the U.S. Postal Service, most of them within 24 hours. In the 1970s, however, the Postal Service began to renege on that promise, with mail delivery taking as long as one week. This was not ideal performance for documents that needed urgent attention. Luckily, the game was about to be changed.

Fred Smith, who had no prior knowledge of how the Postal Service operated except to know that its performance was inadequate, was searching for a topic for a paper he needed to submit in order to graduate from business school. His thesis proposed the formation of a company with a fleet of aircraft that would fly point to point, between major cities and a central hub in Memphis—at night! During the day, an army of small trucks would meet the planes early each morning, collect yesterday's parcels originating from all over the country, and deliver them to recipients in that city "positively, absolutely by 10:30" that morning. In the afternoons, the same trucks would collect parcels from various customers and bring them to the waiting planes that would fly them to Memphis for sorting and then dispatch them to their respective destinations.

This was a radically different concept than the way the Postal Service played the game. In fact, Smith created a brand-new game. A group of investors thought Smith's concept would be so disruptive for the Postal Service that they gave him $60 million in seed capital to get his company up and running.

For years, FedEx mocked and capitalized on the Postal Service's deficiencies, and a full-scale war between the two emerged and went on for over 25 years. Finally, in January 2001, the mighty U.S. Postal Service capitulated. In a rare and public admission of the supremacy of FedEx's strategy, the Postal Service decided to play the game according to rules set by FedEx. It gave FedEx the largest contract it had ever awarded, which calls for FedEx to handle a large portion of the Postal Service's operations. Adding salt to the wound, the "treaty" also gives FedEx the right to place its own pickup bins in every post office in the United States. This could be the first step toward the eventual takeover of the Post Office by FedEx.

Smith's graduation paper? His professor gave it a D minus! Genius is often not quickly recognized—giving strategic innovators the advantage of long lead times before their competitors gradually figure out the new game being played.

STRATEGIC QUIZ

What score would your "professor" give your current strategy?

In order to assess the degree of supremacy you have over your competitors, or that they have over you, you may wish to answer the following questions:

Is your strategy . . .

1. decreasing the gap between you and your competitors?___1

2. keeping the gap the same?___2

3. increasing the gap?___3

Does your strategy allow you to . . .

1. control the terms of play in your sandbox?___1

2. manage your competitors' strategy as well as yours?___2

3. grow at your competitors' expense?___3

Does your strategy . . .

1. put you on a par with your competitors?___1

2. give you a slight edge over your competitors?___2

3. give you a significant advantage over your competitors?___3

4. dominate your competitors?___4

5. make competitors irrelevant?___5

6. eliminate competitors?___6

Total: _____

SCORE INTERPRETATION

If you scored 13 or more, you already reign supreme in your sandbox. You can stop reading at this point, unless of course you want to learn why you are doing so well. On the other hand, if you scored between 10 and 13, you are doing reasonably well but the concepts in the remainder of this book will probably help take your organization to the "next and ultimate" level of strategy.

    If you scored between 6 and 9, you are good but not yet in the "major league" of strategic concepts and processes. A well-developed strategy creation and deployment process could turbo-charge your company into the next strata or above. If you scored below 6, your current strategy is not working and it's time for a major rethinking.

THE STRATEGIC THINKING PROCESS: FROM STRATEGY FORMULATION TO DEPLOYMENT

T he word *process* is often heard in business circles, so one would think that the meaning of that word is well understood. The experience of us at DPI does not show that to be true. In fact, we have noticed that there are several different words used to connote that a process is in place—*system, method, procedure, protocol, formula,* and *practice.* My intent is not to attempt to define each of these words, but I will describe our definition of the word *process.* In fact, in order to define the word *process,* one needs to understand the meaning of the word *concept.*

At DPI, we define the word *concept* as an idea or premise that explains a certain phenomenon or behavior. These would include the following examples:

- Driving Force
- Areas of Excellence
- Controlling the Sandbox
- Stealth Competition

The word *process* is the assemblage of a number of concepts, or steps, into a logical sequence that allows a person to use these processes more effectively. In other words, a process is a series of codified concepts.

However, in any organization, there are two types of processes at work. We call these "hard" and "soft" processes. *Hard processes* are easily codified because they can easily be detected and their sequence of steps can be traced and drawn as a flowchart. These would include processes or systems that exist in most organizations, such as the following:

- Capital expenditure requests
- Personnel recruitment procedure
- Customer complaint reports
- Procurement protocol

Soft processes, on the other hand, occur in the minds of people and are a reflection of a person's thinking. These thinking processes are much more difficult to codify because they occur inside a person's mind—not an easy place to probe. However, at DPI, that is our forte. Our Area of Excellence is the ability to codify "Critical Thinking Processes" that improve a company's ability to formulate and deploy a distinctive strategy; create strategic, new-to-the-market products; and manage strategic information more effectively.

These processes are developed by participating in real work sessions with hundreds of CEOs and their management teams when we discuss such topics as strategy and product development. By listening to their conversations, we have discovered certain "concepts" that seem to be at the root of those discussions. Seeing a concept being employed, usually by osmosis, by several companies, helps us to discern a certain pattern of thinking and the concept is validated. We then organize these concepts into a logical sequence, or "process," which can then be used consciously by the management of any company. The resulting process, as shown in Figure 10-1, enables them to make decisions by design, and not by accident.

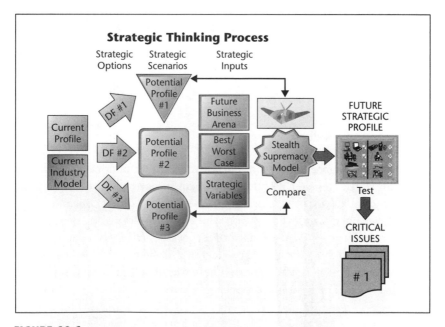

FIGURE 10-1

The first and foremost responsibility of any CEO is to formulate a strategy for the organization in order to give its employees a sense of direction and harness their energy toward the goal of supremacy over its competitors. The process that assists a CEO in this endeavor is one that is proprietary to DPI, which we call Strategic Thinking. The following is an overview of how the process proceeds.

PHASE 1: INTRODUCTION AND OVERVIEW

This first phase is a half-day introductory session with two activities. First, we give the group an overview of the concepts and process so that they are comfortable with these. The second activity is to introduce our Strategic Input Survey, in which the participants are asked to respond to a set of questions prior to the main three-day session that follows a month later. Their answers become the "raw material" for the next session. These responses are sent to us for editing and collating. Our goal is to encourage thoughtful attention to these key questions and extract meaningful answers as opposed to simply "brainstorming" answers on the spur of the moment.

PHASE 2: IDENTIFICATION OF CHARACTERISTICS

This session starts with the construction of a "snapshot" of the company in its present form. This consists of identifying the characteristics that are common to all of the company's products, all of the company's customers, all of the company's market segments, and all of the company's geographic markets. By identifying the characteristics that are common across these four elements of a company's profile, we can then uncover the company's current Driving Force, its current Business Concept, and its current Areas of Excellence. Gaining agreement about the company's current profile is the starting point of strategy formulation.

The next step in this process is to conduct a scan of the external environment and determine what the Future Business Arena, which we will find ourselves in, will look like. Once we are reasonably comfortable with that "picture" of the future, we can more specifically identify the strategic variables that will play for or against us in that arena. This will help us circumscribe the sandbox over which we want to establish supremacy.

Now for the fun part: the creation of a "stealth competitor," a concept that we described in Chapter 1. Which stealth competitor could step into that sandbox and attempt to establish supremacy for itself and create havoc for us? One team is given this assignment and they develop a specific strategy and business model that such a "stealth" entrant would deploy against us with the intent of gaining supremacy.

The next step is then for us to identify which components of our business could be the Driving Force of our future strategy. Companies can usually identify two or three areas that could be the engine of their future strategy. We then take each of these "possible" Driving Forces and develop "profiles" of what we would emphasize more or emphasize less under each one. The development of these scenarios allows the CEO and the management team to choose the Driving Force that will best all current competitors, as well as any new "stealth" entrant into our sandbox.

The final step in this first work session is to bring to the surface the Critical Issues that the management team will need to address and resolve over time in order to attain, maintain, or enhance supremacy in the chosen sandbox.

PHASE 3: SETTING STRATEGIC OBJECTIVES

This one-day work session is dedicated to the construction of strategic objectives. These are different from construction of operational objectives by function, which most companies already do quite well, but are usually extrapolations of past performance—numbers—into the future.

Strategic objectives are different. They do not pertain to functions within a company but rather to a company's future profile, which consists of products, customers, industry segments, and geographic markets. Strategic objectives are the "hills" that we must defend or capture in these four areas that will make our strategy succeed or fail.

CRITICAL ISSUES: THE BRIDGE TO STRATEGY DEPLOYMENT

At this point, our clients get to work on the "Critical Issues." These are the handful of essential initiatives that form the basis of the new strategy. These Critical Issues are one of the most crucial outputs from the Strategic Thinking Process. They are the keys to successful deployment because they have been chosen and agreed upon by those who will carry out the strategy. Once decided, these issues are assigned to individuals to drive them to conclusion. This is where the rubber hits the road—and where the commitment you have developed among these managers will flesh out the strategy and make it happen.

Identification of Critical Issues

Critical Issues are the bridge between the Current Profile and the Future Strategic Profile of an organization that management has deliberately decided to pursue. The direction of the organization has been decided, and managing that direction begins. Managing that direction on an ongoing basis means management of the Critical Issues that stem from four key areas (see Figure 10-2):

- Structure
- Systems/Processes
- Skills/Competencies
- Compensation

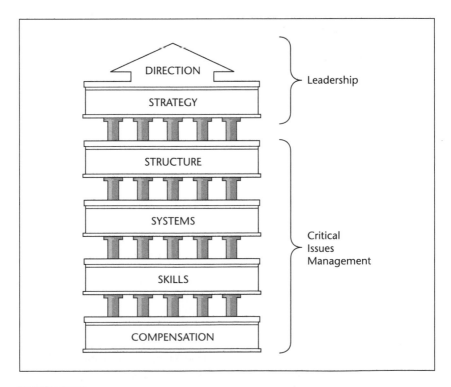

FIGURE 10-2

Critical Issues That Relate to Structure

One of our clients recently asked us a very good question: "Since most corporations are organized in a similar manner, does that mean that they have a similar strategy?"

After all, most companies have a marketing function, a sales function, a production function, an engineering function, an accounting function, an IT function, a human resource function, and so on. Most are also organized in a similar manner geographically, with a domestic operational unit and an international unit separated by country, or groups of countries, into regions. They may further be organized by product, by country, which leads to some form of "matrix" organization. Therefore, similar organization would seem to lead to a similar strategy.

Nothing could be further from the truth! Although organizational structures look as if they stem from the same business model, important nuances exist that make the various functions behave in very different ways. A correlating example is people. Although men wear suits and women wear dresses, no two women or two men behave in the same way.

The same is true in business. Although all companies wear the same clothes—organization—no two organizations behave in the same manner in the marketplace. In fact, if you were to look more carefully, you would detect that, although companies use the same words or titles, they are in fact organized in a very different manner.

The underlying element that determines an organization's structure is the concept of Driving Force, which is at the root of every business strategy.

Take, for example, 3M, Johnson & Johnson, and Caterpillar, examples used earlier. 3M is organized around "applications" it uncovers for its knowledge of polymer chemistry—its Driving Force. As a result, it has a Post-it division, a Masking Tape Division, a Video Tape Division, a Film Division, which are all different applications of its root polymer chemistry. Each division has its own sales, marketing, and manufacturing functions, since these tend to require different skills from one application to another, using different methods to get to market. Some divisions sell direct, some use agents and distributors. Some make end-use products, some make components for other companies' products.

Caterpillar, on the other hand, uses the same titles and words but is organized in a very different manner. Since it pursues a Product-driven strategy—earth-moving machines—the company is organized around different product categories. They have a Large Machine Division, a Mid-size Machine Division, a Small Machine Division, and recently added a Compact Machine Division. The manufacturing is decentralized, whereby different functions are centralized and broken down geographically, with a general manager for each geographic market. This is done to accommodate Caterpillar's unique network of independent dealers, which is their chosen way to market.

Johnson & Johnson is not organized like either of these other two. Its strategy is "satisfying the health needs of doctors, nurses, patients, and mothers"—a User Class–driven strategy. As such, it is organized around where these four groups are accessed. As a result, it has two divisions: a Hospital Division, since this is where doctors, nurses, and patients are found, and a Consumer Division, which is where mothers are found. Manufacturing is thus centralized, while each division has its own sales and marketing organizations. All the products aimed at doctors, nurses, and patients go through the Hospital Division, and all the products aimed at mothers go through the Consumer Division.

There was a fad in the 1970s and 1980s to reorganize and restructure companies. After the reorganization, the most difficult question to answer became: Now that we are reorganized, where are we going?

In our view, structure follows strategy. The organization structure of the business must support the direction of that business. We have further learned that each Driving Force requires a slightly different organization structure.

Critical Issues That Relate to Processes and Systems

The next discussion that leads to Critical Issues is one that revolves around the subject of "systems." Many companies today have purchased sophisticated and costly electronic information systems only to find out some time later that the systems are not supportive of the company's business strategy. Again, our view is that all information systems must be aligned with the direction of the organization and that there are usually issues that surface in the area of systems or processes.

Critical Issues That Relate to Skills and Competencies

When an organization changes its direction, this change will usually require the acquisition of a new set of skills. These skills can be developed, but frequently they do not reside in-house and must be acquired, thus giving rise to another set of Critical Issues. For example, when LandAmerica adopted a new strategy that required more Internet capabilities, one of the most pressing Critical Issues was the acquisition of a company that had the necessary capabilities in that area.

Critical Issues That Relate to Compensation

In spite of all the titles or power you might think you have over people, my experience has convinced me that people do not do what you want them to do; people do *what they are paid* to do. If your strategy says that you want your people to behave in a certain manner but your compensation system rewards them to do something different, I can assure you that at the end of the year they will have done what they were paid to do and not what you wanted them to do.

As a result, another area of discussion that raises Critical Issues is the subject of compensation, to ensure that the compensation of key individuals is geared to supporting the strategy and direction of the business.

Around these four specific areas—structure, systems, skills, and compensation—a number of Critical Issues are identified and assigned to specific individuals for resolution. The expected results are articulated, the macro-action steps are listed, other people that need to be involved are assigned to each team, and completion and review dates are established. These Critical Issues then become "the plan" for the organization, and it is the ongoing management and resolution of these issues that makes the CEO's vision a reality over time. It is how the strategy is deployed successfully.

CLOSING THE LOOP

At this point, you might be wondering how all the concepts presented tie together into a cohesive whole. The rectangle at the top of Figure 10-2 represents the output of our Strategic Thinking Process. The strategic profile is a description of what an organization wants to look like at some point in the future. The inside of the rectangle contains the content of this picture. The Critical Issues are the bridge that needs to be crossed in order to go from what the company looks like today to what it wants to look like tomorrow. Next comes planning time.

The Operational Plan

The next task is to examine the organization's current activities and decide which products, customers, and markets need to be improved or modified.

Moreover, one must identify those that need to be eliminated because they no longer fit the vision of what the company is trying to become.

One of the most difficult decisions we find management having to make, if they do not have what we call a "strategic filter," is not *what* to do but rather what *not* to do anymore. This is because there is always someone telling management to "hang in" a little longer—that the corner 'round which they will turn is about to come but, in fact, it never does. During the operational planning stage, these decisions become easier to make because all participants have agreed on that strategic filter and that those activities no longer fit their aspiration of the type of company they are trying to build.

Said Jack Messman, former CEO of Union Pacific Resources and now CEO of Novell:

> By agreeing to a strategy, you also agree to what you're not going to do. This avoids wasting time and resources on activities that do not support the strategy. After using the DPI process, our people became more focused on success and stopped debating alternatives.

The Strategic Plan

In our view, a strategic plan is one that will alter the "look" of an organization in the future. The key elements that will alter the "look" of a company in the future are the new products, new customers, and new markets that the company wants to add to that look. A plan now needs to be constructed to make these happen.

Our experience shows that if you want to give birth to brand-new activities (products, markets, and acquisitions), it is wise to have people other than those who are running your current businesses "midwife" these projects to birth. The rationale is simple: Those running your current businesses have a locomotive on their hands, and keeping that engine on track will require all their time and energy. As such, it is wise to have new activities managed outside the normal structure of the current business.

The Strategic Profile Is the Target for All Decisions

As illustrated, the strategic profile becomes the target for all the decisions that are made in the organization. Plans and decisions that fit inside the frame of this profile are pursued, and those that do not fit, are not.

PHASE 4: CRITICAL ISSUES MEETING

One CEO client recently said to this author:

> You DPI guys are no more than strategic enforcers. Because we scheduled a meeting with you, we show up. Otherwise, we'd find something else to do. And when we show up, we know what questions you are going to ask. So we work our butts off because no one wants to go to that meeting and report "no progress."

I thought this was a very good way of describing our involvement in the deployment of the strategy as well as in its formulation.

Phase 4 consists of two quarterly, half-day meetings with the CEO and the management team to review progress on the Critical Issues. At these meetings, the "owner" of each issue is expected to give a report of progress. These meetings give the CEO an opportunity to do the following:

- Assess the progress, or nonprogress, on each issue
- Determine whether the issue is "on track" or "off track"
- Judge whether the work on each issue is proceeding at the proper pace
- Remove any obstacles into which the owners and their teams are running
- Make any midcourse corrections

PHASE 5: REVIEW/REVISIT SESSION

Some 10 to 12 months after Phase 2, most clients want to have a review, or revisit, of their previous conclusions. Because these conclusions were based on a certain number of assumptions as to what might or might not occur in the environment, most CEOs want to revisit these assumptions to see which proved to be right and which ones wrong. This reassessment allows the client to fine-tune the strategy and occasionally pick up a Critical Issue or two that were missed the first time through the process.

CONCLUSION

"Thinking," said Henry Ford, "is a difficult activity. That is why so many people don't practice that habit."

CHAPTER 11

ARE YOU USING STRATEGIC INFORMATION STRATEGICALLY?

One of the most frequent complaints we hear from top executives today is: "We're drowning in information. How do we manage our way through all this data?" That frustration is rooted in a phenomenon that has been plaguing humankind since the invention of the written word—the continuous and ever-increasing amount of information available to executives to help them make decisions. Unfortunately, the prognosis is not very promising. This "help" is growing exponentially each day.

Let's review the history of information over the last three or four centuries. Someone has documented that from the mid-1700s to the early 1900s the amount of information in the world doubled. It doubled again from 1900 to 1950. It then tripled and quadrupled from 1950 to 1960 and from 1960 to 1970. With the advent of microprocessors in the 1980s and 1990s, one can just imagine what that multiple has been since then. To put that all into perspective, one page of the *New York Times* contains more information than the average person living during the 1700s received during an entire lifetime!

The same has happened in business. The advent of mainframe computers that spit out mind-numbing quantities of data, and the ever-increasing ability of PCs to do the same, virtually "paralyzes" the ability of executives to make decisions. They are simply inundated with so much information that they cannot separate the relevant from the irrelevant.

In the corporate world, there is another phenomenon at work—executives' inability to recognize the difference between strategic and operational information. One result of this shortcoming has been questionable and very costly decisions as to how information should be managed and what type of IT systems companies should use to manage it.

The difference between the two types of information is simple. Operational information is *how* in nature, while strategic information is *what* in nature. In other words, strategic information is of the kind that helps executives decide what they want the organization to become, while operational information helps them decide how to achieve that goal. Operational data is usually manipulated by IT systems such as

- Payroll
- Accounts receivable
- Accounts payable
- Inventory management
- Human resource management
- Procurement
- Capital expenditure

Strategic information, on the other hand, helps executives decide what they want the company to become in the future. These determinations relate to the following elements of the scope of the company's future:

- Products
- Customers
- Market segments
- Geographic markets

These decisions determine the future profile or "look" of that company and require the assistance of information that is strategic in nature, not operational in nature. There is also another very important difference. Operational information can be managed by generic, off-the-shelf IT hardware and software systems that "plug and play" and are easily available from a large number of vendors. This is so because every company conducts its operations in these areas in the same manner. Every company pays its people in the same way. Every company pays its suppliers in the same way. Every company collects its receivables in the same way, and so forth. As a result, standard IT systems are appropriate.

However, every company does not manage information regarding future products, future customers, future markets, and future geographic areas in the same manner as its competitors do. Each company's strategy is different from its competitors' and, as such, demands that it interact with its customers and markets in a different way. Therefore, generic IT systems are useless in managing strategic information that can help the company realize its future strategic profile. Not only do generic IT systems for this type of information not exist, strategic decisions can only be assisted by IT systems that are designed specifically to accomplish this goal. These systems are almost always proprietary in nature since every company interacts with its environment in its own particular manner. Furthermore, these systems (the information processes, not the hardware and software) must be designed by the company's own experts and not by an outside consultant. No outside consultant understands how a company wishes to interact with its future customers and markets as well as the company's own people do.

STRATEGIC INFORMATICS

At this point, I would like to introduce you to a word that is rarely used in corporate America: *informatics*. Informatics is commonly used in other countries to describe IT systems. In French, the word is *informatique*. In Spanish, the word is *informatica*.

The word *informatics* is defined as "the collection, organization, and dissemination of information." At DPI, we have added the word *strategic* to that definition. As a result, we define *strategic informatics* as "the collection, organization, and dissemination of strategic information."

With the advent of the geographically dispersed corporation, another word needs to be added to that classic definition. A more up-to-date definition for the word *informatics* is the "collection, organization, dissemination, *and transmission* of information." For many centuries, the collection, organization, dissemination, and transmission of information were done verbally or manually. For example, the Pony Express was Wells Fargo's attempt to speed up the transmission of information. In Germany, a gentleman by the name of Urn Taxis received the first contract to create a "postal" system to deliver that country's mail. He fulfilled that mandate by using horse-drawn buggies, which soon became known as "taxis," and thus he gave birth to an entire new industry. This system, again, was an attempt to speed up the transmission of information.

Since the early 1950s computers became the vehicle of choice to accomplish this task. In fact, IT systems were invented to speed up, once more, the transmission of information. Generic IT systems were designed to automate and replace the manual systems that were then in use. It would then make the process more efficient. In other words, IT systems were meant to automate existing processes.

When there is a change in strategy that brings with it a change in the nature of the products, customers, and markets the company wishes to pursue in the future, however, the processes to collect, organize, disseminate, and transmit information do not exist. This situation presents management with a major dilemma: It is impossible to automate nonexisting processes. This dilemma can only be solved in one way. These processes must be created from scratch.

MANAGING STRATEGICALLY SENSITIVE INFORMATION

Before anyone can manage information *physically* he or she must manage information *conceptually*. In other words, a conceptual process is required to design the physical process. That process eventually will help the company's executives manage strategically sensitive information in order to make decisions that will shape the company's future profile.

The first thrust of the process is to determine what information is required to deploy and monitor a new strategy and how that information should flow through the organization.

This conceptual process has the following steps:

1. Validate the company's Future Strategic Profile.

2. Determine the information that will be required to realize that profile.

3. Pinpoint the information that already exists, its source, and location.

4. Determine the information that is required but is not found in the organization.

5. Identify the source and location of this information.

6. Determine the recipients of strategic information.

7. Delineate the timing, frequency, and format of that information.

We call this step the "process architecture," which is required before any physical process can be built. This architecture can only be done by the executive team. The elements they require in each of the previous steps become the blueprint for the firm's IT gurus. This blueprint now provides these internal gurus with a framework to create new processes that are intended to manage strategic information. The following are process questions:

- What is the thrust of our Future Strategic Profile?
- What modus operandi will we use to deploy our strategy?
- What will be the key strategic areas of that modus operandi?
- What information will be required to deploy and monitor our Future Strategic Profile successfully?
- What information do we already have?
- What new information will we need to have?
- Who or what is the source of that information?
- Who or what will be the recipients of that information?

Once these questions have been answered, then the IT group can get together and design the system that will collect, organize, and transmit that information from source to recipient.

CLIENT EXAMPLES

One of our clients is a major producer of fibers for the textile industry. This client considered itself to have a Production Capacity–driven strategy focusing on the sale of high-volume commodity fibers. Their target customer was the textile manufacturer that controlled the sandbox by preventing the fiber company access to the designer or the end user of the garment.

Using our Strategic Thinking Process, this client decided to transform itself into a Production Capability–driven company offering specialty fibers. In doing so, they would attempt to change the game to their advantage by conducting research of end-user needs and selling to the designer instead of the textile manufacturer. This strategy, management felt, was a dramatic change in direction, but it was one they needed to make if the company was to survive and prosper. Using another DPI process called Strategic Product Innovation, they generated over 300 new-to-the-market concepts for specialty products. Yet this company did not have any systems to collect, organize, disseminate, and transmit information necessary to the success of their new strategy. These systems needed to do the following:

- Monitor the progress of these 300 concepts in the new product hopper that are all at different stages of commercialization.

- Control communications with over 400 garment designers located in six different countries.
- Manage the output of their research with 5,000 end users, again in six countries.

Another client is in the trade show business. Trade shows are usually organized by an industry association that handles all the booking details, exhibitor needs, floor space configurations, and so on. In the last few years, there is another market that is emerging. That market is called the "corporate market." More and more companies are starting to organize "captive" shows to which they invite only their customers and suppliers. Our client decided to extend its strategy to include this new, growing segment. However, the client did not have systems in place to do the following:

- Interact with the show managers of the Fortune 2000 companies that were identified as prime targets.
- Interact with over 700 venues where these captive shows can be held.
- Maintain an inventory of the floor plans of these 700 facilities.
- Keep an inventory of the electrical, mechanical, and other standards that these venues use.

In both instances, new systems had to be created from scratch. And again, they used another DPI process—the one described in this chapter. The result has been the effective development of information process "blueprints" that identify which information is strategically essential, who needs to see it, and how it should flow through the organization. This has provided the IT people responsible for creating the infrastructure with a clear set of requirements. The results? Faster, less costly implementation of effective information systems and better deployment of the company's strategy.

MARKETING STRATEGIC INFORMATION

Informatics also brings management another generally overlooked opportunity. This is the possibility of creating new revenue streams by selling information as well as products. This is the second thrust of the process—identifying and commercializing selective information to create new value-added products that bring new revenue streams.

Every company accumulates, over time, a wealth of information about its business, which lies dormant in what I call "data vaults." Like any vault, that information is under lock and key and sometimes is not even available to the company's own personnel. Our experience has shown that some of that information represents value to someone or to some organization that would be willing to pay for access to it. We call this "value-laden information."

The "conceptual" process to do this is different from the one required to "manage" information. This process has the following steps:

1. Identify dormant, but value-laden information.

2. Create new value-added products or services.

3. Identify the value recognizers, the value buyers, and the value recipients.

4. Determine how to package the information.

5. Develop and implement a commercialization plan.

The following are the process questions that need to be answered in order to capitalize on the opportunity that strategic informatics brings:

- What value-laden information do we possess that would be of substantial value to someone or some organization?
- Who would be the value recipient?
- Who would be the value recognizer?
- Who would be the value buyer?
- How much would these people pay for that value?
- What need exists for this information?
- What evidence do we have that verifies that need?
- How can we package this information to satisfy this need?
- How can we show unquestioned, demonstrable value to the potential buyer?

CLIENT EXAMPLES

Another one of our clients is a health-care company that specializes in the treatment of cancer. Over the years, this organization has accumulated voluminous amounts of information about various forms of cancer, all of which has been dormant in a number of corporate "data vaults." Using the process described in this chapter, management identified large quantities of value-laden information that could be of benefit to patients as well as health-care professionals. The company is now in the midst of sorting that information into usable form for new patients who will receive it free of charge, and in a different format for health-care professionals who will be asked to pay for access to it.

Our trade show client also discovered a major opportunity while using this process. As stated above, this company has the floor plans of over 1,500 convention sites together with the traffic patterns of each of the trade shows that are held in these facilities. All that information was dormant, again residing in another data vault. When searching for value-laden information, someone suggested that they introduce a new service similar to that of Ticketmaster and become the "Ticketmaster of Trade Shows." In other words, build a system that would allow them to become the sole booking agent for all the trade shows held in these 1,500 sites. Not only could they book the space that an exhibitor would want, but they could counsel that firm on the location that has the most traffic as well as the best size of booths and other information. These endeavors would create new revenue streams for the company and tighten their control of that sandbox.

In closing, let me leave you with something to reflect upon: The Sabre airline reservation system has a market cap greater than that of all the airlines put together. In other words, people are prepared to pay more for the information about airlines than they are willing to pay for the product itself.

Is there information stored in dormant data vaults in your organization that might be worth more than the product you sell?

CHAPTER 12

HOW STRATEGIC
PRODUCT INNOVATION
BREEDS SUPREMACY

New-to-the-market products are the fuel of corporate longevity.

There was a time, not so long ago, that, when you went to the national sales meeting, you were treated to a barrage of color slides shown through projectors made by Kodak or Bell and Howell. Then along came Power-Point, for better or worse, and those ubiquitous projectors, and the slide-making equipment that went with them, were obsolete.

There was a time, not so long ago, that every desk in an office had a Wang word processor, which promised a "paperless office." Then came the PC, and Wang was out of business almost overnight.

There was a time, not so long ago, that Keds were the leading sneakers for kids. Then along came Nike and Reebok.

There was a time, not so long ago, when there was a Schwinn 10-speed bicycle, or two, in garages everywhere. Then along came Cannon-dale and Trek, with high-tech bikes that ultimately forced Schwinn into bankruptcy.

There was time, not so long ago, that Telex machines were found in every office in the world. And there was a time, not so long ago, that there was a Singer sewing machine in every home in America and many other countries.

There was a time, not so long ago, when these companies and many more such as Addressograph Multigraph, Friden, and Borden's were pow-erhouses in their respective sandboxes, with supremacy over all their com-petitors. Just a few years later, however, their supremacy had disintegrated together with their stock prices, and billions in shareholder value had been destroyed. What did these companies do, or not do, to descend from the ecstasy of supremacy to the footnotes of corporate history books?

LACK OF STRATEGIC PRODUCT INNOVATION

The strategy of most companies is deployed through the introduction and commercialization of new products. Therefore, any company that wishes to perpetuate its supremacy over a long period of time needs to have in place an ongoing and aggressive *new product creation program*. Unfortunately, such was not the case in the companies mentioned above. Many other companies, which had ongoing new product development programs, could extend their supremacy over their competitors for very long periods of time, companies such as Johnson & Johnson, Caterpillar, 3M, Mercedes, Sony, Honda, and Microsoft.

New Products Are Not Always New Products

As noted in a previous chapter, the "profile" of a company is seen in the nature of the products the company offers, the nature of customers to which it makes these available, the nature of the market segments in which these customers reside, and the nature of the geographic markets in which it operates.

If a CEO wishes to change the *profile* of the company, he or she needs to do so by the creation and commercialization of *new* products. During our research into the subject of product innovation, we noticed that most companies concentrate their entire product innovation effort on incremental or marginal improvements to *existing products*. This type of product innovation is not strategic in nature, since there is no attempt to change the "look" of the products the company offers.

In fact, while working with companies considered to be the best at product innovation, we discovered that even these companies had difficulty defining what a *new product* was. Thus our first area of investigation was to identify the various categories of new product opportunities. Over time, we uncovered *five* categories of new product opportunities. These are:

- *New to the market*. These are products that, when introduced, were unique to the market and the world. No similar products existed anywhere. Examples consist of 3M's Post-it Notes, and Sony's Walkman and VCR.

- *New to us.* When Panasonic introduced its own version of the VCR, it was not new to the market, since Sony had done it before, but it was new to Panasonic.
- *Product extensions.* In this category, we find two types: *incremental* and *quantum leap.* An example of an *incremental* extension is 3M's adaptation of the original Post-it Notes into larger sizes, shapes, and colors. Boeing's announcement of a supersonic passenger jet is a quantum leap extension. The technology required is a significant step beyond making its standard passenger jets.
- *New customers.* This category applies to the introduction of current products to new customers.
- *New markets.* This category applies to the introduction of current products to new market segments or new geographic areas.

The Em-phá-sis on the Wrong Syl-lá-ble

The next area we investigated was: In which category did they invest most of their resources? Guess what over 200 companies answered? Right: *product extensions*—of the *incremental* type. The food and packaged goods industries, for example, have perfected the art of "new and improved" products in different colors and sizes. Unfortunately, incremental extensions only bring *incremental revenues.* Only *new-to-the-market* products create new revenue streams. Most companies are putting their em-phá-sis on the wrong syl-lá-ble. In other words, they are pouring their money into the wrong type of product innovation.

THE FOUR DEADLY SINS THAT KILL STRATEGIC PRODUCT INNOVATION

Since new-to-the-market products are the essence of strategic supremacy, we then set out to identify the obstacles that caused companies to spend almost all of their time, money, and energy on product extensions at the expense of new-to-the-market products. Our discovery? Most companies committed one, or more, of four "sins" that killed new product creation and led to a company's loss of supremacy over its competitors. Unfortunately, all four were self-inflicted wounds.

Sin 1: Too Much Focus on Current Customers

Who do most books on product innovation tell you to consult in order to get inspiration for new products? The obvious answer: your customers. Wrong—dead wrong! If a company focuses its entire effort on current customers as a source for new products, it will always end up with *incremental* products. The reason is very simple. *Current* customers are very good at telling you what is *currently wrong* with your *current product.* They can do this well because they do side-by-side comparisons and they identify *performance gaps* in your product relative to your competitors. Naturally, you go back to the factory, tweak the product a little, and come back with an incremental improvement. And the pattern is set and keeps repeating itself.

Worse than that, your current customers can begin to *dominate* your product development process. We often see this scenario when we work with clients. Borroughs Corporation, a company that makes, among other things, checkout lines for retail stores, had gradually gotten itself into this predicament. The company found itself responding to nearly every customer request for tweaks, refinements, and custom designs. Said CEO Tim Tyler:

> It was driving our inventories and engineering costs through the roof. I read an article in *Fortune* about Boeing and how they were faced with the problem of having seven or eight airplane frame models, yet they were offering something like 33,000 different variations of galleys and bathrooms, and that was us to a *T.*

Borroughs used the Strategic Product Innovation Process we describe later in this chapter to analyze the problem and come up with a game-changing solution: a standardized product that meets all its customers' essential needs. That product is also easily customizable to fit each customer's unique "look"—all at a very competitive cost. Customers readily embraced the concept, and Borroughs's margins recovered nicely.

You cannot depend on current customers for your new product ideas because they are *not* very competent at telling you what they will need *in the future.* The following are some examples.

Not one of 3M's millions of customers ever asked 3M for Post-it Notes. Not one of Chrysler's millions of customers ever asked for a minivan. Not one of Sony's millions of customers ever asked Mr. Akio Morita, the founder of Sony, for a Diskman or a VCR. No one on this planet ever asked Steve Jobs and Steve Wozniak for an Apple computer or an i-Pod. And the list goes on. These are all products that originated in the minds of the *creator, not the recipient.* There is a very good reason for this, as articulated by Morita:

Our plan is to influence the public with new products instead of asking which products they want. The public doesn't know what is possible. We do.

Another person who said it as eloquently was the recently retired CEO of 3M, Livio DeSimone:

The most interesting products are the ones that people need but can't articulate that they need.

In order to breed competitive supremacy and create new *revenue streams*, it is imperative to concentrate a company's product innovation resources on *new-to-the-market* products.

These are products that satisfy *future implicit needs* that you have identified and that your customers cannot articulate to you today. In this manner, the result will be products that will allow you to *change the game and perpetuate your supremacy.*

Sin 2: Protect the "Cash Cow" Mentality

Every company, over time, has products that become cash cows. *Never worship at the altar of the cash cow.* You will lose your supremacy. IBM is a case in point.

IBM's cash cow, as we all know, had been its mainframes–once the workhorses of the computing industry. In 1968, in its Swiss laboratories, IBM invented the first microchip—the RISC chip—with more processing capacity than its smaller mainframes. A small computer prototype, powered by this chip, was built and could have been the first PC the world saw. IBM, however, made a deliberate decision *not* to introduce that chip, because it could foresee the devastation it might have on its mainframe business. In 1994, 26 years later and maybe 26 years too late, IBM finally introduced the RISC chip under the name PowerPC. In the meantime, IBM lost the opportunity to be the powerhouse in the *consumer* market that it is in the *business* market.

The same happened at Xerox. The company worshiped so diligently at the altar of large copiers that it did not see the advent of a stealth competitor—Canon—with small copiers. Furthermore, it failed to capitalize on unique inventions that were developed in its Silicon Valley laboratories, such as the mouse and inkjet printers, both used successfully by Apple later.

General Motors' fixation on large, gas-guzzling cars of questionable quality caused it to fail to foresee the entry of Toyota and Honda into the U.S. market with small, high-quality cars that have reduced GM to half the company it used to be.

Sin 3: The Mature Market Syndrome

> Our industry is mature. There is no more growth in these markets.

Many people would claim that the reason products become generic, prices come down to the lowest levels, and growth stops is that the "market is mature." Mature markets, in our view, are a myth.

Consider some examples. Who would have thought 15 years ago that people would pay $300 for a pair of shoes? Running shoes at that! After all, everyone had a pair of $10 sneakers, and the market was mature. Then along came Nike and Reebok, and the "mature market" exploded.

Who would have believed a few years ago that anyone would pay $4 for a cup of coffee? Yet Starbucks has revolutionized the takeout coffee business by introducing unique products and marketing in a "mature" industry dominated by Dunkin' Donuts for decades. Dunkin' Donuts had mastered the perfect 50-cent "bottomless" cup. A cup of coffee, after all, was just a cup of coffee.

Who would have thought 15 years ago that people would pay $5,000 for a bicycle? After all, everyone had a $100 bicycle, and the market was mature. Then along came Shimano, Cannondale, Trek, and others with 18- and 21-speed bicycles and a new type of bike called a "mountain bike," and the "mature market" exploded.

Two CEOs who have based their success on debunking the notion of "mature" markets are Jack Welch, General Electric's famous ex-CEO, and Lawrence Bossidy, formerly CEO of Allied Signal. Jack Welch preaches that "mature markets are a state of mind," while Bossidy says: "There is no such thing as a mature market. What we need are *mature executives* who can make markets grow."

Sin 4: The Commodity Product Fallacy

"We're in the commodity business" is another mindset that can bring down a company's supremacy. This is also a state of mind. Products become commodities when management *convinces* itself that they are. It's a self-fulfilling prophecy.

An example is baking soda, a "commodity" product that has been around since the days of the pharaohs. One day someone placed a small quantity in a refrigerator and noticed that it absorbed odors. Not so long after, we had baking soda deodorant. Then came baking soda toothpaste and, recently, baking soda diapers.

Frank Purdue pioneered the concept of branding chicken, promising more tender, better-tasting chicken. Before Purdue, chicken was chicken, and the only price factors were supply and demand.

Then there is the "mother" of all commodities—water. Yet, look at what the French can do with water. They have mastered the marketing of this mundane commodity by branding it under a variety of names such as Vitel, Evian, and Perrier. Knowing that people are becoming more concerned about the quality of the water they drink, they began to market *bottled* water at exorbitant prices. This concept was immediately successful even in places where tap water is excellent and essentially free. Through brilliant marketing, they made water "trendy," creating "designer brands," and they charged even more.

Beverage manufacturers are now taking the concept a big step further, adding *nutrients* to water to create a new category: *sports* water. One of these even incorporates the "grandmother" of all commodities: *oxygen*.

NEW-TO-THE-MARKET PRODUCTS BREED SUPREMACY

Sony, 3M, Canon, Microsoft, Johnson & Johnson, Caterpillar, Schwab, and many others maintain their control of the sandbox not by introducing "me-too" products but rather by focusing their resources on the creation of new-to-the-market products. These have three inherent characteristics that contribute to breeding supremacy over their competitors:

- *A period of exclusivity.* When you are the only product in the market, you are the *only one*.
- *Capability of charging premium prices.* During this period of exclusivity, you can obtain *premium prices*, as opposed to me-too products, where every transaction comes down to haggling over price.

- *Ability to build in barriers.* Being first to the market allows you to build in barriers that make it very difficult for competitors to gain entry into your game.

After all, that's what supremacy is all about: changing the game and creating the rules to which competitors who wish to play your game must submit.

THE STRATEGIC PRODUCT INNOVATION PROCESS

Strategic supremacy is highly dependent on the organization's ability to create and bring to market new products more often and more quickly than its competitors. We view new product creation as the *fuel of corporate longevity*—3M, Johnson & Johnson, and Sony introduce hundreds of new products every year. The secret of these product innovator superstars is a deliberate process that causes product innovation. This systematic process is known and used by everyone in the company.

Observing this phenomenon, we at DPI went on to *codify* this process being practiced *implicitly* at these kinds of companies. The result is a unique process called "Strategic Product Innovation," which makes new product creation a learnable, *repeatable* process. This process can be used by an organization to create and commercialize new-to-the-market products (not seen before) that leverage the company's Driving Force and Areas of Excellence, and to generate new revenue streams, allowing the company to grow faster than its competitors.

This conscious, repeatable business practice consists of the following four steps:

1. *Creation.* Carefully monitor the 10 sources in your business environment, which are listed in the next section, from which you can create a broad range of opportunities for new-to-the-market products.

2. *Assessment.* Measure the new product opportunities in terms of costs, benefits, strategic fit, and difficulty of implementation. These criteria will let you know which opportunities should be pursued further—and which should be abandoned.

3. *Development.* Once a commitment is made, try to anticipate the critical factors that will cause the new product to succeed or fail in the marketplace.

4. *Pursuit.* Develop a specific implementation plan that promotes success and avoids failure.

For a visual representation of these steps, see Figure 12-1.

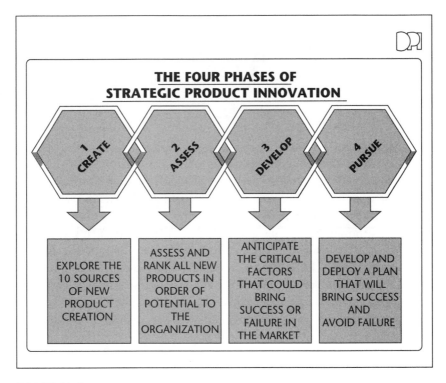

FIGURE 12-1

THE CREATION STEP

Our research in this area of corporate endeavor has uncovered 10 sources from which can emerge new-to-the-market product concepts:

1. Unexpected successes

2. Unexpected failures

3. Unexpected external events

4. Process weaknesses

5. Industry/structural changes

6. High-growth areas

7. Converging technologies

8. Demographic shifts

9. Perception shifts

10. New knowledge

The following paragraphs give some examples.

Unexpected Successes

McDonald's unbelievable growth since the 1960s began with Ray Kroc's curiosity about why he had been selling so many milkshake machines to a small hamburger stand owned by the McDonald brothers. By examining the cause of an unexpected success, as Kroc did, we are able to uncover opportunities to create new-to-the-market products.

Even though Steve Jobs and Bill Gates may claim differently, I am convinced that neither expected their first products, the Apple PC and Microsoft's original PC software, respectively, to be as successful as they proved to be or that they would lead to an entire new universe of new-to-the-market products. Bill Gates even offered that software to IBM for $75,000 but IBM refused, which, in hindsight, has probably proven to be IBM's biggest strategic mistake.

Unexpected Failures

Failures, large and small, happen every day. They are generally viewed negatively, yet in many of them are the seeds of a success. The failure of the Ford Edsel, for example, led to the development of its highly successful, and game-changing Mustang.

Unexpected External Events

The world throws unexpected curve balls at us all the time. Two such events, the Asian financial crisis and a sudden decline in IT growth, threatened the previously very successful strategy of DPI client Teckwah, a Singapore-based commercial printer. These changes caused management to rethink the future, particularly since the IT industry was their primary market. Teckwah decided to provide a range of printing-related services that no other printer offered. This rethinking of their strategy and the offering of these new "products" evolved into a very successful new business model—supply chain management—and expanded Teckwah's market scope, enabling future expansion into new segments such as pharmaceuticals.

Process Weaknesses

Federal Express was created to exploit a major weakness in the U.S. Postal Service—its inability to deliver all the mail within 24 hours. If the Postal Service ever corrected that weakness, it would be the death of FedEx.

One of our clients mentioned earlier, Roberts Express, exploited a process weakness in Just-in-Time (or JIT) deliveries to the auto industry to create a game-changing service in the trucking business. It was so successful that none other than FedEx decided to make Roberts part of their business.

Tom Siebel, CEO of Siebel Systems, noticed another process weakness—the disconnect between the many, and increasing, channels through which customers buy a company's products. His company developed products called CRM (Customer Relationship Management) software, which enable a company to coordinate information about a customer's activities in all channels simultaneously.

Industry/Structural Changes

Changes such as the deregulation and internationalization of many businesses have led to new product and service concepts. These changes have given rise to companies such as MCI, Sprint, alternative local telephone carriers, electric power resellers, satellite dishes, and peripheral products such as decoders.

High-Growth Areas

The stupendous growth and penetration of PCs over the past decade created nearly endless opportunities for innovative *software* for business and entertainment uses. This trend continues, despite the leveling off of demand for PCs. Have you noticed unusual growth in an area of your business or *somebody else's* that might create an opportunity for you?

Converging Technologies

A lot has been said in the media about the convergence of computer and telecom technologies. Many of the predictions have come to pass with a wave of various personal communications devices. Much less has been said, however, about the convergence of electronics and biotechnology—a scientific trend that began with the now-archaic-looking Jarvik heart. The pacemaker and other similar devices are products that have emerged from this incipient branch of science. Much more sophisticated advances are on the horizon. One surprising player in this relatively new field is Motorola, which is developing products for use in applications as diverse as bioinformatics, molecular and cell biology, and genetics. That's a long way from cell phones. The situation is somewhat unique in that both electronic information processing and biotechnology are sciences in which new knowledge is emerging at an accelerating rate, opening an unprecedented range of new product and market opportunities.

Demographic Shifts

The aging of the baby-boom generation has given rise to a wide assortment of new products. One of the most profitable is the "new-age beverage" category championed by start-ups like SoBe. Knowing that the boomer generation is struggling to hang on to youth and vitality, SoBe has mixed various strange-sounding herbs with water and flavors, enticing the consumer with promises of greater physical and mental well-being. So successful has SoBe been, in a market assumed to be controlled by the distribution networks of Coke and Pepsi, that Pepsi recently acquired a controlling interest in the former cottage business for just under $400 million. This, after a heated bidding battle with none other than Coca-Cola.

Perception Shifts

One of the twentieth century's most enduring brands—Oldsmobile—fell prey to this type of change. Once a symbol of stature and upper-middle-class solidity, the perception of Olds gradually came to symbolize "old, stodgy, and boring" to younger consumers. Realizing this, apparently too late, GM tried to reposition Olds under the slogan "Not Your Father's Oldsmobile." It didn't stick, and the division flailed about looking for a way to revive its popularity until its demise was finally announced in 2001. Meanwhile, Toyota is *leveraging* the same type of changes in perceptions about cars—they have to be "cool" to appeal to a youthful driver—to create a new product line called "Matrix." This line has its own "youth-friendly" areas at dealerships that cater to some of the same consumers that Oldsmobile failed to attract.

New Knowledge

The latest new knowledge that holds immense implications for future products is the mapping of the human genome. This remarkable advance promises to open far-reaching new avenues of treatment of a wide variety of diseases. New knowledge concerning the effects of nutrition on human health is creating the opportunity for a wide variety of new products called wellness foods, nutraceuticals, and medical foods.

Opportunity's Constant Knock

Although many executives tell us, before they use our process, that there are no new product opportunities for their companies, we have never found that to be true. The problem is not that opportunity knocks but once, but it is knocking every day in the multitude of changes facing organizations. We have found—initially to our surprise, and always to the surprise of clients—that organizations have a surplus of opportunities. They just don't know where to look for these in a systematic manner. One of our clients generated over 1,200 and another, over 400, new-to-the-market product ideas in businesses that thought themselves to be in commodity, low-price, low-margin, mature market industries.

By exploring each of these 10 sources and their derivatives, management can generate dozens, if not hundreds, of new-to-the-market products. Once the ideas are in the hopper, the real challenge for management is to discriminate among them in order to select those that promise the most potential within the company's strategy.

THE ASSESSMENT STEP

The second step consists of ranking all these new product concepts in terms of their potential for the company. This is done by anticipating the relationship among the following:

- Cost
- Benefit
- Strategic fit
- Difficulty of implementation

Judging all concepts on these criteria allows management to rank them in order of attractiveness to the organization. Some of the new concepts with lesser potential are abandoned after this step.

Cost-Benefit Relationship

The first two criteria are obvious enough—*cost and benefit*. Each opportunity needs to be assessed in terms of its relative cost versus relative benefit.

Anyone engaged in product creation and introduction should want to know fairly concisely and rapidly, what will be the cost of implementing this opportunity? And, what will be the benefit of implementing this opportunity? The following are two of the generic questions usually asked:

- What is the cost of this new product or market opportunity?
- What is the benefit of this new product or market opportunity?

The following is a checklist of considerations that contribute either to the potential cost or potential benefit of an opportunity. An evaluation of each will allow you to create a framework within which the cost-benefit relationship can be clarified and scrutinized.

Checklist: Cost/Benefit

Cost	Benefit
People	Market share
Materials	Return/profit
Equipment	Prestige/image
Research	Service/satisfaction
Marketing	Earnings/dividends
Legal	Fallout/residuals
Promotion	Safety/security
Time	Quality
Pilot	Morale/motivation
Contingency	Growth/size

Strategic Fit / Difficulty of Implementation Relationship

The next two assessment criteria are less obvious: *strategic fit and difficulty of implementation*. These two criteria are probably more important than the cost-benefit ratio, but unfortunately they are almost always overlooked.

Strategic Fit   How well does this new product or market opportunity fit the strategy of the business? This is a key question that is often not asked but should be. Experience has shown that organizations that try to innovate *outside the strategic framework* of the business usually do not succeed.

By strategic fit, we mean the degree to which an opportunity fits a company's direction. The opportunity need not fit exactly at first, provided that it promises to fit well in the near future. So the issue concerns not just today's strategy but also the direction that the company is pursuing.

When an opportunity is pursued irrespective of strategic thrust, the results are usually disappointing or even damaging. Several years ago, Exxon decided to enter the office information business and began an operation known as QXT. Despite the infusion of massive amounts of money and the work of some highly talented people, QXT was a disaster, and Exxon eventually dissolved it. The office products market simply was not a part of Exxon's direction and strategy as a company. That is, it could not be *made* a part of the nature and direction—the fabric—of Exxon's business. Consequently, it was doomed to failure from the start. A senior executive of Exxon recently told us that Exxon executives did not understand the office equipment business as well as they did the "trivia of the oil business," and thus they could not manage or even judge the opportunities of the former. There was *no strategic fit*.

New product or new market creation is not a question of unbridled enthusiasm spinning off into every direction of the compass at once. It is a question of organized, purposeful, and *focused* attempts to create new products that fit the organization's *business goals*. Consequently, new product innovation must be undertaken within the purview of corporate strategy and its *future strategic profile*.

Assessing Strategic Fit   If the Driving Force of a company is not entirely clear (the company hasn't used the Strategic Thinking Process), we can still assess strategic fit by asking the following questions.

Questions: Strategic Fit

- How similar are the products this opportunity brings compared to the products we currently offer?
- How similar are the markets (segments or geographic) this opportunity brings compared to the markets we currently serve?
- How similar are the customers this opportunity brings compared to the customers we currently serve?
- How similar are the production capabilities and/or processes this opportunity brings compared to the production capabilities we currently have?
- How similar is the technology this opportunity needs compared to the technology we currently know?
- How similar are the sales/marketing methods this opportunity requires compared to the ones we currently use?
- How similar are the distribution/delivery methods this opportunity requires compared to the ones we use currently?
- How similar are the human resources and skills this opportunity requires compared to those we have currently?
- How will the size/growth and return/profit criteria compare to our current levels of achievement?

The more similarity there is in each of the above areas, the closer the strategic fit. The more dissimilar, the more remote the fit, unless of course the discrepancy is that the opportunity represents higher size/growth, or return/profit potential than that to which the company is accustomed. We have found that better than "normal" financial expectations are more the rule than the exception simply because the new products often represent a change from me-too commodities to unique, differentiated products.

Difficulty of Implementation   The fourth criterion is *difficulty of implementation*. Again, we have seen many good opportunities fail because management had simply understated the degree of difficulty in trying to capitalize on an opportunity.

The relative ease or difficulty of implementation really refers to the "organizational immune system" that every company seems to possess. We've seen numerous cases of good ideas that presented high benefit at reasonable cost within the organization's strategic framework but that were rejected by this immune system.

A case in point was Honda's marketing of its Acura automobiles when they were first introduced. These cars represented Honda's entry into the luxury auto marketplace. Honda made a decision at the outset that these luxury cars could not be sold through the same dealerships that were handling the rest of the Honda line. It was apparently felt that the Honda "sales culture" would not be conducive to selling these high-end automobiles. So Honda's decision was to market these new cars only in separate dealerships, and even then, only in those dealerships that maintained a certain physical distance from any nearby Honda dealerships. This decision was taken even at the risk of offending current Honda dealers. Honda clearly believed that its *organizational immune system* was not ready for the luxury auto.

Even IBM, with all its success in the mainframe business, had some initial difficulties when it entered the PC field. The reasons were obvious. The customer base was not the same. Mainframes are sold to companies, PCs to individuals. Thus, the selling and distribution methods were different, and IBM had no experience selling directly to consumers.

The degree of difficulty encountered in introducing new products or entering new markets is directly proportionate to the number of changes that the organization will need to make from its current modus operandi. The more changes, the greater the degree of difficulty; the fewer changes, the less difficulty.

To assess the degree of implementation difficulty, the following question needs to be asked: *How much change will be required in each of the following areas to implement this new product or market opportunity?*

Checklist: Implementation Difficulty

- Organization structure
- Processes and/or systems
- Skills and/or talents
- Manufacturing methods and capabilities
- Selling and/or marketing methods
- Distribution or delivery methods
- Technologies
- Capital and financing
- Legal and regulatory issues
- Image, reputation, and quality
- Compensation systems
- Raw materials
- Customer services
- Corporate culture

Once the changes have been identified, the element that will determine the degree of difficulty is the amount of control the implementors have over those changes. The more control, the less difficulty; the less control, the more difficulty. Another key question then is: *How much control do we have over each of the changes we will need to make in our current modus operandi to implement this new product?*

By assessing each new product on the basis of these four criteria, we can rank them in terms of their overall potential for the company. And, like milk and cream, the best new product opportunities rise to the top of the list, and the balance are discarded or saved for future reworking.

THE PURSUIT STEP

New product introductions succeed or fail based on management's ability to anticipate the *critical factors* that will deliver one or the other result. The development step is the *transition* to the formal pursuit, or introduction, of the new opportunity. It is the organization's ability to *think* through the implementation *beforehand*.

Best-Case and Worst-Case Scenarios

The first part of the pursuit step is to construct scenarios. In other words, management must try to foresee what would be the best possible set of outcomes as well as the worst possible set of outcomes for each new product opportunity. These scenarios can be captured in the following format.

Each new product, starting with the best one first, is now examined, and best- and worst-case scenarios are constructed using the results we could expect if we were to pursue this opportunity. The following are the questions to ask.

Process Questions

- *Best-case scenario.* If we pursued this opportunity, what are all the best results this opportunity would bring?
- *Worst-case scenario.* If we pursued this opportunity, what are all the worst results this opportunity would bring?

The second part of the pursuit step is to start *thinking* about how we can achieve the best-case scenario while avoiding the worst-case scenario.

In order to do this, we must now attempt to identify the *critical factors* that will lead to one or the other of the two scenarios. The following are questions to ask about critical factors.

Process Questions

- What critical factors will cause the worst-case scenario?
- What critical factors will cause the best-case scenario?

Having listed the outcomes that would produce the worst-case and best-case scenarios, you're now in a position to list the critical factors that will tend to bring about the best case and the critical factors that will tend to bring about the worst case.

After the identification of all the critical factors of success or failure is completed, we are now ready to proceed into the last, and final, step of new product or new market innovation—the launch.

The next step takes us from *transitional thinking* into the world of *implementation*. For new product and market concepts to be successful, the implementors must concentrate on two key elements. One is containing or *preventing* the worst-case scenario from materializing. The other is assuring or *promoting* the best-case scenario. Thus, the need at this stage in the process is to introduce the concepts of *preventive* and *promotive* actions.

Preventive and Promotive Actions

The pursuit step concentrates on taking special actions to remove obstacles to the effective implementation of the opportunity. The fundamental premise is to now think of specific actions that will *prevent* the critical factors that would cause the worst-case scenario while also thinking about actions to *promote* the critical factors that will cause the best possible outcome. Promotive actions seek to maximize the benefits of a new product while preventive actions seek to mitigate the effects of the potential problems that might be encountered.

Building the Implementation Plan

Pursuit is the process of formulating an implementation plan and then beginning the actual implementation of opportunities. It relies heavily on the critical factors that were raised in the development step. It is a step that is specifically designed to focus on individual opportunities and to bridge the gap between the *conceptualization* and the *actualization* of these opportunities. It allows you to analyze those factors that will determine success or failure for your opportunity and to assign *specific* actions that will help to enhance success and avoid failure. Pursuit is begun "on paper" before energy, resources, and reputations have been committed. Once the plan takes a coherent shape, implementation begins. Although the pursuit is not an absolute guarantee of success, it does function as an insurance policy, one designed to provide the greatest protection for you and your plan.

STRATEGY AND PRODUCT INNOVATION AT FLEXCON

A company with whom DPI has had a long-term relationship dating back to 1985 is FLEXcon, based in Spencer, Massachusetts. The company is a world leader in the manufacturing of laminated substrates and adhesives for a wide variety of applications across many industries. Here is what CEO Neil McDonough says about DPI's SPI process:

> New products are the lifeblood of our company. We put DPI's Strategic Product Innovation Process into place about 18 months ago. And after 18 months *30 percent of our sales come from new products*. We started with a goal of 30 percent in three years. Obviously, we blew that away. Through the first four months of this year, we came up with 179 products, using combinations of materials we had never made before. We made *and sold* them. So this has been very successful for us!
>
> It all comes down to getting agreement on the Driving Force, and the business concept, so that you can develop the Critical Issues from there. It's very straightforward. You've just got to invest the time and do it. And do it with a facilitator who has the experience to force you through these questions and keep the process on track. Then, once you've gotten down to the Critical Issues, give people the tools to make the right decisions and get things done. If you're going to tackle complex issues, you've got to embed these concepts in your company's culture.

PART TWO

CEOS AROUND THE WORLD EMBRACE STRATEGIC THINKING

Over the last 25 years we have worked with over 500 CEOs and some 600 companies, divisions, and business units. During this period of time we have interviewed over 100 of them and asked them to tell us why they decided to use our Strategic Thinking Process and what results they got. There are a number of themes that emerged from these interviews.

Why Did They Decide to Use DPI's Strategic Thinking Process?

Many reasons were cited by different CEOs why their companies decided to use the Strategic Thinking Process. But there seems to be three big themes:

- There was a lot of "turmoil" in their sandbox. They wanted to "stop the world" for a few days, take stock of the changes happening, and decide how to position the company in view of the dynamics that were occurring.
- They wanted to make a significant change in the direction of the company and they were having difficulty convincing their executive teams to do so. So, they were looking for a tool, vehicle, or "catalyst" to help their management teams see the world "as they saw it" and convince themselves of the need to change the company's direction.
- They didn't want an outside consultant to tell them what needed to be done nor how they should do it.

What Results Did They Get?

Although all used the process for one or more of the reasons mentioned previously, almost all CEOs praised the process for some of the additional *intangible* results that the process generated:

- They all spoke about the total *consensus* and *commitment* that the process created around each key decision taken.
- They all spoke about the *speed* with which decisions were implemented.

But don't take our word for, read for yourself. The following pages contain a broad selection of client companies that represents the spectrum of small, medium, and large firms—private and public—across various industries and located in different countries operating under different regulatory, cultural, and linguistic constraints. Thinking seems to cut across all these elements.

CHAPTER 13

CHARLES FOSTER, CHAIRMAN TED CHANDLER, CEO LANDAMERICA FINANCIAL GROUP RICHMOND, VIRGINIA

Title insurance. To most of us, it's just one of those details that comes up in the blur of closing a real estate transaction. But, to LandAmerica, it's their bread and butter. Or it was until a startling revelation occurred as the company's managers went through DPI's Strategic Thinking and e-Strategy Processes.

Back in 1998, LandAmerica was the second-largest U.S. supplier of title insurance policies, with $2 billion in revenues. The company was the product of the merging of two large competitors, Lawyers Title and the Commonwealth family of companies, in February of that year.

As mergers go, this one went quite well, as Chairman Charlie Foster describes: "There were some good cultural fits, and we brought them together. We went through a year of a robust economy, which helped, but then the world had been changing and continued to change. I believe our entire management team was looking for more cohesion than we had been able to articulate. We completed a lot of projects with regard to the merger and what systems and organizational structures needed to be changed, but we weren't sending a consistent internal message regarding growth strategies in the face of emerging technologies. We were just saying, here we're two companies that used to do something, how do we do it together? We got by that, and there was this companywide hunger, this need, this management imperative, to be clearer about the future."

In addition, there was a pressing need to deal with some fundamental shifts in the industry. Other mergers. The effects of the Internet. The very nature of how real estate transactions were being done. How would they react? Could they find a way *not* to be reactive, but to be more in charge of their own destiny?

As Foster explains: "It really boiled down to the competitive environment of what was going on in the industry, with how real estate transactions come down. The mortgage originators began to behave differently because of consolidations and capabilities afforded them through the Internet. There were consolidations going on in our industry and talk of further consolidation. But the state of our business really had to be characterized as one that was more *reactive* than proactive. We were dealing with the world as it was shifting, and *responding* to it."

Adds CEO Ted Chandler: "We began to see the limitations of our historical focus on being a single-product vendor of title insurance. We were concerned that this singular focus in a rapidly shifting market positioned us more on the *periphery* of the action than we used to be and than we wanted to be. We saw the opportunities, but we were not clear on how we should alter our positioning to take advantage of them."

The management team decided to look for objective outside assistance to work out a strategy. But unsatisfactory results from previous encounters with "traditional" content-based consultants led them to look for another solution. DPI's Strategic Thinking Process seemed to fit their needs.

"We first concluded that we would like to have a facilitator-enhanced process," Chandler says. "We had experience with consultants who came in and attempted to provide domain expertise, but we always knew that the real answers were locked up within us. We were looking for a set of professionals who could help us pull those ideas out. Really, the DPI Process, led by a facilitator who transfers the process skills that you need to continue and give momentum to the process, was exactly what we were looking for."

Adds Charlie Foster: "If I could characterize it another way, we were responding to the outside world, including our shareholders and the investment community. And we concluded, I guess, that we lacked clarity of direction. We needed clarity of purpose first of all—what it is we wanted to do, what our mission really *should* be—and then clarity of thought as to how to approach that goal. We were looking for a discipline, a structured process, not an *answer* by the guru du jour."

They gathered a LandAmerica management team from a cross-section of locations and disciplines, 25 in all, to participate. Right from the start the Strategic Thinking concept clicked.

Chandler continues: "The reaction from our people was very positive. I think there was a desire for this. We, like most companies, had a strategy. We were executing on a strategy, but it tended to be more of an implicit strategy—not one being aggressively communicated beyond the executive suite. The reason is, as Charlie said, there was a bit of a lack of clarity as to how boldly we should be taking advantage of emerging opportunities. When we brought the people together for the work session, I think there was a real buy-in that it was appropriate, and needed."

Despite the fact that the participants had come from many parts of the company and country, the process quickly got them on the same page and moving toward a surprising conclusion. It became immediately apparent that the company might make a major change of direction and Driving Force—creating an opportunity to drastically change the game in their sandbox.

As Chandler explains: "Because this business is largely locally driven and because real estate laws are different, and customs and practices are different, when you pull these people together, you find that it takes a while to talk the same language. This is because the business, even though it's under the rubric of title insurance, is actually executed differently depending on your geographical market. So the effort to identify the Driving Force brought on a lot of discussion. We actually, I think, are unusual among companies that have gone through the DPI process because we have changed our Driving Force. After we identified our current Driving Force as Product—title insurance policies—we realized we could really *change the game* if we moved to a *new* Driving Force: Market Category."

To put a finer point on it, they would be moving away from being simply a title insurance company and moving toward providing a wide range of services, all related to the *real estate transaction market*. Instead of selling a single piece of the puzzle, they would eventually manage the entire transaction—a radically different business model.

"The simple truth of the matter," says Charlie Foster, "is that we had been very oriented toward something called a 'title insurance policy,' which, if you peeled it back, had 95 percent *information* value versus 5 percent *insurance* value. But our current thesis is to try to respond to what the customer *really* wants. And the customer, no matter if it's a lender or a Realtor, a builder-developer or an attorney—our basic customer sets—what we think they want is a facilitated transaction, not just the title insurance. And so we're putting ourselves in a position to be that concierge, to be the facilitator, to provide that *seamless transaction*. And we're starting to call ourselves a *transaction manager* as a simple phrase as opposed to a title insurance fulfiller."

"The primary piece of it is that we had to get away from thinking of ourselves as just a title insurance company," Chandler says. "So our sandbox is that *we proactively provide services in the information, assurance, fiduciary, and settlement segments of the real estate business. And we intend to be the preeminent provider of seamless transactions and value-added knowledge through economical, time-sensitive, and customized solutions.* That combined statement of our future strategic profile does a number of things. It focuses people on the fact that when we talk about *information, assurance, fiduciary,* and *settlement,* then *title insurance* tucks into *assurance.* It's just one of a series of guaranty products that we can provide. And when we speak to a sandbox that encompasses providing the information needs of the real estate industry, we're talking about, in fact, a *very* large market opportunity. That description of the new sandbox and aggressive development of multiple products for that space, coupled with our intent *to be the preeminent provider of seamless transactions,* led us into the need to build a different profile than we had been pursuing."

A change of Driving Force mandates a corresponding change in the Areas of Excellence to be developed and nurtured. LandAmerica's people do not perceive this to be a major problem, as these areas are not entirely new to the company's culture. It simply means a change of emphasis.

As Chandler sees it: "Our main Area of Excellence is Market Knowledge—which is really an aggregation of local market knowledge. To support that, we will also need to concentrate more on Information Management and Technology. Even though we're in the 'insurance business,' that is very much misleading. We're an information management company, and that is really our business. And then, thirdly, is Internet Technology, and that is a skill set, not just purchased goods. It is an area of focus, and it is highlighted under our future strategic profile management because we need to leverage it to a significantly greater degree."

To get their arms around the role that the Internet might play in the future, they decided to use DPI's e-Strategy Process, again with surprising results.

Says Foster: "We didn't realize, going in, the kinds of things we'd come up with and how central they would be to our new strategy. I looked at it as a scenario of, 'Gee, I don't know enough; this is an education opportunity. Let's do it!' You have these natural anxieties and fears that somebody knows something you don't know. So that's why we went into that process. The almost immediate outcome of that is now we don't even call this e-strategy. *This is just strategy.* It was its own separate project at the outset. In fact, now it's one of our major Critical Issues to the overall development of strategy. So we're attempting to learn and to build and develop strategy based upon the evolution of Internet.

"We had, in our previous, fragmented approach to the Internet, responded to one of our customer sets by building a part of our company, which we called LandAmerica One-Stop, to try to respond to what the customer was saying. But we were doing it looking through the eyeglasses of a title insurer. So we hadn't thought of everything. In fact, we weren't, from a technology standpoint, very far along in terms of connectivity. We had struggled with that. Because of the DPI Process, we immediately recognized the need to look at it in the broader context."

That broader context, of course, was the new, more expansive strategy the company had embarked on. Given that their products are essentially information products and that the thousands of potential customers are located literally everywhere, e-commerce would play a central role as the concept developed.

The process allowed them to create a realistic and comprehensive design for an e-commerce solution that would precisely fit their new business model—complete with definitions of specific applications and their requirements. What really made the whole e-commerce concept gel, though, was the transformation they saw taking place through the "Killer.com" segment of the process.

"Part of what we had done during the Process was to engage ourselves in two or three exercises. But one of them was much more than an exercise. It was something about building a whole new model. And through Killer.com we came up with an approach that turned the light on and said 'this sounds exotic,' but it really is what we're trying to do. It's just a way of explaining it, of giving it a complete definition," Foster states.

The result is the game-changing "Transaction Manager" concept brought to market. This breakthrough model will take years to bring to fruition, but LandAmerica wasted no time getting started. Within weeks, they made a strategic acquisition that would supply a critical piece of the new business model.

Chandler explains: "We, almost immediately out of the box, after having our phase-two session, once our future strategic profile was set, once the strategic filter was delivered, applied that filter to several pressing opportunities. We zeroed in on this one particular target company named Primis. We very boldly acquired the company, and we have incorporated that business into one of our most important market segments. So there was this absolute direct, not indirect, linkage between the development of that Strategic Filter and us pulling the trigger on a major initiative.

"Primis embodies our movement into this transaction management space in a key market segment. What we got with that company was a whole array of valuation products that we were not offering and market knowledge of where innovation was needed. We also were able to get technology that was specific to those products. But what we had, and what we saw, and what has proved out is that the acquired technology was readily adaptable to be our primary e-commerce front-end with respect to this one very large market segment. So when we bought Primis we merged it into one of our companies that was operating in the same market but didn't have the same set of tools. And, combined, we are very, very well positioned to be the transaction manager for our largest, most demanding customers.

"I can actually say, unequivocally, that we would not have bought Primis but for the DPI process. I mean just flat out, because prior to DPI, we were not looking to expand into, essentially, another line of business— the valuation products line of business. And even if we had been, we would not have done it at this level of financial commitment.

"Because of the complexity of the new LandAmerica business model, it will take some time to develop and mold it into a complete, integrated operation. Primis is an important piece of the puzzle. Yet despite the challenges inherent in creating a new game, Foster and his team are confident that the concept is sound and that the market is moving toward using this type of service. The journey has also completely changed their perception of the game, the rules, and the nature of competition in their space.

"We haven't completed them yet, but the transaction management tactics that we're bringing to the table will have the effect of changing the game. We're doing business in a way that's different than any of our natural competitors. We are actually, counterintuitively, positioning ourselves so that we will even sell our competitors' products. We are moving into the transaction intersection to manage the transaction, and, if our customer wants to use our competitor for the title order, then we're going to do that. So what changes the rules of play is that all of a sudden when a customer chooses us, they're not making a choice on one major title company versus another where the differences across the country may not always be apparent, or real. They're making a choice that they want a manager of that transaction who will then use the fulfillment entities that are best in class—best in class being defined by the customer, or in the absence of being defined by the customer, defined as quicker, better, cheaper. This will fundamentally change the game and the rules of play because we do not see our traditional competitors positioning themselves in a way that they would forgo the title insurance order.

"As a result, we are less obsessed with our traditional competitors than we were before. I think one of the benefits of going through the Process is that you become more confident in the direction of the company, and, therefore, you're less reactive to their 'me-too' type strategies. And the other piece of this is that we recognize that our traditional competitors, in this brave new world, are perhaps not our real competitors. That comes out of the Killer.com evaluation. So we are much more going to go in *our own direction*, full of 'competitors be damned,' than we were prior to the DPI Process."

Throughout the next couple of years, a new type of company will emerge, although pieces of the model may change as ideas are tested and adjusted to fit the evolving marketplace.

Says Chairman Foster: "We have come up with what we think is a pretty good game plan. Now it isn't proven out and it changes from time to time. In fact, one of the beauties of this whole DPI effort is the fact that it is a continuum. Strategic thinking is just that, a continuum of thinking."

Where would they be had they continued on their former course?

Foster puts it succinctly: "We probably would have been much more on the target end of the range than the shooting end."

Robert Burgess, CEO
Mark O'brien,
President and Coo
Pulte Corporation
Dearborn, Michigan

In 1996, Pulte Corporation, a major national homebuilder, set out to "change the rules of play in the homebuilding market," as CEO Bob Burgess then stated. Through DPI's Strategic Thinking Process, the then-$2 billion company committed to several ambitious goals, including doubling the size of the company by the year 2000, which it has successfully accomplished.

The guiding mantra through the ensuing years of extraordinary growth has always been "delight the customer." Most people who have been through the process of building a home know that the experience can be fraught with delays, blown budgets, and disappearing contractors. It can be anything but delightful. Pulte was determined to change all that.

First, they trimmed down the company by shedding businesses unrelated to homebuilding. Pulte got down to a solid foundation—its homebuilding and home mortgage businesses. Then it worked to apply more sophisticated marketing techniques for understanding its customers and markets and focused on delivering the highest quality home possible. This work evolved into a strategy Pulte calls Homeowner for Life, which seeks to extend the strong customer relationship Pulte develops over the course of building a customer's new home. The ultimate goal of Homeowner for Life is to sell additional products and services by maintaining that customer relationship long after the house sale is complete. These concepts required the integration of skills not always found in homebuilding—market research, consumer marketing, and an obsession with quality improvement throughout its complex value chain and sales process. Pulte's exceptional growth in sales and profits as well as consistently high customer satisfaction marks attest to the success of its strategy.

ENTER THE INTERNET

It may be possible to build a house without a blueprint, especially for experienced builders if they have built a similar structure before. They know what it will look like, what materials to use, what it's likely to cost, and what kinds of problems they may run into. While it can be done, it's certainly not the most intelligent way to build a house. Unfortunately, a lot of companies have tried to do the same thing with their Internet initiatives, with disastrous results—cost overruns, overlapping applications, and projects that seem to go on endlessly. The fundamental difference between building a house and undertaking an Internet initiative is that there are no proven Internet models for the business. No one's ever built one like it before. No one knows what it should "look like," how long it will take, what problems will be encountered, what it will cost—and, most importantly, whether it will do what's needed to support the business strategy.

Pulte Corporation had been quite involved in the Internet over the past three-plus years, implementing a reasonably well-developed plan. Yet early in 2000, the people at Pulte—a homebuilder that *does* use blueprints to build their houses—saw that the time had come to design a comprehensive blueprint for an Internet strategy that would fully support their *business* strategy. They elected to use DPI's e-Strategy Process to do it. But let's step back a bit in time to see how they arrived at that conclusion.

In the midst of all this change, Pulte, as early as 1995, had recognized the emergence of information technology (IT) as an important tool to improve and grow the business. Its embrace of IT was ahead of many companies in the homebuilding industry. This trend continued as Pulte was an early adopter in using the Internet to support its business operations. As IT and the Internet became an increasingly important part of the business, they felt the need for a cohesive overall strategy and opted for DPI's e-Strategy Process to help them create it.

As president and COO Mark O'Brien recalls: "We began to develop a long-range e-business plan that would help guide us for the foreseeable future. As part of this process, we formed an e-business team to develop a more comprehensive Internet strategy. The preliminary work of this group provided a pretty solid foundation that we brought into the DPI process. The DPI process helped us define and validate the strategy and prioritize some of the underlying tactics. That's the junction in the road we found ourselves in. Seven or eight years ago, Mike Robert and the DPI team assisted us in developing a strategic plan. That experience was positive, and we thought Mike could provide some of the same assistance in developing our e-strategy. By coincidence, DPI had just developed a process to help companies formulate an e-strategy.

"Pulte had already developed a number of e-business initiatives focused on capturing B-to-C [business-to-consumers] and B-to-B [business-to-business] business opportunities. We had established an e-business team that reported directly to senior management, guiding and implementing our process. We really saw the DPI process as a tool to help us focus and prioritize our Internet-related activities that are designed to support Pulte's core home-building business."

People from a wide array of disciplines within Pulte were assembled to hammer out their new e-strategy. One of the most critical steps in the process is to bring the group to a common understanding of the Internet's potential effects. To accomplish this, DPI has developed a set of 12 *e-nablers*, which represent the Internet's basic business models. These e-nablers demystify the Internet for businesspeople by identifying specific capabilities of the Internet that can be used to leverage a company's key strengths.

"Understanding of the Internet varied widely," says O'Brien. "We assembled a group of about 60 people to go through this process. Some had great knowledge of the Internet and e-business, while others are more focused on our traditional homebuilding activities and thus less exposed and conversant with the powers of e-commerce.

"The e-nabler framework is a great way to present a complex series of concepts. I know the participants in our group who were unfamiliar with Internet-based business models found the information helped focus their thoughts and ideas as we advanced through the subsequent stages of the DPI process."

Once the e-nablers were understood, the core business and information processes that tie the company together were then mapped in detail. The process then allowed the work teams to identify the points of impact where these different e-nablers might affect these processes, positively and negatively.

A list of specific potential Internet applications was then developed that would leverage the positive impacts and mitigate the negative ones. These applications were then filtered for strategic fit, cost, benefits, and ease of implementation. The resulting short list was deemed to be the applications most crucial to supporting the business strategy.

As O'Brien comments: "One of the interesting results having gone through the e-strategy process was that each of the teams came up with applications working independently which had a lot of common characteristics. There were several overlaps and links among them. As we developed our Internet blueprint, we were able to merge all of our various disciplines and visions into a real value chain of e-commerce.

"We are in the very final stages of a comprehensive Internet blueprint that will address all aspects of our homebuilding value chain from managing the customer experience to efficiently linking our contractors, vendors, and suppliers. We're now working to set priorities and establish the teams that will drive the implementation as we go forward.

"I don't think there's any question but that as a result of going through the e-strategy process we eliminated some applications from our previously articulated strategy, added some others, and, in fact, identified a lot of enhancements that will have value. Fully implementing this program will take place over a period of months and maybe years, but at least we're beginning with the end in mind.

"Having gone through the Strategic Thinking Process seven years ago and arriving at a clear strategic direction for the company, and now exploiting the e-nablers together with our strengths and understanding the competitive environment that we were in, there is every reason to believe that we will get the same positive result from our e-business strategy that we got for our corporate strategy."

A LOOK AT E-COMPETITION

The process then gave Pulte the opportunity to look at the Internet from their competitors' perspective. The "Competitor.com" Team used the process to determine how competitors might use the Internet.

"The Competitor Team did a great job of providing insight into where the industry is likely to head, and how specific competitors might respond to our various initiatives at Pulte. Working independently from the rest of the teams, I think the Competitor Team validated many of the strategic initiatives that we are considering, while at the same time highlighting some of the opportunities and risks inherent in our approach. Overall, I think it was a very valuable contributor to the process and a necessary one," O'Brien states.

In a similar vein, the "Killer.com" Team was given the assignment of designing a new e-competitor whose purpose would be to invalidate Pulte's business model and possibly put Pulte out of business. What form would it take? How vulnerable would Pulte be? What can the company do now to mitigate such a threat?

Though he understandably provides no specifics, O'Brien says simply: "With respect to the Killer.com Team, they did some very interesting work. I think as the result of their work, we are incorporating some features into our strategy that will insulate us from The Killer. We have a vision of that Killer.com, but I don't think we got absolute clarity because that Killer may manifest itself in varying ways over the years to come. But I think we have an idea where it would come from and what we might do about it."

Indeed, the flexibility of both DPI's Strategic Thinking Process and e-Strategy Process may be what gives these processes strength and longevity within an organization. As they become part of the fabric of the company's thinking, they provide a basis for continuous re-evaluation as the world changes. This is particularly crucial with the Internet, since the future is filled with unknown developments.

Says O'Brien "On the other hand, I think there are some knowns. The Internet has touched every one of us. It is changing the way we live on a daily basis. I don't think there is any question but that it is changing the homebuilding landscape, as it is many other businesses. I think we just need to be prepared to develop with it. We're obviously excited about the future. I think the process we've been through added clarity to our e-business strategy. As we go forward, we will continue to apply many of the tools that are in the DPI kit to varying opportunities that the e-commerce world presents to us."

Perhaps the most important result is that Pulte now has an agreed-upon e-strategy that fully supports its business strategy, which has proven to be successful throughout the last decade.

"Our vision is to effectively link the entire homebuilding value chain from customers to contractors and suppliers," O'Brien states. "We recognize that this is an ambitious undertaking. It will require an enormous investment of people and financial resources. The DPI process helped us be more specific and precise about the potential benefits associated with these various programs, as well as how best to prioritize the initiatives.

"Pulte Corporation is a homebuilder. We will continue to focus on our core homebuilding business, delighting our customers with every house we build and the entire home buying, building, and ownership experience; e-business is not a separate activity. It needs to add value, must add value in fact, and be integrated into our day-to-day operations and support our core homebuilding and mortgage businesses. It's the function of technology to support and enhance communications with our customers and our business partners before, during, and after the home is built. And I think the DPI process helps ensure that we will retain that focus."

CHAPTER 15

DAVID HOOVER, CHAIRMAN, PRESIDENT, AND CEO BALL CORPORATION DENVER, COLORADO

The name Ball has been associated with container making since two of the five Ball brothers borrowed $200 from an uncle in 1880 to make wood-jacketed tin cans. The company grew, adding three more brothers *and* their most famous product—the Ball home canning jar—which the company produced and sold for about a century.

But since the early 1990s, the company has gone through a major transition, spinning off the jar-making business and a group of other businesses. Ball hasn't made those jars for a decade. In fact, Ball makes no glass containers at all.

What it does make are metal cans and plastic bottles. Lots of them. In fact, last year Ball made about 32 *billion* beer and soda cans, as well as food cans and plastic bottles. In 1999 the container business accounted for about $3.3 billion in sales, with about $400 million coming from an aerospace subsidiary.

Ball got into those high-volume container businesses through a series of acquisitions over time, as they also sold off other companies. As the new Ball took shape, management knew they were on the right track, but performance wasn't where they wanted it to be. They wanted to refine a strategy for growth, and selected DPI's Strategic Thinking Process to catalyze their thinking.

Says CEO David Hoover: "In '98, the year that we moved our corporate headquarters to Colorado from Indiana, we knew, of course, that the beer/beverage can business had consolidated, that we were at about 17 to 18 percent market share along with four or five other companies, and that there probably needed to be more consolidation. We also knew that either we had to try to make something happen or something might happen to us.

So we acquired the can business that was owned by Reynolds Metals, and doubled our size. Ball became the largest beer/beverage can maker in North America, and probably in the world, at that time. We make about 35 percent of the beer/beverage cans produced. That was a big lift, because there were consolidation and rationalization savings to be made.

"We had also entered the PET plastic bottle business. We had invested in China. The company was getting along but not doing real well. After we moved to Colorado and hired some folks, including our Vice President of Corporate Planning and Development, John Hayes, we thought that we were at a stage where we were getting better performance but we thought we really needed to take a look at the planning process that we used, and try to think about 'How do we move this thing forward?'

"It was then that we ran across one of Mike Robert's books on Strategic Thinking. From that we made contact with Mark Thompson, one of the DPI partners, and we decided to go through the Strategic Thinking Process with Mark. At the same time the company had been changing, and our management was changing. I became CEO in January 2001, was chief operating officer before that, and was an advocate of this kind of strategy approach. We had other changes within the management team, some new people and others who were doing new jobs. So it was a good time to make a critical thinking assessment. The Strategic Thinking Process allowed us to make sure that we aired all relevant points and talked freely and openly, so we could decide where to go in a structured way."

What most interested the Ball team about the DPI process was the concept of enabling the company's own people to contribute their ideas and experience, and develop a strategy they could agree on and more importantly, gain ownership of that strategy.

"I think what attracted us first, just from reading the book, is that DPI's process is based on clear thinking. What you don't get with DPI is some gray-headed guys who come in from a consulting firm who sell you the job and then send all the kids out to take your watch and tell you what time it is. We didn't need an army of 25-year-old MBAs crawling around. It wasn't that we were in deep trouble, but it was that we wanted to get better. We knew that *we* had to do it.

"The great thing about the DPI process is that it's largely a facilitation. A lot of it is done by example. It creates understanding. It gives the facilitator an interesting way of saying to you, 'Okay guys, what are you going to do? Here's one way to think about it. Let's identify what your Driving Force is, what are the critical factors affecting your business and what are the issues that come out of that.' It just resonated with us. So we had a group of close to 30 Ball people across the disciplines come through the process."

The process enabled Ball's managers to assess the company's current profile, to understand their current Business Concept and environment, in order to make specific decisions about where they wanted to take the company in the future and how to create new opportunities for growth. Among the decisions central to creating that picture of the future was gaining agreement on the company's Future Driving Force.

Two of the choices they considered were Production Capacity or Product. Under the Production Capacity scenario, the company would strive to maximize capacity utilization by finding additional products, possibly unrelated to present products or markets, to keep the plants "full." A case could be made for this, and was. A more obvious choice would be Product-driven—metal cans and plastic bottles. After all, the company was among the world leaders in both categories. Yet, after intense debate and playing out the future scenarios for each, they came to the conclusion that a third choice, Market Category, built upon their current capabilities, was a better option, and would create new growth opportunities through innovative new products and processes.

As Hoover explains: "As the facilitator, Mark helped us to understand the difference between these different Driving Forces. He showed us examples of companies with different Driving Forces and how that shaped their businesses. He guided us through that very well. If you read our Business Concept, it says, basically, what we are—*we're a supplier of metal and plastic packaging products to food and beverage manufacturers.* And so we decided to focus on that market concept, which is a different answer than one might have expected and opens up new avenues to explore beyond our current products."

The key implication of that decision is the concentration of effort on cultivating the Areas of Excellence implied by a Market Category–driven strategy which all revolve around understanding and serving a specific set of needs of a market—in Ball's case, food and beverage companies, which have an ongoing need for innovative packaging solutions.

"As a result we have dedicated more resources to understanding where our customer is going," says Hoover. "We think that's where we've got to follow, and it's our lifeblood, so we need to understand what they're doing. The whole idea is trying to think through—What is our customer doing? Where is the market going to go? And what do we need to do to improve our performance and capability? Do we need new products? If so, what should they be? Should we get into a new kind of business and how would we do that? I know that people here now think about these things a lot. I think the DPI process has helped us get focused, and, in an organized way consider all the relevant facts and factors in reaching a conclusion about what we should do. If I were to sum it up, it helped to get our management team on the same page. When you spend these few days together in an intense environment and you break into teams, it fosters communication about the things that are important. It also helps newer people become part of the team much quicker."

Out of the process, the Ball management group outlined what they now call "Five Keys to Success" to help communicate the basic principles of the new strategy to people throughout the company.

Hoover explains: "These Five Keys come right out of the DPI process. The first is to be close to our customers to understand their needs and their future direction and what they're trying to do. And it's all the way up and down the organization, from the senior management to the people on the manufacturing floor in our plants.

"The second is this whole idea of creativity and imagination. And that's where DPI's Strategic Product Innovation Process comes in. And we're taking advantage of that to create new products, new processes, and new businesses.

"Third is attention to detail. We tend to be relentless at managing our business. At Ball, that starts with housekeeping. I mean, you could eat off the floor in one of our can plants, and we don't have any janitors. We think that's where it starts. And then you manage the entire operation like that to yield high productivity and low cost.

"The fourth key is to build on our strengths, which is where a lot of the DPI process comes in—our historic strengths of high quality and greatest value to the customer, and to couple that with this rigorous approach to managing the business.

"Finally, and I saved the most important for last, we want to behave as owners. I talk a lot about that. We expect our employees to act like true owners of the business. What does that mean? Well, it means you show up when you're needed and you go home when the work's done. It means that you care so much that you don't want any customer to be disappointed, that you care about the other people in the business because they're your co-owners. I want you to think this is your place. And that's a powerful thing. And actually if everybody behaves like an owner, those other things that I talked about, they're going to happen."

The part of the process that converts those conceptual goals into tangible actions is the development of a list of Critical Issues that are assigned to individuals to manage to completion.

"We agreed to five Critical Issues," Hoover recalls. "Once you've done that and given ownership to individual managers, that becomes how you *behave*."

A few months later with those issues well on their way to completion, top management again met with DPI to refine the strategy. The result was a slight redefinition of the business concept and a couple of new Critical Issues.

"Before, we would have said we were only a supplier of rigid metal and plastic packaging," said Hoover. "We decided the containers don't necessarily have to be rigid. It's subtle, but it opens up new opportunities. We also added an important Critical Issue—innovation—new products, new concepts, which led to us using DPI's Strategic Product Innovation Process. We've done that two or three times and come up with 11 excellent ideas to work on."

Ball found that the SPI Process was a more structured approach to product development than they were accustomed to.

Said Hoover: "Most ideas before had been based on an engineer's idea of something he could make, but the customer wouldn't necessarily want or need. Since we are much more focused on our customers and where they and their markets are going, we now have a process in place that helps us turn that knowledge into successful new products. It helped bring order to what most of us think of as chaos."

The results over the last few years are impressive, and Ball executives now feel their strategy—understanding their customers' needs and providing innovative new products—is a key component in their growth.

"We've grown in the food can business, for example. We've grown that business in a flat market, not by cutting prices and taking other people's business, but by finding new applications, by having customers who are growing. We grow right along with them. Those are some of the reasons we're doing well."

Well indeed. Even in the bear market of 2001–2002, Ball has received a vote of confidence from the market, with its share price *tripling* in about a year.

The Ball, as they say, is rolling.

CHAPTER 16

LAURIE DIPPENAAR, CEO FIRSTRAND LIMITED JOHANNESBURG, SOUTH AFRICA

Even Horatio Alger would be impressed.

Two men set out with $10,000 and in less than 20 years parlayed that investment into a world-class company with a market cap of over $7.5 billion.

To make the accomplishment even more stunning, they didn't do it in the usual places—Silicon Valley, Wall Street—or with some Internet meteor. It happened in South Africa, a relatively small country beset for years by internal strife and external economic pressures.

They did it, the CEO says, by consistently looking for ways to change the rules in their markets and exercising a combination of fiscal savvy and an entrepreneurial management style.

The two original partners were Laurie (pronounced *Low-ry*) Dippenaar and G. T. Ferreira. A third partner, Paul Harris, joined them a year later. All are the senior management with what is now known as FirstRand Limited, with Laurie Dippenaar as CEO. FirstRand is reported to be the largest financial services organization on the African continent. But these men have never forgotten their small-company roots.

"We started out offering finance to public utilities for their capital equipment with $10,000 in the bank," Dippenaar remembers. "Now I promise you that one can't compete with that amount of money and those resources unless you've changed the rules of the game *completely*. And that's what we did over and over throughout the years."

The idea that got them started was a unique opportunity in a tax break offered to public utilities by the South Africa Tax Act. Says Dippenaar: "There were tax incentives for capital investments in public utilities, but of course the utilities couldn't take advantage of them directly because they don't pay taxes. So commercial leasing companies could come into these deals as participants and then be able to enjoy a part of the tax allowances. We weren't the only ones to get into this, but we did it a little differently than anyone else. Normally, participants in these deals would be advisers who would go to a bank or another finance company, tell them how to structure the deal, and share the profits. But we were brave enough to quote as a principal, a very important difference. We were then able to control the distribution of the profits to the participants. We *made* the price instead of being a price taker.

"Obviously, to accumulate capital you either take capital from outside or you generate it yourself through earnings. We did that by simply using a structure that nobody else had used, and it took our competitors a long time to cotton onto what we were doing."

Profits from this stratagem enabled the group to build their initial investment into a growing portfolio of financial service entities over the next few years. The company grew quite rapidly.

"We started with this idea of residualizing capital equipment for public utilities," Dippenaar relates. "And then seven years later, in 1984, we acquired control of a small merchant, or investment, bank called Rand Merchant Bank. We grew that to become one of the preeminent merchant banks in South Africa. Then our next milestone was in 1992, when we acquired control of Momentum, the fifth largest life insurance company in South Africa. It was ailing when we bought it, and it took us five years to turn it from an ailing situation into South Africa's most admired insurance company. In 1998 we acquired joint control of one of South Africa's biggest four banks, called First National Bank, and also the fourth largest insurance company, Southern Life. In between these big takeovers, we grew our existing business rapidly and started a number of new businesses—'seedlings' as we call them. We believe we're quite good at starting new businesses from grass roots. In fact we make very few acquisitions, but when we do make them, they're extremely large. Our group now covers virtually every facet of financial services. In banking we do commercial banking, investment banking, private banking, and finance. In insurance we have life insurance, health insurance, property and casualty insurance. We're also in fund management and mutual funds. Our market capitalization currently makes us the largest financial services group in South Africa. Just before the meltdown in world financial markets last year, for a brief spell we were South Africa's largest listed company. Not large perhaps by American standards, but we are probably the largest financial services group in Africa today."

Dippenaar and his partners have become widely known for their decentralized management structure that encourages prudent innovation and outside-the-box thinking. At Momentum Insurance, for example, they changed its monolithic structure, breaking the company into profit centers so that profit could be measured in small units, not as massive net numbers. Creating an "owner-manager culture," as they call it, produced very successful results at Momentum.

As Dippenaar explains the concept: "One of our core philosophies is that we try and break up big groups into smaller little units. We refer to it as 'chunking.' We are great believers in not having monolithic structures. Instead of having a battleship, we prefer to have a hundred destroyers. Even if it's a large market, we believe in doing that. We like lots of captains commanding, with minimal input from the center. That's part of our philosophy. It's really born out of our history. Because we started as a very small company, we still have a lot of faith in the small-company mentality. But at the same time we realized that you want to get the benefits of a large-company balance sheet. So often our legal structure will be one balance sheet and a lot of entities operating with different brands within that legal structure."

Discussing the role of the central management group that binds these independent units together, Dippenaar refers to the top management team as the "foxhole at the top."

"We didn't use any other management style except the one where you place a great deal of trust in your own people, because that's the only one we knew," he says. "Those were our roots. So we, almost by accident if you will, applied that management style to Momentum, the first insurance company that we took over. And we just found the people responded very well to it. It unleashed creativity—people being held accountable, being trusted.

"At the top, we don't have a command and control mentality. We rather see ourselves as being strategic enablers and facilitators. That's the role. Because we feel that, if you really believe in an empowered, autonomous, owner-manager type of culture in your operating company, the only style that fits in well with that at the center is if you style yourself as a strategic enabler and facilitator. We like to think of ourselves as, not a 'rule-driven' group, but a 'value-driven' group. I explain this to people as follows: Do you want to establish a rule for everything for your children, or do you just want to give them a set of values and then they conduct themselves according to that value system rather than by reference to the rule that father and mother have lain down? This filtered down to all levels and we found ordinary people doing exceptional things."

BOTTLING THE SUCCESS FORMULA

In early 1997, a year before Rand Merchant Bank and Momentum took over Southern Life and First National Bank, the company was brimming with organic growth. It was time, they said, to step back, arrive at a clear definition of strategy and to gain an understanding of that strategy across these many units—in effect to extract their success formula and "bottle it."

At the time, one of the traditional management consulting firms was being considered for the job. But it just happened that one of Rand's executives was sick in bed and picked up *Strategy Pure and Simple*, a predecessor of this book. He recognized the Strategic Thinking Process it described as a natural extension of the participative style of management Rand had cultivated. He took it to the CEO when he returned to work.

"I was quite pleased about it," Dippenaar recalls. "Normally you would think this kind of thing would come from the chief executive. I was delighted that it came from a guy in sort of second-tier management. I thought it was quite telling for the group that we all had the openness of mind to say, 'Let's try this.'

"In our first exposure to DPI's process," Dippenaar explains, "we actually used it to get the captains of our different operating units, the CEOs, to arrive at a common understanding of our business philosophy. So, it wasn't really what the DPI process was primarily designed for. We weren't trying to necessarily find our Driving Force, as DPI puts it. But we just thought: If we go through this process, we're going to get a common understanding and buy-in into our business philosophy. And it definitely achieved that objective. Obviously, what's affected us more than anything else is the fact that it systematically extracts the thinking and ideas from the executives' heads, rather than imposing the consultant's thinking. I think it almost *forces* it out of their heads. That obviously leads to the strategy being owned by the company rather than by the consultants."

The Strategic Thinking Process with this group and subsequently with various FirstRand units was facilitated by an international team of DPI partners, South Africa's Rex Glanville and Mark Thompson of the United States. Senior executives from the various operating units were able to come to a common understanding of the unique structure and management culture that the company had been practicing and cultivating for nearly 20 years. In such a decentralized structure, particularly one involving a number of acquisitions, there is always the danger of disconnects between the central management's philosophy and objectives with those of the operating units. One way to avoid that is living the values from the top, and certainly part of the CEO's job is to continuously reinforce the code of goals and beliefs across the many units. But, as Dippenaar found out, those efforts are far more effective if the people in charge of those units have arrived at those conclusions themselves, developing ownership in them and conviction about their importance.

"Remember, our objective here was to get an alignment of thinking from executives in the group. Of course we have this decentralized process, or 'chunking,' because we'd rather have a hundred companies than one big one, but we need to be sure they're all heading in the same direction. Alignment of thinking is very, very important. And DPI's process is extremely useful for that. You can use it to align thinking within a business unit or you can use it to align thinking within a group of businesses. And it does it very quickly. You can get to the same alignment of thinking over years, but with this, in a matter of days you get there. At the time we used it, we had bought and started a number of new companies. It was extremely useful for them to acquaint themselves with each other, and get familiar with what the whole group was all about.

"We're not great users of consultants, I must tell you. Consulting firms have a great deal of talent and intellectual depth in them. Often, simply because of that inherent strength in consulting firms, any strategic plan or strategic thinking is often *their* thinking, and ownership of that plan or strategic thinking is never embraced by the company. So if there's no ownership, there will be no implementation. In fact, implementation of the strategic thinking is even more important than the thinking and planning itself. If it's not owned by the company, implementation has almost no chance at success, and you've wasted your money.

"We've started using DPI's process, not just for getting a common understanding and buy-in on our business philosophy, but actually getting the individual companies to identify their Driving Force and develop plans of their own. We're now using it extensively in all of our businesses for the purpose for which it was originally designed.

"As I said, we've never been great users of consultants. Can I just say that it's a credit to DPI that we've used them so extensively. It was partly because the style suits us. We don't want our business run by consultants."

CREATING ADVANTAGE BY CHANGING THE RULES

With its key managers now firmly on the same wavelength, FirstRand continues to search out ways to innovate in all of its key markets by looking at them from its unique viewpoint.

Dippenaar and his team are convinced that the concept—changing the rules—that got them their start, has been the secret of their success for over 20 years and will continue to be so.

To illustrate the point, Dippenaar gives an example from their insurance business: "In our life insurance company we saw a big swing away from traditional life insurance investment products to unit trusts, or mutual funds. Clearly, at that stage in the industry, mutual funds were regarded by life insurance companies as Enemy Number One. We concluded that the market was moving that way. At the time, our life insurance company had a 5 percent market share. So we moved into what we call the mutual funds packaging industry. It means packaging different mutual funds into groups of funds. We moved into that early, well ahead of our competitors. That's a new game in town as an alternative option to life insurance—investment products at the upper end of the market, not the lower end.

"We're great believers that when there's a paradigm shift, when the rules of the game change, everybody goes back to zero. And if you go back to zero, the race starts again. It's the same as if you had 80 percent of the Telex market, and faxes come along. You may have 80 percent, but its 80 percent of nothing. The race starts all over again. In our new game, we went to 25 percent market share in just a few years. Companies who, collectively, had the 60 percent market share of the traditional life insurance market now only have 25 percent of the packaged unit trust market, which is a big swing. Originally they had 60 percent, and we had 5.

"The shift, or the balance of power as it were, is just dramatic. We *thrive* on that. We *thrive* on these situations. And we are *alert* and *watch* for ways that the rules of the game are changing."

FirstRand has found that DPI's Strategic Thinking Process has helped them to differentiate between opportunities and identify those with the best strategic fit.

"One of the most valuable contributions to our thinking from the DPI process is that it provides a filter for the opportunities that you're swamped with," Dippenaar observes. "You can easily choose the ones that fit strategically so you don't go chasing hares across the plains."

"The last merger that we did is now just a year old. Part of the rationale was to take full advantage of this convergence that we see taking place between the products of banks, insurance companies, and mutual funds. In recognition of that, we've put together a group that has, as wholly owned subsidiaries, all these components. We'd like to think that in the next four to five years, we may rewrite the rules of financial services companies in South Africa. And if we rewrite the rules here, there will be a consulting company—DPI—that will be able to take some of the credit."

CHAPTER 17

KURT WIEDENHAUPT, CEO
AMERICAN PRECISION INDUSTRIES
BUFFALO, NEW YORK

"**M**anaging companies is like standing with your management team in a valley, and you're surrounded by many beautiful and challenging mountain peaks. The strategic objective is to decide which mountain to climb," says Kurt Wiedenhaupt, CEO of American Precision Industries (API), in discussing his approach to creating and implementing strategy.

"Now, there are various ways of doing it. Number one is you sit in an armchair as boss and you point at one peak and say 'charge.' The people are charging up and they come to the first difficult spot. They say, 'Do you think this guy is serious? Why don't we take a rest here? He's still down in the valley.' And then after a while they say, 'We're not crazy,' . . . and then, 'forget it.' They come back to the valley and say, 'It was too difficult, it was too dangerous, and it didn't make any sense.' Then the boss gets upset and everyone wonders what comes next.

"The second way is that the boss says 'charge,' and then he goes out in front of these guys. Then the only difference is that when they come to the difficult spot, the boss makes the decision that maybe that wasn't the right mountain to climb, so they go back into the valley and try another one, and another one, and another one. They are very busy and expend a lot of energy and money. And the reason they turn back this time is that they are not sure that it was the right peak to climb in the first place. But with DPI's Strategic Thinking Process you get conviction because you very carefully select the mountain you want to climb together, and everyone knows the reason why you want to climb that mountain. Then you start working your way up together, and if you hit a rough spot, a crevasse or overhang, you will find a way around, and you will get to the top. The team will think it out, because everyone is convinced and *knows* it's the right peak to climb.

"They know the logic, the logic that says to everyone: It's the right thing to do. There's ownership, there's pride, there's determination. And the team is united in it. As an alternative, you only have a strategy that is developed by the boss, or by somebody from the outside. So in the team of 20 you might have two or three who are enthusiastic, then you have four or five who are followers, and the rest are leaning back."

When Kurt Wiedenhaupt came to American Precision Industries as the new CEO in 1992, he saw no lack of mountains worth climbing. The questions, of course, were: Which ones? And how? Wiedenhaupt had such consistent success with the Strategic Thinking Process in previous assignments as a CEO that he resolved early on to use it to identify the mountains and the means.

API was then a "miniconglomerate," a collection of three technology-driven divisions with no real strategic connection to one another. One is in precision motion control, one in industrial heat transfer, one in electronic components. Each has a unique technology at its core. But no synergy potential exists among the divisions, given widely divergent technologies, and applications, and markets.

"The three businesses had nothing to do with each other," Wiedenhaupt explains. "That's the way I inherited the company. There had been others, but these divisions were the ones that remained when I arrived here. It was a dormant company, which at one time had grown but was not growing anymore. There was no clear strategy for future growth. Sales had moved from $38 to $50 million in the 12 years before—below the inflation rate. The company was profitable. There were good products and good people. But there was no R&D, no vision of the future.

"So, I had to give the company a vision, a future. That was my main job, to define the future, to communicate it and get the company moving. And I knew only one effective way of doing it—the Strategic Thinking Process. Within the first month I took three groups separately off-site, and we developed strategies for each of them."

Kurt Wiedenhaupt is a strong believer in the ability of the process to draw out the knowledge, experience, and honest thinking of the participants, as long as the CEO doesn't try to dominate the discussion or manipulate the outcome.

"I was a very attentive listener," he says. "The only thing I told the people before we started each session was that the good news is I cannot interfere in the process. I do not have a preconceived idea of where we will take this company. The only thing I know is, we're going to grow the company. But you are the ones who will decide the strategy, not I. The bad news is, whatever you decide, I will make sure you implement, so you better make the process yours, and that's what happened. The three technology groups developed strategies. Then, based on that, I developed my own thoughts with Mike's help, for the company as a whole."

This is a somewhat unusual application of the Strategic Thinking Process since most companies are looking for a way to coalesce the various and sundry business units together into one synergistic dynamo.

"One thing I recognized immediately was that I was not running one company," Wiedenhaupt states. "I was running three companies. And it would have been wrong to push all the three groups through the same filter."

In sorting out the future strategic profile of the units, and ultimately of API as a company, the key question became: By what route would profitable, stable growth be achieved? By building on each individual technology? Seeking further unrelated technologies? Looking for synergistic, interrelated technologies? As a Technology-driven company, the teams decided to focus API's growth on the diversification of products and markets based on the three core technologies. By combining the R&D strengths of all the business units, the company could begin to generate new, differentiated products based on leveraging of each unit's technological strengths. These products would provide opportunities to strengthen API's position in current markets and offer opportunities to break into selected new markets. This two-pronged expansion would then be bolstered by acquiring companies with a direct relationship to these core technologies, thus opening up new geographic and market opportunities.

On the macro-strategy level, the plan would be that when these core technologies begin to run out of growth at some point down the road, *interrelated* technologies would then be added to create new growth, building on the strengthened foundation of three original business units.

"So we did it," Wiedenhaupt says, "and got the Critical Issues moving. The board approved the strategy in December, when I presented it officially, and we started implementation in late 1992, early 1993. And the rest is really history, because we grew the company in four years from $50 million to $250 million in 1998."

COMMUNICATING TO THE TROOPS

API's *management* had a clear understanding of the Critical Issues and their role in resolving them. But what about the worker in the plant, the machine operator, salesperson, administrator? How did the CEO assure that the company's direction and purpose would be understood at *all levels* of the company?

"After the strategy was done, the team members who were part of the strategy group, together with me, presented it to every single employee," Wiedenhaupt recalls. "We went in and we had meetings from the shop floor to the corporate office. Everyone was exposed to it. We went in at night, at eleven, to get the second shift and the third shift, we went in at six in the morning. We must have had over a dozen meetings to communicate the details of the strategy to all people. I also have what I call 'coffee with Kurt' sessions, where people who were interested were invited, to chew on a donut and have a cup of coffee, and ask me questions. I gave them a brief update on the state of the nation. We communicated regularly. Otherwise, you lose momentum.

"And, of course, on some days we hit some hard spots but we got through these because we were solidly committed to our strategy. We didn't change course. This is another item which is important in the DPI process. People have to see their role. You have to define it. And they must know what is expected of them. You have to define clear targets—set the crossbar at the height you expect to jump. We announced that in five years we wanted to be a $250 million company. These people thought I had smoked something on my way from New Jersey to Buffalo. It was pure lunacy in the eyes of many. We hung big banners in the factories, and posters in the offices, saying, '*We* are the company. *We* can do it.' But then you, the management, have to act consistently and people start to believe it."

As any leader knows, setting ambitious goals is critical to inspiring exceptional performance. API's leader illustrates the point with this analogy:

Running a business is like going into a track and field meet, and you have to make a decision how high you put the bar for the jump. If you put the bar at three feet, no problem, you step over it. You put it up to six feet—well, you have to train a little bit, and then you jump. Put it at seven feet, then you have to change your style but you can still make it. And now comes an idiot who puts the bar up to 14 feet. What do you do now? There are some people who give up and turn away and say this guy is crazy, and there are others who go around back to a shed and pick up a pole and jump the bloody thing.

So my role is to manage processes in the company, make sure the processes are being followed, and help people to find the pole to jump the bar, and put the bar up as high as realistically possible. And then encourage and not tell them. You put the bar up and say, "Okay, now let's figure out how we get over it," and it can be done.

AN EXPERT'S VIEW OF THE STRATEGIC PROCESS

As the first client of Decision Process International back in the 1980s, Kurt Wiedenhaupt has a unique perspective on the Strategic Thinking Process. An acquaintance of Mike Robert at the time, he learned of the process when Mike visited his home in the United Kingdom.

"It was at my rustic dining room table in England," says Wiedenhaupt, looking back some 25 years. "That's where Mike first revealed to me that he was going out on his own. He was full of enthusiasm for this new process he had developed. So I asked him if he had a client, and he said, 'Not yet.' And I said, 'Okay, let's start.' I was the first one. At the time, I was with AEG, which became part of Daimler-Benz.

"Mike had looked at what was available in the market and he was frustrated with what he saw there," Wiedenhaupt remembers. "He believed the standard consultant told the client what the strategy should be and then watched as their recommendation got gracefully placed on a shelf even though the company might have paid that consultant a few million dollars. What intrigued me was Mike's commitment, not so much about going into business—he was interested in delivering a better result, to the client. And that, combined with the simple wisdom of the process he had developed, convinced me to go along with him. Number one, there is no mumbo-jumbo. It is straight, may I say, street wisdom. It's not an academic challenge to the participants. It is clearly, simply, an application of sound, basic business knowledge."

So Wiedenhaupt tried out the DPI process on the management team at AEG. It was so successful in creating a cohesive strategy that he used the process several more times to help management teams sort out strategies in subsequent assignments. He had identified something new in the process, and the Strategic Thinking Process was a refreshing change from other methods of strategy creation he had encountered.

"I have been exposed to McKinsey, Boston Consulting Group, and to Bain & Company. They are all very capable and I'm sure they have a good product that's extremely impressive," he says "and I'm sure intellectually they're also very sound. The only problem is their product is not of the people, by the people, through the people. It's not owned by the people who later have access to it. It is an alien product, no matter how well it relates to the company. That's why it fails. I think, *intellectually*, they might even come up with a better product than the process we are using. But when it comes to executing it, they are miles behind DPI. It's simply ownership. We as human beings do what we *believe* in, and we do that with *enthusiasm*. If somebody else tells us something to do, we might do it, but don't expect any enthusiasm.

"But anyone who is considering using the process should not see it as a one-time exercise; it has to become part of the company, part of the everyday life, language like Critical Issues, Driving Force, Areas of Excellence, Strategic Thinking, this is part of our daily verbiage. This is part of our language, this is part of our culture now. This way people start to adopt it, to live with it, and it gets stronger and stronger."

STRATEGY AND THE NEW CEO

Having been called upon several times in his career to take the reins of businesses he did not know as an insider, Wiedenhaupt has come to recognize that Strategic Thinking can be an especially valuable tool to the CEO coming into a new situation—either as incoming chief executive or in the integration of a new acquisition.

"This process, I have found through my own experience," he says, "can be beautifully used by *any* new CEO coming into a company or business he is not fully familiar with. You have the opportunity in a very short period of time to immerse yourself into this new business. You get a deep understanding of the issues. You get a very good feeling for the players in your organization who are participating in this process. And I have to say it took at least half a year out of the learning process in my last assignment. I feel much more secure in the path I'm walking because my own people have described that path and they are walking with me.

"No matter what industry you come from, what industry you go into, the fact is that when you enter a new company, you enter a different culture, a different and new business environment. The most important thing for you is to learn to listen and not to tell people what to do until you really know what you're talking about. And going right away into the strategy session and sitting there and listening affords you getting to know the people, their thinking, their emotions. You get to know the issues, the real issues the company has to address. So by just going through the Strategic Thinking Process you get tuned into the company much faster than any other way I know."

From 1993 to 1999 API generated a compound annual growth rate of 23 percent in sales and 29 percent in net earnings. API's stock went from $6 to $22 for an increase in shareholder value of $112 million.

In fact, the company was so successful that it attracted the attention of the Danaher Corporation which bought the company in 1999 at a substantial premium.

NEIL MCDONOUGH, CEO FLEXCON SPENCER, MASSACHUSETTS

One hundred million. $100,000,000. Eight zeros. For some of today's mega-companies, a $100 million year may not seem like a lot, but for Spencer, Massachusetts–based FLEXcon in 1986 it was an important milestone, one they had been working toward for 30 years.

As FLEXcon President Neil McDonough recalls: "My father started the company in 1956, and it took 10 years to grow it to a million. It took another 10 to grow it to 10 million in 1975. So from that point we had it as a long-held goal to get to 100 million and to do it in 10 years. When we got there in 1986, the whole company gave a sigh of relief. There were celebrations and congratulations. But there was no sense of what we should do from there."

Then director of marketing, McDonough and the rest of the management team were looking for a way to create new goals for the company and a means to reach them. In other words he was looking for a way to develop a growth strategy to take FLEXcon to the next level, whatever that would be.

"I happened to read *The Strategist CEO*, Mike Robert's first book," says McDonough. In it, he read a description of the Strategic Thinking Process. He immediately recognized it as the means for FLEXcon's management to leverage its knowledge and experience, creating its strategy together. He passed the book along to CEO Myles McDonough and then-president Mark Ungerer, who agreed they should give it a try. "It was obvious this was what we needed to help us understand our future direction."

So they had Robert take his management through the process, and today McDonough sees it as a critical turning point in the company's history. In McDonough's estimation, the company had been very strong from an operational standpoint, but it lacked the future vision it needed. The Strategic Thinking Process changed that for good.

"As a company," he says, "we always had a cultural sense of our strategy. We could describe ourselves as a pressure-sensitive films manufacturer. We had always done a pretty good job of declining opportunities that would drift us away from that. But we didn't have a good sense of what we needed to do to grow our core strength.

"We were very department oriented. Although we had monthly staff meetings, they tended to be presentations from the departments, not about where we were going in the future. It became very difficult to do new things. Each idea had to be sold to the people who would implement it. But once we went through the Strategic Thinking Process, any new ideas were in effect presold. The result was that everything was easy to accomplish, if it was part of what we said our strategy would be. Everybody was on board, no explanations needed."

The Strategic Thinking Process enabled the management to agree on a Driving Force and a better definition of what FLEXcon would be and become. As McDonough describes it: "Deriving from the Strategic Thinking Process, our Driving Force is Technology/Know-How. Around here we talk more about the Know-How than the Technology because everybody thinks technology is high-tech. The Know-How is combining a customer's applications needs with our coating and laminating and film selection know-how, or material development expertise, to make a product that works on that application. Given that as our core strength and our Driving Force, it leads us into so many different areas."

CHANGING THE RULES— JUST IN TIME

It was 1987, not long after FLEXcon had finally reached its $100 million milestone, and a serious threat suddenly emerged. A Japanese company had bought a coating company just down the road. It quickly became obvious to FLEXcon management that the new group would be going after their market aggressively.

"So we went through a mini–Strategic Thinking Process," McDonough remembers. "We said, 'If *we* wanted to go after the heartbeat of our business, how would we do it?'—particularly if we used Japanese manufacturing strategies. We were producing all of our products on a custom basis, hundreds of them. We always thought it was a great strength to provide that kind of variety. But if I were going to compete against us, I would come out with a few standard products that had superior quality and consistency of performance, price them low, and get UL approval, which for us is like the Good Housekeeping Seal of Approval. So we decided we'd do it before they had the chance. We knew that the company the Japanese had bought didn't have the equipment to compete with us yet. But the rumors in the industry were that they immediately ordered the equipment so they could go right after us."

FLEXcon management sat down and hammered out a plan in mid-January to launch by April, whittling down 168 products to a dozen standard products that would meet all of their customers' needs then served by all those custom products. They were priced to make it very difficult or impossible to underprice FLEXcon profitably. They planned the production to run on two of their newest machines and geared up quality teams for zero defects.

Mark Ungerer believed that if the new competitor were successful, it could cost them more than 20 percent of their sales almost overnight.

"We weren't about to let that happen," says McDonough. "They were about to change the rules of play on us, so we went full out to change the rules on them."

McDonough carefully designed the program to avoid cannibalizing its own products and set prices to thwart countermoves.

"The pricing ended up being 20 percent under the pricing for the custom equivalent. I learned from Procter & Gamble that customers will not switch to an unknown product unless they see at least a 20 percent advantage in pricing. In our industry it takes about a 10 to 15 percent difference to cause the customer to switch.

"So the program was set to launch in April. We used DPI's Potential Problem Analysis to look for things that might become obstacles later, and decided that resistance from the sales force might be a problem. They're compensated on dollar volume, not units."

In anticipation of those objections from its own salespeople, McDonough placed an ad in trade journals with *the new price list*. Three weeks before the ad would run, he announced the new program to the sales force.

"We told them they had three weeks to look like heroes with their customers," McDonough recalls. "We said, 'Go out there and hit every customer. Make sure everybody knows.'"

The program was a huge success. The new competitor was caught flatfooted. By the time they had a product line the following September, it was too late.

"The fact that we were able to develop the idea in January and launch the product in mid-April without a hitch shows how well the Strategic Thinking session worked. You think of all the time it takes for a brochure to be printed, for data sheets, not to mention setting up the manufacturing, getting approval from UL, it was an amazingly tight time frame.

"Not only did we not cannibalize existing lines, we got a ton of new business. Customers started coming to us with significant pieces of business. Business that had gone to lower-priced competitors started coming back to us. Two major competitors got out of that segment of our business, and the new competitor never really got going, although they're still around.

"It was from this that we started talking about ourselves as our own best competitor. Now we offer the best competitive choice, within one house, of short custom runs or standard products. Two entire product lines came out of the new manufacturing capabilities, we had learned. The Eveready Battery business we have today, we wouldn't have thought we could take on efficiently. The whole glass bottle business that we developed, we wouldn't have thought we could take it on and develop it. If we hadn't realized this threat and moved swiftly to change the rules in our market, we'd be a much different, much smaller company," says McDonough.

GROWTH CONTINUES

In the ensuing years, FLEXcon has charged ahead. Sales have swelled to over $350 million, a new plant has been added in Scotland to serve the European market, and products now range widely from labels for shampoo and wine bottles to membranes for touch pads, and holographic security indicia. Yet these products all stem from its agreed-upon Driving Force— its specialized know-how in the development of adhesive-backed materials. And Strategic Thinking as well as other DPI Critical Thinking Processes have become an important part of the culture.

As McDonough remembers it: "For the first three years or so after going through the process, our way of applying it as a decision-making filter was not as formal as taking (which we've done since then) our Business Concept and turning it into a literal filter of yes/no answers to seven or eight questions. All we had to do was describe an opportunity in terms of what we had said in the Strategic Thinking session and make a decision based on that.

"Today when we're evaluating each situation such as developing a new product, we're looking at strategic fit and ease of implementation. To determine the strategic fit, we have taken our Business Concept, two paragraphs long, and turned it into eight simple yes or no questions, such as, 'Will this bring us closer to the customer? Will this allow us to fragment the market? Will we bring new materials to this application?'

"It's not a matter of right or wrong," he continues, "and you don't have to have a perfect yes on every single one. It just gives you the tools to compare various alternatives. If you've got one with six yesses and two no's, and another one with two yesses and six no's, it doesn't take a genius to know which one to pick.

"The other thing it does is that it forces people to ask those questions, and it opens up the idea to challenges. It enables us to say not just *whether* it will bring us closer to the customer, for example, but *how*. It puts all those issues on the table. It takes the idea beyond someone's opinion and allows open questioning."

McDonough also recognizes that even the best strategy needs to be evaluated on a regular basis. He feels that the right time frame for his business in its particular environment is six years for a complete review of the Strategic Thinking Process, with a "quick gut check" every three years.

"We've gone through the full-blown process actually three times, with different numbers of people. These sessions haven't led to any changes of direction. What it has allowed us to do is to really refine our Business Concept, make it better and more clearly delineated."

FLEXcon management has even done the ST Process *from the standpoint of its competitors*. "By putting ourselves in our competitors' shoes, we got a much better understanding of how they may react to any given situation. They have different strategies and different Driving Forces than ours." In his pocket, next to his company's Business Concept card, is *another* card, which carries *his competitors'* concepts, better enabling them to anticipate future competitive moves.

"The real value in revisiting the strategy on a regular basis is not in changing direction but in getting our Business Concept more and more refined, understanding our situation better, and developing the list of Critical Issues to bring us closer to that vision that we've got for our future," McDonough states.

Critical Issues, in the parlance of DPI's process, are initiatives that must be accomplished for the strategy to succeed. Having a strategy is one thing, getting it done is another. The disciplined management of these Critical Issues drives the deployment of a successful strategy.

Ask Neil McDonough what the Critical Issues are, and he knows them off the top of his head. So do his key managers. "The Critical Issues are blended into our monthly staff meeting," he explains. "Each is broken out into small assignments. Each has a Key Champion responsible for it. It's never been a problem of people neglecting those issues because these people are all a part of coming up with the agreement that those *are* the key issues."

CRITICAL THINKING PROCESSES— PART OF THE FLEXCON FABRIC

Through the past 20 years, the people at FLEXcon have worked with Mike Robert and DPI Partner Craig Bowers to fully embrace the concepts of several Critical Thinking Processes, Strategic Thinking being one, developed by DPI. These processes provide a common framework, and logic pathways for evaluating various kinds of opportunities, problems, and decisions in a rational, disciplined manner. DPI's Decision Making Processes, Continuous Process Improvement (CPI), Business Process Improvement (BPI), and Strategic Product Innovation (SPI) are all part of FLEXcon's culture and common language.

Because employees have not only the authority but the *tools* to make decisions, it is visibly apparent that this is an exceptional company. As one visitor to FLEXcon's facilities recently said, "When you walk into their plants, you can see immediately how well run they are. These are plants handling all kinds of adhesives and you can practically eat from the floor."

The company also uses DPI's Strategic Product Innovation process to direct the use of its new product development resources. Most companies use SPI to continuously search out and evaluate new products, customers, and markets. But FLEXcon uses the process somewhat differently, because its customers supply a steady stream of new ideas for products. FLEXcon, therefore, uses the SPI process as a strategic filter to evaluate these many opportunities. "Filtering" each product opportunity by several measures, the company's people are quickly able to make decisions as to which products should be emphasized in terms of timing and resources, and which should receive less emphasis.

As McDonough explains: "Most of our product developments aren't thought up in the lab. They're actually thought up by the customer. We want to respond quickly, and our previous processes were flawed in that they *created obstacles* to getting things approved and implemented. Now people can quickly evaluate Strategic Fit, Ease of Implementation, Cost/Benefit, and everybody has the right, if not the obligation, to get working on the project. Approvals now may come as *dis*approvals and they're usually done by the people involved. They have the tools to evaluate the criteria themselves and can then get access to resources to pursue the project.

"New products are the lifeblood of our company. We put this process into place about 18 months ago. And after 18 months *30 percent of our sales come from new products*. We started with a goal of 30 percent in *three years*. Obviously, we blew that away. Through the first four months of this year, *we came up with 179 products*, using combinations of materials we had never made before. We made *and sold* them. So this has been very successful for us!"

DRIVING FUTURE GROWTH

As FLEXcon continues to grow, the Business Concept stays constant, but of course, new challenges lay ahead.

As part of its goal of reaching $1 billion by 2010, FLEXcon is expanding overseas. Its recently built plant in Scotland is part of that drive. Getting the new staff there on board with the FLEXcon strategy and management methods is key to the success of that new facility.

Says McDonough: "We built the manufacturing facility and hired some key people in Scotland who have not been part of the FLEXcon organization for very long. As a company, we tend to have low turnover and try to promote from within. In our key staff group, I don't think there's anybody with less than 15 years of experience. Then we got over there and didn't have that. They're very bright, capable people, and they understand our business, but I don't believe they'll have it in their blood until they've gone through the Strategic Thinking Process. They'll have their own list of Critical Issues, yet we still share the same Business Concept.

"We also need to get them involved in these other thinking processes. One of our managers was over there and some issue came up and he asked, 'Have you done a Decision Analysis on that?,' and they looked at him like he had three heads. So we want to get to the point where when there's some issue, major or minor, to talk about, we use the same language.

McDonough looks confidently toward that objective with expansion plans into new markets and the further development of the ever-increasing stream of new FLEXcon products.

To what does he attribute his company's exceptional focus?

"It all comes down to getting agreement on the Driving Force, and the Business Concept, so that you can develop the Critical Issues from there. It's very straightforward. You've just got to invest the time and do it. And do it with a facilitator who has the experience to force you through these questions and keep the process on track. Then, once you've gotten down to the Critical Issues, give people the tools to make the right decisions and get things done. If you're going to tackle complex issues, you've got to embed these concepts in your company's culture," McDonough concludes.

PETE SAMOFF, PRESIDENT AND COO T. D. WILLIAMSON, INC. TULSA, OKLAHOMA

For several decades, T. D. Williamson, Inc. (TDW), has been the world-wide leader in pigs. No, not that kind of pig. These are specialized pigs, equipment that cleans and measures the geometry of a pipeline. Beginning with pigs, this 80-year-old privately held company has developed equipment to perform maintenance, without shutdown, on pressure piping systems. The company is the recognized leader in hot tapping and plugging products and services worldwide. Business had been good; the company was stable. But management realized that significantly greater growth was essential if they wanted to remain so. Yet efforts to charge up the engine had fallen short of where they wanted to be.

"We had few competitors and we certainly had the lion's share of the business that we were in," says Pete Samoff, president and COO of the privately held Tulsa, Oklahoma, company. TDW currently has about 700 employees living in 20 different countries. "We're the company that developed the technologies and marketed them, bringing something to the pipeline marketplace that's truly needed, and we're highly respected for the quality of our work. But the market for those products was getting mature. The company could only grow at the rate of the market segment. We had done all the right things to find new growth, searching out new markets, pushing the organization for growth. We ran harder, invested capital, developed new markets. We did all those things but really couldn't outpace the market itself. We just weren't getting the *level* of growth that we felt we needed as a company.

"We also wanted to see a company that would look more for opportunities, a company that would be more aggressive, that would assume a little more risk in the way we approach things. Not risk in the marketplace, not risk in what we do as a company, because you can't have risk when you're working on live gas pipelines. I'm talking about that risk that would allow people to say, 'Okay, I think this is a good idea and we should pursue it and I'm willing to go forward with it.' And that just wasn't something that we had."

Samoff and his top managers had tried to tackle the issue of growth, or lack of it, in their annual strategic planning meetings, but they didn't seem to be able to break out of their current business's confines.

Says Samoff: "I had been president for three years, and when I looked at what we'd accomplished in these planning meetings over that time frame, I realized we'd gone over the same issues every year, and they were much more operational than strategic in nature. We really needed to get beyond that. That's when we set out to find somebody who could bring some discipline to the process, to get us on the strategic side of things and off the operational issues."

After a thorough search of strategy consulting options, the DPI Strategic Thinking Process rose to the top, as it represented a means to mine the knowledge and experience of TDW's own managers, collectively amounting to hundreds of worker-years. The process, which systematically extracts a complete picture of the company, its products, markets, and view of the future business arena, would allow them, they felt, to draw on their deep understanding, to envision a new future for T. D. Williamson, Inc.

"The fact that the DPI process uses *our* people to develop *our* strategy, that it's not people coming in and doing it *for* us made a whole lot of difference," Samoff states. In assembling the group that would go through the process, Samoff and his senior managers were interested in extracting the best thinking of a diverse cross-section of the company. "We brought in 35 people from 10 different countries, people with different backgrounds, and different markets—some from developing markets and others from markets that were very mature."

DPI partner George Spiva facilitated the process, keeping the discussion on track and assuring that all points of view would be heard. Says Samoff: "I think having a facilitator like George Spiva, who's experienced at this process, was important. An outside facilitator makes sure that you stick to the program and that the most vocal or most senior people don't take over the discussion."

As they went through the sequence of the process, they quickly found that this crossbreeding of ideas led to lively debate, with new perspectives emerging. "It was interesting to see how, in fact, we didn't always agree on everything, but in the end we came out with 35 people who were on board as to where we're heading."

The turning point came, as it often does, during the debate over their Driving Force, which, in the parlance of the DPI process, is the specific set of skills and capabilities at the core of the company that propels it toward a given set of products, customers, and markets.

The discussion at T. D. Williamson, Inc., brought about a surprising conclusion. Most of the team *thought* they were Technology- or Know-how–driven (pipeline maintenance technology) but soon realized they had gradually *become* Product-driven (niche suppliers of equipment and services) and determined they *should* be Customer Class–driven, offering solutions for the maintenance needs of owners/operators of pressurized piping systems.

Samoff describes the discussion this way: "When we got into the Driving Force we all *knew* we were a Technology/Know-how–driven company—the know-how being the specialized ability to service pressurized pipes. We'd been doing it for 80 years. But when we got into talking about it, and we did have some heated discussions, all of a sudden we began to question if that's who we truly were. It was interesting to watch the discussion evolve as we realized that we had probably become, over many, many years, more of a *Product*-driven company and not what we *thought* we were. We were market leader in hot tapping and plugging equipment for a long time, but after a time the equipment was in broad use. And we came to the conclusion that our customers weren't really looking for us to be just an equipment supplier any longer.

"So we found that who we thought we were, we really weren't, and realized our customers were looking for us to be more. So we decided to shift our Driving Force to Customer Class-driven and expand the services we offer to our customer base. We already had most of the capabilities we needed to do that. But what we would really need to do to make this change was to develop a new Area of Excellence and spend a lot of time with our customers to find out more about what they're doing and what else we can do to help them in their businesses."

As a result, the group hammered out a concise new Business Concept that would reshape the company and provide a blueprint for the future: "*We will anticipate and respond to the maintenance needs of owners and operators of pressurized piping systems with innovative solutions that leverage our unique operating and technical capabilities that have application in all of our geographic markets. By partnering with our customers we will enable them to minimize their risk and maximize utilization of their assets.*"

As Samoff explains: "There are about a half-dozen key words in there and our managers understand it. We use it as a filter for what we *will* and will *not* do."

To illustrate the difference between the new concept and old, Samoff recalls an incident that occurred a few years ago: "I was listening to one of our guys telling a customer how to go about doing a particular type of job. He was telling this engineer exactly what he needed to do to clean his pipeline, and how he needed to do it. That's just how we supported our customers who'd bought pigs. I think that pig sale was $3,000 or $4,000. Today, we're doing the *whole* cleaning job that could be *$300,000* and the pig sale's still $3,000. So we really do it from beginning to end now, rather than just selling the products."

This has grown the field of opportunity dramatically, enabling T. D. Williamson, Inc., to drastically alter their view of the future possibilities.

"We've got a much larger sandbox, a much larger opportunity. Now we're in the process of learning more and more about our customers. We need to understand them well enough, that when they're out there trying to decide what to do next, and they get to a decision about where *they* want to be, we're already standing there ready to serve. That's where *we* want to be."

CRITICAL ISSUES: A PIPELINE TO IMPLEMENTATION

As any CEO knows, creating a strategy is only the first step. It's a crucial step, but only the beginning. Making sure it happens requires a disciplined approach, the backbone of which is a list of Critical Issues—an essential output of DPI's Strategic Thinking Process.

"The greatest thing about it for me," Samoff says, "was that we came out of the DPI process with a clear list of Critical Issues. Issues like customer research, maintaining our brand equity, breaking new markets. We had the people who took part in the strategy sessions design and pursue these. We have a lot of ownership in the process because a lot of people have been involved."

Samoff believes this *involvement* in these issues has been essential to getting commitment to the strategy and effective implementation.

"We selected the Critical Issue teams very carefully and, as time went on brought in more and more people. By the time we'd been through the first meeting or two, we had somewhere between 80 and 100 people directly involved. That led to a lot of buy-in throughout the company around the *world*—and a focus on getting it done."

One of the most pressing Critical Issues was to prepare TDW's 700 people for the changes that would be taking place. After all, these highly skilled workers had been doing the same types of things for many years and the company seemed to be doing well, enjoying a sterling reputation in its field. Why change? Why now? How?

"One of the things we had to do was to change the culture in the company that really resisted change," Samoff explains. "Any kind of change caused a great deal of anxiety. In addition to directly involving people in the changes, one of the tools we used is a set of videos to explain change. In the first one, we used the lemonade stand to try to put the new strategy in terms everybody would understand. It was about a lemonade stand that only sold lemons and water and sugar, and you made your own lemonade, versus one that made the lemonade (complete solutions). Another video was about the Critical Issues and another on progress and successes.

"Our personnel were told that there would be organizational changes, and there were. We told people we were going to change who our customers were, that we were going to change how we do business, bring in new skills. And we *did* all those things. People are beginning to recognize that change is here, that it's going to happen, and can see the positive results.

"Now when we're talking about making a change or coming up with a new breakthrough capability, people want to be a part of those teams, teams like the lean manufacturing team. They see that this new strategy is really what's *driving* where we're headed and want to be a part of it. They now understand that change isn't necessarily bad. That change can make things better. This could never have happened two or three years ago. The process would have just faded away. Now when I walk through the shop and offices around the world, people all want to talk about the strategy and how we're doing, not just where the next order's coming from."

Another Critical Issue team's charge was user research—learning everything it can about relevant customer needs to flesh out future products and services. Another was assigned to researching and creating a plan to handle a burgeoning customer need, called "pipeline integrity." "It's a new market that's emerged in the United States, and we're there already, ready to support our customers," Samoff says.

As these and other Critical Issues have progressed, the much-needed growth has followed along exceptionally well.

"One of the things we said was that we wanted to *double* the size and value of the company in five years. That would have been a big stretch for our company historically," Samoff states.

"Right now, in the first full year of our new strategy, we're *way* ahead of where we thought we'd be. We've had a very good year—the best in our history. Our sales volume increased by 20 percent versus the typical

6 percent over the past several years. This put us ahead of our five-year target, and expected revenue growth and total company value is continuing to exceed our projections.

"We can actually measure and see how much of that growth has come from the new strategy and how much from our traditional market niche. So being able to pass that along to all of our people has been a real shot in the arm for everybody."

As a private company T. D. Williamson does not disclose its revenues or profits. However, from December 2000 to December 2004, the company more than doubled its shareholder value.

Richard Stephenson, Chairman Steve Bonner, President and CEO Cancer Treatment Centers of America Shaumburg, Illinois

Anyone who has been seriously ill or gone through the experience with a friend or relative knows the stress and frustration that often accompany dealing with today's health-care system. Most of us do the best we can with the situation and move on. Dick Stephenson felt compelled to change it.

In the early 1980s, Stephenson's mother was diagnosed with cancer. So dissatisfied was he with the way her treatment was handled that he decided to research and create an effective alternative to the established system of treating the disease. His dream became a reality with the opening of the Cancer Treatment Centers of America's two hospitals, or "Centers of Excellence," one in Zion, Illinois, and one in Tulsa, Oklahoma. CTCA, as it is called, has gone on to provide new hope, a unique array of healing options—and excellent results—for many "late-stage" cancer patients.

"This all started when my mother was stricken with the disease and we observed how she was treated," Stephenson recalls. "She ultimately succumbed to the disease in 1982. It took us six years of research to discover more and more about the values of cancer patients—what are their values, what are the best treatments, and what are they prepared to pay someone to do? This led to the formation in 1988 of the Cancer Treatment Centers of America that has become the treatment center of choice for thousands of patients, a world leader in providing second opinions on cancer treatment, and a high-quality source for cancer information. We get over 5,000 phone calls a week, easily 200,000 phone calls annually. We also host over 1.25 million unique visits to our www.cancercenter.com Web site.

"The first step is helping those who call us to understand what their options around the world are today for the cancer that is threatening their lives."

CTCA grew rapidly as it provided an effective alternative to the standard medical options. In its "Centers of Excellence" it provides not only the most sophisticated forms of "standard" therapies but also a wide range of alternatives.

"The business for us is 'patient empowerment medicine.' That's something we've framed, and coined, and used. *It is all about the patient.* It is *not* about the providers to the patient of any good or service. It is *only* about the patient," Stephenson says.

"We are talking first about the strongest set of shoulders in conventional medicine that you can imagine—advanced radiation therapy programs; advanced, complicated, but nonmutilating surgery; very clever and advanced chemotherapy regimes; immunotherapy programs and vaccines; cell biology programs, genetic medicine programs, and a range of programs on the shoulders of so-called modern medicine.

"Then we are blessed by a bridge that has been formed—and we're the only ones doing it—through Chinese medicine and Ayurvedic medicine, both of which stand on 5,000 years of experience, and 2,000 years of natural medicine. We have a wide range of highly qualified professionals in psychological care, physical therapy, pain management, and more nutritionists on board in our facilities than anywhere else, that provide really differentiated, make-a-difference nutritional support. We serve the finest food, including organic food, that is nutritionally beneficial to the patient."

CTCA's regimens of treatment are yielding excellent results in pancreatic, breast, prostate, and several other cancers.

"As an example," says Stephenson, "many of our patients with pancreatic disease are outliving the next best by 100 percent, although too many are still dying from that disease. Yet we have planted numerous trees for pancreatic cancer survivors, as a celebration of their five-year survival."

The CTCA approach became so successful that they felt the need to deliver their unique brand of cancer treatment to a wider geographic area than the original facilities in Illinois and Oklahoma were practically capable of reaching. One way to extend that care and to gain referrals from physicians, they thought, would be to acquire oncology practices in various locations around the country. The approach ultimately proved to be flawed, however, as they were unable to adequately convert these traditional providers to their unique methodologies. Expected referrals never materialized, and the company's financial situation was eroding as a result.

About that time Steve Bonner was brought in as CEO, and he immediately saw the need to clarify the company's strategy. Having used DPI's Strategic Thinking Process in previous situations, he and Stephenson agreed to go ahead.

Taking a cross-section of key managers through the DPI process enabled the group to totally reassess CTCA's direction, and pointed them back to the enterprise's original concept—focus on the patient—in a hospital-based setting, and sourcing patients directly.

"When I came in, it was clear that we were strategically out of focus and I thought the DPI process would be the best way to get us back on track," Bonner explains. "I had used the process at two other companies and what I like about it is that it's simple—it forces you back to the soul of your business, to the things that truly set you apart from your competition.

"As I think back on my first exposure to Strategic Thinking," says Bonner, "the financial services company where I worked had hired one of these armies of consultants from one of the Big Five firms who sweep through an organization and come back and tell you what your strategy should be. Then at another company, [the consultants] came in and did the same thing. I thought what they did was very provocative but not relevant. It never really converted to action.

"When I first saw Michel Robert's book *Strategy Pure and Simple*, I thought it was an oxymoron. I thought the words that went together were *strategy, complicated* and *expensive*. DPI's concept really resonated with me—their view that all the knowledge you need to create a strategy resides in the heads of your executives, and that what you need is a process to extract that and look at it differently and then translate that into an actionable set of tools. It just seemed so logical, and in Mike's word, simple, that it was clearly worth a try. I think it's a *powerful* concept, and it's the *right* concept for *every* organization. I've used this process in three different organizations, and in each case, the results have been spectacular!"

The most important revelation to emerge as CTCA's management team progressed through the process was that the company, particularly as a result of its acquisitions, had wandered away from its founding principle—the complete focus of all the company's resources on providing their unique type of care to its patients.

"We realized that we have to live by a Customer Class Driving Force—it is always and only about the *patient*," says Stephenson. "During the DPI process there was some healthy discussion about that. Some thought we could be Technology-driven. After all, don't we really need to be on top of the latest technology? But we already are—we're famous for that—we have the most modern of everything that's needed. But the process helped us to see we don't want to be in the business of *developing* the latest medical technology. That's somebody else's business. Technology for us is a subset of our Driving Force—which is *the patient*."

Says Bonner: "The process really allowed us to reexamine this issue of a hospital-based delivery system as opposed to an oncology practice–based system. It became clear for a number of reasons how important it is to do this in a hospital setting. We have inpatients and outpatients but we need a critical mass and a nucleus of patients to be able to have all these integrative therapies and practices available on a highly convenient basis to the patient. That became very clear. That made these oncology practices nonstrategic assets."

The first major decision to come out of that conclusion was the divestiture of the oncology practices CTCA had acquired.

"We immediately did a number of things," Bonner says. "We started either selling or shutting down these practices. We also completely resized the corporate office because it had been sized to handle this big network of physician practices. And that then allowed us to take a deeper look at what we really meant by *the patient as the strategic driver* and what we meant by *patient empowerment*. We pulled back to the top of the list the importance of being very close to the patient, of really gathering market research, which we had given lip service to but hadn't really done much of.

"We also were able to see clearly how we could redirect the resources that had been going into these other facilities and focus them on constantly improving our understanding of the needs of our patients and the treatments that will benefit them the most. So in the roughly four years since we used DPI's process, we became much more tightly focused, and the financial impact has been amazing."

A set of essential actions—Critical Issues—were agreed upon by the group, with ownership for each assigned to an executive to shepherd to completion.

"We're way down the road on the Market Research Critical Issue," Bonner states, "which was a key issue. In our divestitures, we had 13 practices at one time, and now we're down to one. We're also doing very well on the Integrative Approach to Medicare Critical Issue and I think the issue of Upgrading Technology in our treatment capabilities is coming along very well. Then there's the whole area of Talent, and we've focused our very sophisticated marketing expertise on that so that we will continue to have the high level of staff we'll need in the years ahead."

Looking toward the future, CTCA management has a clarified vision, and with that, a concise Strategic Filter to screen opportunities as they arise.

Of this capability, Bonner says, "We're a very entrepreneurial organization, and that's *good* news. But the flipside of that is that if you don't have a strong filter in place, you get all these ideas coming along and they all look like good ideas. We now have the ability to run these through a process. We've built this filtering process in advance to decide what's relevant and what's not. We're still entrepreneurial and opportunistic, but much more strategic than we were prior to the 1999 run through the DPI process.

One "opportunity" that these filters helped CTCA management to turn down was a very large acquisition that was tempting but would have been a strategic step backward.

As Stephenson describes it: "We had the opportunity to buy the biggest network of radiation oncology centers in the nation. It looked like another way to develop a distribution point for our comprehensive care. We'd be the nation's biggest in cancer treatment. But we reinforced, through these filters, that it isn't the 'biggest' that counts. It would have been another clash between a *Physician*-driven organization and a *Patient*-driven organization, and it would have put us in the middle of a *Technology*-driven organization. Did that meet the requirement of serving the values and needs of our patients as *they've* expressed it? No. It would have been a huge mistake."

DECODING THE FUTURE

As an additional "filter" on CTCA's strategic assumptions, in 2002 Bonner decided to pilot DPI's Decoding the Future Process. They found that by examining future trends in each key segment of the business (for example, technology, demographics, and professional talent) in terms of each of five "futures," they were able to detect changes in their future business environment that they would otherwise have missed. This led them to utilize an extensive range of internal and external data and market research to look for ways to improve the care of, and build a stronger bond with, their targeted set of cancer patients.

"We explored the trends in the world around us with respect to how cancer patients are making decisions, and more importantly how they're *going* to make them in the future. People are taking a much more active role in their health-care buying decisions. Through the Internet and other places, people have much more access to information. So we went down that road and said, if there's going to be a lot more of that, then what is information access going to look like in the future? It got us more focused on what we intuitively knew was an issue, but it's front and center now. It's an extension of our key driver—the way we provide invaluable information to cancer patients and their families," Bonner says.

"It also took our gaze out of strictly health care and allows us to look for other meaningful trends. There were some very creative connections made, some of which were counterintuitive. A lot of creativity is not logical looking forward. But looking back, it looks logical. The Decoding the Future Process helps you move ahead to look back. We looked at a variety of factors against all five futures. For example, one team looked at Technology and another team looked at Markets and Customers.

"Can we predict exactly how the world will look in 5 or 10 years?" asks Bonner. "No, but we've now got some great tools that will make us better at that. And more importantly, we've got a process that will enable us to look at these futures periodically and sharpen our ability to anticipate what's coming at us and be able to respond to it.

"The greater power of this is the general shift in thinking. A professor once expressed it well when he said, 'A fish doesn't know it's wet.' That's the way we were—swimming around in this medium, but we weren't paying attention to it. It goes right along with the shift we've been trying to make in an organization that had been too inwardly focused. Part of the power of the DPI process is that it gets you thinking more about the sandbox around you, and the adjacent sandboxes, and so forth. We've jumped a couple of levels in getting people to look outside for new sources of information, and recognize the power of, and importance of, making sure that we look and keep looking at the world around us as we go forward."

As many hospitals struggle to remain profitable, CTCA is now doing exceptionally well financially, which enables them to continuously develop their effectiveness in fighting cancer.

"In these four years," says Bonner, "we have really accomplished a major turnaround here. We're now just finishing our fourth consecutive year of record earnings and we've got double-digit top-line growth.

"We live in a world of finite resources, and if you're not real clear about how you allocate them, you're going to spend some of those resources on things that won't give you the result you're looking for. The DPI process has allowed us to be very clear about what's at the center of the bull's-eye at CTCA."

And the bull's-eye, in Dick Stephenson's words is "our expertise in treating third- and fourth-stage cancer patients more comprehensively, more empoweringly, and more definitively than they have been told they can expect to be treated anywhere else."

CHAPTER 21

WALT HAVENSTEIN, PRESIDENT, INFORMATION AND ELECTRONIC WARFARE SYSTEMS BAE SYSTEMS NASHUA, NEW HAMPSHIRE

The most technologically sophisticated fighter plane ever built, the F/A-22 Raptor, is now rolling off the production line. This "stealth" aircraft gives U.S. fighter pilots unprecedented offensive and defensive capabilities. Offensively, it is the first fighter to provide pilots with "first look, first shot, first kill"—a combination that ensures air dominance and survivability. It also has an exceptionally acute sensing system that warns of potential threats, enabling the pilot to take defensive actions. Its unique self-protection system is being designed and built by a Nashua, New Hampshire–based company called Information and Electronic Warfare Systems. The business unit accounts for nearly a third of BAE Systems North America's $3.7 billion in annual sales.

IEWS, as it is called, is headed by Walt Havenstein, a former marine and president of the business unit. IEWS develops and manufactures systems such as electronic jammers and acoustic countermeasures, radar warning receivers, laser warning systems, space electronics, and other sensor-based systems that give air, land, and sea forces a distinct advantage in combat situations. It is these products that, as the company's motto pledges, "Protect Those Who Protect Us."

When Havenstein became president several years ago, he joined a company with undisputed technological proficiency. Yet he sensed that the company, with its many different businesses, lacked focus and that this could be causing resources to be spread too thin. To resolve this strategic uncertainty he decided to take his key managers through DPI's Strategic Thinking Process.

"The whole purpose of Strategic Thinking for us was really to facilitate understanding of our strategy," says Havenstein. "Our company environment had many products with a common technology base, but they weren't focused into particular lines of business, nor was there any prioritization *across* them.

"The company is 51 years old. It evolved over those years into 'stovepipes' both operationally and strategically. The Strategic Thinking Process helped align everybody's understanding of the markets we serve, our *unique* and *relative* strengths and weaknesses in those markets, and then to come to a realization as to where our focus *should* be going forward. Ultimately it helped us to simplify what was a very, very complex operating environment.

"That *understanding* assured that when I set the strategic course of the enterprise, it would be understood why we were going in that direction. There may not have been total agreement, but there was *understanding*. I'm not a believer in consensus management in the sense that everybody has to be happy. But I certainly expect feedback and expect people to have their own opinions."

DPI partner George Spiva facilitated the process at IEWS. In describing the need for a skilled objective facilitator, Havenstein says: "The facilitator, for one thing, keeps the process from being dominated by the most senior people. You've got to be careful about that. I equate it to the story about a marine general's visit to a military base. He's just arrived and as his jeep is approaching headquarters, he notices a fire hydrant near the flagpole. He says offhandedly, 'Gee, that's a funny place for a fire hydrant.' The next morning he looks out the window and there are 20 marines out there moving the hydrant, and that's not what he intended at all. So you have to be careful not to overwhelm the process. The facilitator is there to assure that every voice is heard. We operate under the theory that everybody's opinion is valid. That gives you *valid* information to create the understanding. George kept the process pure."

As the top management team proceeded through the Strategic Thinking process, participants were able to systematically examine every aspect of the business—products, markets, technologies, competitors, strengths, and weaknesses. This self-analysis enabled the individuals in the group to gain a deep understanding of how the company was generating and deploying resources and how the configuration had evolved over many years. Armed with this knowledge, they were then able to look to the future and determine the Driving Force and Business Concept that would make the most of those resources, taking them to the next level of technological and financial performance.

As they looked at the various Driving Force choices, three possibilities rose to the top—Market, Product, and Technology/Know-how. Under the first scenario, they would serve a wide range of needs of their market, however they chose to define it, broadening the scope of products they would offer to their clientele across several military and commercial markets. In the Product-driven mode, they would produce a specific set of products, each a direct genetic extension of the last, thus limiting their product scope. The third, however, won out in the end.

"We played out the different scenarios," says Havenstein. "We kept asking the hard questions, looking at our history, and more importantly at our 'future strategic sandbox,' as George would call it. How did we want to expand our role in the future sandbox? It became pretty evident, and our people quickly understood, that the real Driving Force behind the enterprise is the Technology base—our Know-how. Once we completed the process, I don't think the other Driving Forces were even an option. What drove us to that decision was not only our legacy but the realization that, in the market we serve, our technology is really what differentiates us. It's a *unique* strength, not a *relative* strength. It enables us to avoid a 'me-too' scenario in the future. By being Technology/Know-how–driven, we know we will bring something different to our customers than what we see in the rest of the marketplace."

From that understanding, the process participants constructed a concise Business Concept that would guide their future decisions on products, customers, markets, and resource allocation.

"Our Business Concept is formed around what we believe is our *world-class understanding of electromagnetic phenomenology and signal processing*," Havenstein explains.

The resulting Strategic Filter led IEWS to completely review its business portfolio, deciding on areas of the business that would be emphasized and *de*emphasized. They divested a business that was focused on commercial electronics and reduced investments in certain components that were clearly "less-emphasis" areas of the enterprise.

"We stopped investing in some commercial activities and even some military product lines," Havenstein explains. "They just didn't play to our technological strengths. We also made an organizational change. We elevated our *advanced systems and technology* organization up to the senior leadership ranks of the enterprise, under a chief technology officer. The chief technology officer is a direct report to me, and he's responsible for advancing the technology that is critical to enabling and discriminating each of our lines of business—often common technologies that can be used for different products and purposes across several business areas."

These decisions have allowed the company to redeploy resources to more effectively nurture the development of its core technologies and the advanced new products they make possible.

Indeed, this singular focus has enabled IEWS to gain a clear lead in the technological sandbox in which they participate. One significant outcome is that IEWS was selected as the supplier of electronic warfare systems for two of the highest-tech warplanes ever built.

"We were selected as a supplier to the F/A-22 Raptor Fighter and the Joint Strike Fighter, the F-35," Havenstein states. "So, we are the electronic warfare systems provider for the world's most advanced fighters. We were chosen as the supplier for *both* teams competing to build the F-35. The fact that we were selected by *both teams* was clearly based on our unique technology.

"That's the kind of strategic situation you want to create—where you are *clearly leading*. We want our customers to understand that when they want solutions in information-based warfare, electronic warfare, and electronic protection, when they need sophisticated solutions to sophisticated problems, then we're the people they should come to see."

A CULTURE OF STRATEGIC THINKING

Walt Havenstein had used the Strategic Thinking Process before joining BAE Systems—experiences that had shown him how unified thinking can maximize an organization's effectiveness as a world-class competitor. As a result, he has come to view Strategic Thinking as an essential element of managing a company.

"I'm a three-time participant in the DPI process," Havenstein explains. "We used it at two other companies before I came to BAE Systems and now we're using it here. I'm a believer in the Strategic Thinking approach. I'm a believer in having a commonsense vocabulary, and I think the results are evident.

"It gives people a sense of direction. In a short time, our strategy and Strategic Thinking itself have been institutionalized across the enterprise.

That makes our job in managing and leading the business much easier. There is less debate throughout the year as to the important priorities for the company. That's all settled early on in the Strategic Thinking Process, so you're not constantly asked to make *strategic* decisions. Provided there aren't significant changes, the business tends to flow pretty smoothly. I think that's the most important thing. Everyone gains a clear understanding of where the business is going. That, in turn, impacts the level of precision you can achieve in allocating discretionary resources.

"As for Critical Issues that arise from the process, we just tee them up as items that we assign action and closure to, and then we look at them as a leadership team regularly to ensure we're making progress on them. This fundamentally lays out the framework from which we establish our goals and objectives at the top of the company. We have what we call our Top Ten List. We establish the top 10 objectives for the enterprise, and each one of my direct reports has a similar list for their part of the business. We spend a lot of time getting those aligned, and they're all driven as a result of Strategic Thinking."

Because the business environment is dynamic, each year the IEWS team goes through a "strategy refresher," using the process to reassess its strategic situation. The conclusions reached in those sessions then provide the basis for the year's planning. If, in the course of the year, a major change takes place in their environment, a segment of the process is used to determine if any adjustments should take place.

Havenstein explains: "We use the Strategic Thinking Process annually in advance of our normal strategic planning to allow me to issue what I call 'commander's guidance' to the business area leaders. We have seven lines of business managed by vice presidents, as well as the functional vice presidents across the enterprise. So, as we go into strategic planning, I issue commander's guidance that says, 'Here's what I expect to see in the strategic plan.'

"If we then have what we refer to as a 'strategic inflection point' either caused by technology or caused by changes in market conditions—September 11 is a good example—then we run what I call a 'mini-Phase 5' and relook at all the critical Strategic Thinking elements. 'What is happening in the marketplace? What is happening relative to our customers? What is happening relative to our competition? What is happening relative to our Driving Force? What has happened in terms of our relative and unique strengths and weaknesses? Are there any changes in emphasis that we need to make? Should there be any change in the Strategic Filter?'

"It just gives you a *ready template* for quick assessments of strategic inflections. There are strategic initiatives that come out of these sessions but, by and large in the last three years at IEWS, we haven't had to make big rudder changes. I think our last annual Strategic Thinking session resulted in probably an 80 percent solution. We tend to work on the other 20 percent across the course of the year, as we deal with the different levels of strategic issues."

To assure that Strategic Thinking is perpetuated throughout the organization, Havenstein has introduced the key concepts for promising managers coming up through the ranks. The segment is part of a "management boot camp" called the North American Leadership Development Program, or NALDP.

Havenstein says the NALDP "typically involves people who are 5 to 10 years into their careers. It's an 18-month program for selected people—high-potential managers, future leaders. We've just started a pilot program this year. Among other things it will involve understanding the concept of Strategic Thinking—getting exposed to the vocabulary, going through a couple of exercises. We want to expose them to this so that when they do get involved in the process as they assume more senior leadership roles, they'll recognize the need for, and methodology of, Strategic Thinking.

"We've also rolled down the idea of Strategic Thinking to all the directors at IEWS, so we probably have about 125 people that have been exposed to the full process or are at least introduced to the vocabulary and ideas around Strategic Thinking.

"It's important that when we talk Driving Force, everyone understands the relevance of a Driving Force. When we talk *more or less emphasis*, people need to understand what more or less emphasis means. When we talk Strategic Filters, everybody understands the value of the Strategic Filter and how it manifests itself at the different levels within the business unit. And when we talk about the Business Concept, there is a common understanding of the Business Concept. What you see is that, everywhere in the organization, people become familiar with the vocabulary. They start to express themselves in terms which contribute to a common understanding."

A high level of focus throughout the organization has also led to excellent performance. Says Havenstein: "The business is growing. The last two years have been record years for getting orders. This year will be another record-setting year—and that's the bottom line."

Says Stolzenberg: "Before thinking it through, we all, including myself, thought we were a *Product*-driven company. After all, we spend everyday thinking about our *products*. This was probably the most difficult part, but the DPI facilitator took the time to help us think it out."

As a small company in a very fragmented business, the central question became—what Driving Force has enabled, or will enable, the company to compete and grow against competitors as large as L'Oreal and many others? Through the DPI process, the group came to the unanimous conclusion that they are not *Product*-driven at all, but rather, *Know-how*–driven. Its unique edge in the marketplace is its exceptional know-how in creating high-end skin care products, primarily in the anti-aging niche. It is this particular know-how, the team reasoned, that has resulted in its most successful products, created a loyal consumer following, and set Juvena/LaPrairie apart from other cosmetic companies. This know-how stems from an in-depth understanding of skin cells, the stresses they undergo in aging, and effective treatments to counteract these damaging elements. This difference would at once define what kinds of products, markets, and customers it would—and would *not*—pursue in the future.

Of Juvena/LaPrairie's unique know-how, Stolzenberg says: "It's mainly in R&D, where the D is bigger than the R. It is basically product development, including marketing know-how. So we had to define that and say for instance, 'Our parent is one of the leading companies in the world for basic scientific research in this area. How can we leverage that and cooperate better?' As a result, we decided to hire people, who we called 'hunters,' who now work with our parent company to discover what new know-how we can gather in this specific area and turn into products. Instead of just saying we want to develop whatever products our competitors do, we decided to really expand our know-how to create *unique* new products.

"A lot of this know-how comes from discovering the thousands of ingredients that are already there, where the potential has not been recognized, or by finding new combinations that help deal with skin problems. That is because the ingredients are quite regulated and new ones do not come along very often. That is where we want to become an excellent or even *unique* know-how company.

"The other thing we said was we have so much know-how in our company, maybe we can use it in cooperation with other partners. Maybe we can have strategic partnerships where we are more than a third-party manufacturer, which we always did because we have quite an effective factory. That has now resulted in two major companies cooperating with us, where we develop, consult, produce, and sometimes even take on the logistic part.

That has had an enormous effect. For instance, the R&D costs, which are very high for a smaller company, are distributed better and we can afford more highly qualified people, which again, will help our own brands.

"We have expanded our R&D as a *clear result* of analyzing our organization through the DPI process and realizing what would be critical to our future. We have rebuilt the laboratories and hired four or five additional people in the meantime. We are building up the R&D know-how as part of our long-term strategy. We really said, even if we have to overinvest, this is essential to our long-term survival.

"That is the core of the strategy. And that's where we have really invested. Now we are much ahead of where we were a year ago. Probably the *next* most important part is that *everybody accepted* that and stopped criticizing when we invest money there. Everybody realized that this is necessary to our survival in this environment. Everybody is behind the investment in R&D. Absolutely."

Another important step in the process is the forging of a concise Business Concept. Everyone has seen mission statements that all seek to communicate what the company's all about. Most fall short of a useful definition. But the DPI process requires the construction of a Business Concept that defines a future direction in detail and creates strategic filters for decision making companywide.

"We could have easily written down a five-page Business Concept," says Stolzenberg, "but the DPI process drove us to get it down to a few sentences. When we really condensed it we saw why this part is so important. This is the precise expression of our strategy. It guides us in knowing what we have to do about it."

The Business Concept is as follows:

> We will leverage our unique know-how by searching or combining technologies to produce and market innovative face care products with emphasis on anti-aging. We will do this by cascading to other care-related categories, faster and better than the competition. We will cater only to demanding women with beauty and well-being needs that buy in selective distribution worldwide.

The practical value of creating such a statement of purpose is that it serves as a strategic filter for differentiating between essential and nonessential projects and expenditures. Stolzenberg explains: "We now have *strategic filters* and *financial filters*. The strategic filters we arrived at quite fast.

For the financial filters we needed a little bit longer. Now all of our projects go through these filters. We are quite tough with ourselves. That means we are sometimes fighting with our own filters, which is good. And I personally think that the *strategic* filter is more important than the *financial* filter, because some of the things we did in the past would have never passed the strategic filter we now have. If you have that kind of self-critique of what you have done, it helps in deciding about new projects. Now when an idea comes up we ask ourselves, 'Should we really do that, is it in line with our filter?'

"I'll give you an example. We could ask ourselves, 'Should we develop a new fragrance?' Some of our competitors make fragrances, and it's possible for us to do, but it doesn't fit into the filter created by our Business Concept. It doesn't leverage our Know-how Driving Force. In the past we might have just done it, maybe out of enthusiasm or because competitors are doing it. There is always a reason, such as it complements the business, we can use our synergies, and so on. Now we would probably say that product doesn't fit our strategic filter. And of course, from time to time we may have to review the filters. They shouldn't be dogma; they shouldn't be the Bible. On the other hand they should not be changed daily."

Since the completion of the Strategic Thinking Process, the company has been diligently working to resolve a set of Critical Issues—the specific steps to implementing the new strategy. The action most central to the strategy was the increased emphasis on product and market development. Much of that effort is well underway. As a next step, Juvena/LaPrairie has decided to use DPI's Strategic Product Innovation Process to "keep the hopper full" of new ideas for growth. The company's Business Concept once again will serve as a filter for determining which ideas should be pursued.

"One of the other issues," says Stolzenberg, "was changing our attitude toward classic trade. That was one of the things that we ingested for the first time within the whole group. The marketing people and some others had dealt with it before. But now the whole group knows that this is a threat and opportunity at the same time. Again, I think what you learn is very often just two sides of the same coin. For example, concentration of trade can run in your favor or can run against you. Last year we had the abolishment of the duty-free business in Europe. It was considered a Critical Issue and we have learned how to take advantage as a growth opportunity."

As the company continues to work the Critical Issues, Stolzenberg now feels that Juvena/LaPrairie's people are far more united in their focus than before.

"One of the advantages of this process is that the people who were present and those they have spread the word to are taking a more corporate view of where we should go and invest. They now can look at the company as a whole, not just at their own brand. I can say, very clearly, that has happened. That alone was worth the effort.

"We are doing well at cooperating and seeing our interdependence," Stolzenberg states. "We all know that if you want to reach a common goal, all the brands have to do well and everybody has to do something for the other. Very obviously the formulation of the strategy did a great job of that. We can't put it into numbers yet, but there's a general feeling that we all know where we want to go, and that has made many things much easier."

ANDRE HEROUX, PRESIDENT AND CEO MAAX, INC. MONTREAL, CANADA

"Changing the rules of play, for a company such as ours that was a little Quebec company with $6 million in sales back in 1987, has always been our strong belief," says André Héroux, president and CEO of MAAX, now a $750 million force in the North American market for bathroom fixtures, spas, and kitchen cabinets. "As an individual, being a Canadian who has traveled a lot and worked in the United States and elsewhere in the world, I've always believed you can't be a 'me-too.' You have to bring something different. Because we have a small market here in Quebec, in order to grow and be successful, we have *no choice* but to go into new markets. And to do that, we need to offer something different. We can't just do what American Standard and Kohler are doing. We need to go out there and change the rules of the game."

Founded in 1969 by entrepreneur Placide Poulin as Modern Fiberglass, Inc., a small producer of fiberglass snowmobile components, the company shifted gears in 1973 when they diversified into making fiberglass showers and tubs, which would become its main business. The name was eventually changed to MAAX and over the next couple of decades grew through a series of acquisitions, 13 in all. They broadened their offerings into all kinds of tubs and showers, shower doors, tub enclosures, spas, and other related products.

The result of all of these acquisitions was a major company with more than 20 plants and over 3,000 employees spread out across the United States and Canada—all doing well, but doing business as separate entities.

Then, in 1999, André Héroux was brought on board as COO to integrate these 13 acquisitions into one coherent company. The next year or two were spent with the individual general managers working on an integration plan.

"When I was hired as COO, my first mandate was to integrate all of our facilities and distribution centers which were operating as separate companies," says Héroux. "So we built an integration plan with each of those general managers. When you work on integration, you're actually cutting costs, eliminating duplications. You're evaluating everything. So once you get out of that, you need to decide where you go from there, and that is very, very exciting. What I felt we needed then was to bring all the general managers together into one room and get everybody thinking about where we would *all* go in the *future*—what we would become as we grow up. We needed to have a strategy, and most importantly to have these people work together to build that strategy."

On learning of the DPI Strategic Thinking Process, Héroux recognized its methodology as the kind of approach that would draw upon the ideas and expertise of the leaders of all the MAAX companies. Because they had been operating independently, this he hoped would lead to a common understanding of each unit's business, and how each would fit into an overall MAAX business, creating *one*, more competitive company.

Says Héroux, "It's a process where I'm not being bombarded by 10 consultants, and with all kinds of theories and buzz words. What it offered us was a vehicle that is very rigorous, that has clear parameters, and that would have us working with one consultant who was the facilitator. And what it meant to me was that I was able to involve our top executives, including myself, using *our* brains and *our* input to develop the strategy.

"I knew we had very good people with a lot of passion. But I also knew that we needed someone to guide us in how to develop our strategy. The ease of working with a facilitator like Michel Moisan through a very vigorous process was something I had never seen before with other strategy consultants. That was what attracted us to DPI's approach."

So in late 1999, Héroux got his team together to go through the Strategic Thinking Process. For most, it was the first time they had any direct interaction with one another. The goals were clear—mold this group of individuals into a coordinated team, and develop a game-changing strategy that would enable the combined entities to take MAAX to the next level of success, competing with the best-known names in the business. This would be particularly important in the U.S. market, where sales were healthy but the company had no corporate identity, organization or coordinated distribution.

"Everybody was very pleased that we were at the point of developing an overall strategy, which we didn't yet have. This was a very major step.

Of course I think there was some question in people's minds as to whether their input would really be considered. But as we got into the process, those question marks went away. That's behind us, and our people are very, very pleased with the output. The bonding that took place between these executives was extremely positive.

"The basic challenge was to develop a concept of the business that would not only combine those individual units into one company, but to do it in such a way that the combination would bring a unique advantage in the marketplace. As the process progressed, the path to that result began to become clear.

"We were a company that grew our sales, but didn't have a Driving Force defined. So when we talked about that, we had some people in the group that thought we were Production Capacity–driven. We had people who thought we were Profit-driven. We needed to select a Driving Force that would help eliminate duplications and confusions within the organization that had resulted from all these acquisitions and find a common strength that would take us forward. So looking ahead, we needed to define what we would do to maximize all these assets together for the future. The selection of the Driving Force was very important. Looking back, if we were Production-driven, we would have thought, 'How am I going to fill up each plant with volume?' But that wouldn't necessarily be in the interests of the whole or differentiate us, and each plant would still really be working on their own to make and sell whatever their plant was producing. What we needed to do was to select a Driving Force that would enable us to deploy all of the different MAAX product categories, especially in the United States, where we just did not have a strong MAAX presence. We were very strong in Canada, with the 45 percent market share we had. But as we tried to deploy in the United States, we didn't understand the market very well. We didn't understand the distribution networks."

Their future Driving Force, they realized, would be the key to a unifying concept. They found the answer in their vision of a Market Category Driving Force, which would direct all of their activities to fulfilling the needs of bath and kitchen wholesalers, retailers, distributors—even consumers. This would bring a unique product range, unavailable from other single sources, to the market. It would also require a number of major changes to make the idea a success.

"Actually, it implied a lot of significant changes to the organization, the first being how we are structured, the roles and responsibilities of our sector heads, and use of corporate resources. Once we had a clear definition of our Market Category Driving Force, we then could focus on our two Areas of Excellence—Market Knowledge and Customer Loyalty. It allowed a shift of investment toward developing a clear brand strategy and establishing a much more complete sales organization and distribution network. This brought us to the value proposition we are building on today, which is a *total package* we offer, as opposed to just offering a product and a price," says Héroux.

"So this Market Category–driven strategy was a big change but at the same time brought clarity. It gave us focus as to what we would do and how we would do it. Today it is easy for our people to make decisions—where we should manufacture products, what channels to use to sell them, and, importantly, how we go to deploy that throughout North America"

The goal of the new strategy is to continue to develop MAAX's dominant position in its markets in Canada while developing into a strong number two in the United States, as an alternative to the dominant players.

As Héroux puts it: "Our mission statement is that we want to be a leader through our innovative products *and* through our business propositions, through the *total value* that we offer to our customers. The big thing for us is that we're positioning ourselves on value propositions. Our strategy against the big guys is to have multiproduct categories offered in one shipment through one P.O. The big guys don't do that. Instead of just talking about price and product we talk about our value proposition—'Here's how I can make life easier for you Mr. Customer, and how I can reduce the total cost of doing business together.' If my products are easier to install, don't need to be repaired, and we offer an integrated package of products, there's a tremendous advantage to them. This makes us a solid alternative to those big guys, and MAAX is perfectly suited for that.

"And the other part of that is, of course, product innovation. We have designed new, I'll call them Euro-design, products, and other systems such as whirlpools, body jets, the back jet system. Last year at the Kitchen and Bath Show we introduced a new translucent bath product that won first prize in its category. So we're showing people we can come up with premium designs. And already today we are influencing what is happening in the markets. People are taking notice of the confidence and credibility that we have created with the customer base. We will become number one or number two by region, by product category, wherever we have penetration through our products and services."

The bridge from the past to this future vision was a set of five Critical Issues—a roadmap of actions that would alter the organization and give it the capabilities it would need to make the vision a reality.

"We had been a company that was trying to do too many different things at the same time," Héroux explains. "The development of these Critical Issues through the DPI process forced us to identify five things we needed to accomplish and focus on them within our common theme, which is 'Committed to Our Customer's Delight.' And that theme, no matter what sector you're in, no matter where you are geographically, everyone can relate to it and everybody knows what their individual objectives are within it. So this team of 12 managers has been addressing the Critical Issues together as a team. It's been a great thing. Everyone understands all of our sectors of activity today, which was not the case before going through this process."

The first Critical Issue was to develop a comprehensive coordinated marketing plan for North America.

"We had been individual plants selling in their regions. What we found out was that we needed to implement a business plan, per sector, per distribution channel. There are three sectors—bathroom fixtures, spas, and kitchen cabinets—and we needed to define our strengths and weaknesses, where the markets are going, what our competition is doing. That was the first *big* priority," Héroux says.

"The second issue was that we, of course, didn't have a supply chain that would give us the necessary tools to deploy our products throughout North America. Now we do, and that's gone extremely well. This is what makes it possible for us to make one delivery, one P.O., and it has met with great acceptance by our customers."

The third Critical Issue was to establish a North American organization. Although more than half of its sales were in the United States, MAAX as a company had no presence or organization there as it did in Canada. MAAX now has sector managers in each product segment who coordinate the activities of those markets.

The fourth was to establish a system to understand profitability for each activity in the company, which had never been done on that scale.

"What we did not have in the past was that breakdown so we could understand the impact of each activity on our overall results. In doing this exercise, it became very, very clear, by product category, by distribution network. So today this enables me to influence where we should invest our resources and our efforts," Héroux states.

This led to an incentive program based on the mix the company seeks to improve margins, called the "MAAX Index."

"That's worked very, very well and it's enabled me to benchmark, and to see where one group has been successful at something and help the different groups to learn from each other," Héroux states.

The fifth Critical Issue was perhaps the most crucial to the growth of the essential U.S. market. Recognizing that MAAX lacked a sufficient distribution network to implement their new strategy, they decided on the spot to make a major acquisition that would provide the needed capability.

"We decided to acquire Aker Plastics, our fifteenth and largest acquisition. It's a $150 million acquisition, and we used the filter created during the process to make that decision. It gave us the U.S. wholesale distribution network, where we were very weak. They had a strong positioning at number one and number two in the Midwest and Northeast. That entire process is influencing our presence in the U.S. in our other facilities. We're converting our MAAX facilities to the Aker distribution process. We needed this very strong distribution. I call it the 'horse to the market.' So this is absolutely exciting to us."

The filter Héroux and his team now have in place is a set of concise guidelines for strategic decision making. It contains a short list of parameters that allow managers throughout the organization to test new ideas and choices against the tenets of the strategy.

"This Strategic Filter today drives not just capital investments, but it drives decisions about opportunities and it has eliminated a lot of what I call 'the seduction effect.' Let's take the example of a high-potential volume customer at very low margins. It doesn't meet the filter. So people know to fix what doesn't fit or stay away from that. So it's financial *and* it has to fit our two Areas of Excellence. We don't want to be *avoiding* opportunities. But that filter, on the other hand, is a tool that makes sure that you actually *accelerate* the thinking process on opportunities *within* the filter, the decision to acquire Aker, for example."

As the filter has been applied to decisions throughout the organization, the strategy has been implemented quickly, with strong, tangible results.

"The acceptance of our strategy, especially in the United States, has been very, very good," Héroux states. People take the time to listen, and they want to know more. Once we've proven to them that it can actually be successful, they become key partners. And the financial results—our last year has been the best year ever, and I'm not just talking 5 or 10 percent. Our earnings will be up in the range of 35 to 40 percent. Is that *all* related to the strategy? No, but what I'm saying is that not only are the results fabulous, but these results allow us to take advantage of opportunities now that will make us even better in the years to come. So that's very exciting. The market is reacting extremely positively to the new MAAX strategy! And the passion of our people, who are the ambassadors of this strategy to our customers, is really exciting. I think that is what I am most proud of."

THOMAS CHUA, GROUP DEPUTY CHAIRMAN AND MANAGING DIRECTOR TECKWAH INDUSTRIAL CORPORATION LTD. SINGAPORE

The story starts this way: Two guys in a dormitory room write an ingenious software program. People like it and want to buy it. They start a company to market it and develop future enhancements. The company grows. Pretty soon, they're spending a lot of their resources on activities unrelated to software and customer support. Package development. CD production. Order fulfillment. Retail distribution. And on and on. Profits lag, and innovation loses momentum as the business gets bogged down in more and more complicated logistics.

Then along comes Teckwah, an entrepreneurial Singapore-based company that provides complete supply-chain services, from packaging design through shipping and distribution. The two guys heave a sigh of relief and get back to what they do best—creating software. Their company starts growing again.

TECKWAH: FROM CARDBOARD BOXES TO SUPPLY CHAIN MANAGEMENT

The idea of becoming a "complete supply-chain management services provider" to the IT industry didn't come to Teckwah out of the blue. The concept developed in stages, with the help of DPI's Strategic Thinking Process.

Teckwah first opened its doors in 1968 as a printer of cardboard boxes. Under the guidance of founder Chua Seng Tek, father of present managing director Thomas Chua, the company did well in Singapore's thriving manufacturing-based economy. After all, most manufactured goods wind up in cardboard boxes. It was a good niche, and the company gradually moved on to more sophisticated commercial printing and packaging products as their customers' needs changed.

The company eventually served a variety of markets such as food and beverage, toys, consumer electronics. Fast-forward to 1994, when the company went public.

For a while after the offering, Teckwah continued to prosper. But times were changing, and the company was in danger of being left behind. As one packaging printer among many, it found the competitive environment heating up while Singapore was gradually diminishing its emphasis on manufacturing and moving into the era of the "knowledge-based economy." With a hefty overhead in printing facilities, the company was feeling the pinch.

As Thomas Chua recalls: "In the early nineties we were working very hard to get listed on the Singapore Stock Exchange. We were at the peak of our performance in both top and bottom line at the time of the listing. But we really had not addressed what we would do next. Our planning for the future had all been done based on what we had done in the past—commercial printing and packaging materials. We expanded geographically into China and other regions. But after a while we felt we had lost our direction and that something had to be done. But what—and how? Coincidentally, a letter from Andrew Sng, a DPI partner in Singapore, hit the right note and we decided to call DPI in. We liked the idea of a process that would guide us to think logically and strategically. I was also looking for a platform where I could involve other levels of staff."

So in 1997, the top three tiers of Teckwah management went through DPI's Strategic Thinking Process.

"It was a session that involved all the right people," Chua recalls. "It was because of this team involvement that top management and the next two levels down could understand one another's opinions and thinking better. This enhanced the communication between the top management and the next levels since we were able to use a common language when talking about strategy. The interrelated questions led us to think through the implications of our past, present, and future internal and external environments and finally arrive at a consolidated picture that captured all of these."

The sessions resulted in a major shift in the focus of Teckwah's business, culminating in the agreement among the management that their Driving Force should change from *Capacity*-driven to *Market*-driven. They would concentrate on one rapidly growing customer segment—the IT industry—and provide those customers with new services that were logical extensions of printing and packaging.

"As we went through the DPI process, we finally realized that in the past we had just banked on our production capacity," Thomas Chua recalls. "But expansion in that kind of business is difficult and expensive because you have to buy more machinery and keep it running at top capacity. So to fill capacity, we would serve anybody we could offer our services to. It became so competitive, and all our competitors were doing the same thing. There's no point to trying to keep up the capacity if you don't have the business. So we decided to focus on one or two industries and expand our range of services to them. We studied among the industries we knew and decided that the emerging information technology industry, which we were already involved with, had the most potential. So we changed our Driving Force to *Market*-driven. We concentrated on providing higher-value services to that niche market, and it worked."

At that time, the IT business was in a rapid expansion mode, with an explosion in product development and marketing. Teckwah saw a need for a growing list of services, all related to printing—activities that are not core competencies of its customers. The opportunity was there for the taking— *if* they could effectively make the needed changes in their organization. So, as part of the process, they developed a list of Critical Issues—actions that would be essential to the successful implementation of the new strategy. Foremost among them were attracting top-notch people with knowledge of the industry and discovering and developing the services that would be most valued by this burgeoning segment.

The business concept that emerged was right on target, the Critical Issues were effectively accomplished over time, and the company's range of services—and top and bottom lines—grew. Management today feels that the successful deployment of this strategy was greatly enhanced because of participation in the DPI process by several levels of Teckwah managers.

Says Chua: "Our middle management level understood our strategic profile better because they were involved, and so there was *ownership* in the action plans, and they cascaded the action plans down to their subordinates. Now we have a set of documents, a strategic filter, for us to refer to. Whenever we want to invest or make some major decision, we check whether it is in line with our business concept and strategic profile. A good example is that we decided to divest a subsidiary which, although it is profitable, did not fit our strategic profile anymore."

Thomas Chua describes the new strategic direction that emerged from the Strategic Thinking sessions: "To a certain extent we changed the rules in our sandbox. As a packaging printer, usually you produce your packaging box in your factory and deliver it to your customer, and they do the final packing. Now, as one example of how we have changed that system, our customers could send their finished products to our factory and we would do the final packaging and fulfillment for them. So this is not a standard practice. We even do the sourcing for the customer in some of the accessory items. So we made a transition from printing to what we now call the supply-chain business."

As the new concept took hold, profitability improved dramatically, as expansion was now far less capital-intensive than growing the printing business had been.

"First of all," Thomas Chua says, "the supply-chain business is more service oriented compared to printing and packaging, which is more production oriented. And when the supply-chain business expands, we don't have to invest heavily in equipment. Investment is more in people and computer systems. So when the business grows, expansion is much less costly."

STAYING AGILE IN A RADICALLY SHIFTING ENVIRONMENT

Yet, despite all of this success, two unforeseen shifts in Teckwah's external environment—the Asian financial crisis and a sudden slowdown in IT industry growth—prompted a strategic review in 1999.

Again, Andrew Sng led the Teckwah managers through the DPI process, with a very unusual result—a second change of Driving Force! Recognizing that growth in IT and the economy in general had diminished, *and* that Teckwah had developed a sophisticated supply chain management expertise, they decided to change their Driving Force to *Capability*. The capability, of course, is supply-chain management. The main difference would be the development of an even deeper set of service offerings and the ability to eventually expand the range of customers to include new markets.

Says Chua: "We did our second review in '99. We had been doing okay when we changed from Capacity-driven to Market-driven. We saw the strength in our results. But when we saw these major, unexpected changes happening, we started asking ourselves if we should still focus on the same model, or should we change? We were supposed to have a review in 2002, but because of the Asian financial crisis, a lot of things had changed. It was time for us to look into all the fundamental assumptions. Our competitors were also beginning to imitate us because they saw how well we performed. As a result of going through the process a second time, we decided that if this new supply-chain capability proved to be well received by the IT industry, one day we could have the same capability to serve other industries such as pharmaceuticals."

The strategic refocusing has enabled Teckwah to once again forge a new direction and new growth without having to abandon its existing skill base. They are simply building onto it to find profitable opportunities.

"So now we are a total solution provider. We offer complete solutions to customers. We take over the customers' responsibility in the area of supply-chain management. It's high value and they pay us for that. Now that's *totally* different from an ordinary, traditional printing and packaging company. But there is still a genetic connection between where we started and where we are now. We are still very much linked to printing and packaging. These are core competencies. But this new strategy gets us out of our old sandbox," Thomas Chua states.

"The business performance, the growth and the bottom line are all positive," he says. "In 1997, almost 100 percent of our business was printing and packaging. In 1998, the supply chain business was 6 percent of the total business. In 1999, it was 19 percent; in 2000 it was 49 percent. Today, it is almost half and half. Last year our turnover, compared to 1999, almost doubled. The top line doubled from 70 million Singapore dollars (41 million U.S.) to 130 million (76 million U.S.). The bottom line doubled from 7 million to 14 million Singapore dollars."

Looking back, he says: "We could have engaged a consultant from our industry, but we chose not to. DPI's tool is applicable to *all* industries. The DPI process emphasizes changing the rules and controlling your sandbox. This intrigued us very much, and we have done that.

"Also," he concludes, "I think that this process is very complete. It is not difficult to apply or understand. It is a process that *teaches you to fish*; it doesn't give you a fish! It's our own input. At the end of the day, we feel it is *our work* and not that of a consultant. This makes implementation much easier. Through the DPI process, we changed our mindset. In the past, our slogan was 'Good Printing for a Good Image.' Now our slogan is 'Best People, Best Solution.' From the 'pre-DPI' time to the end of 2000, Teckwah's revenue has grown 250 percent. Along with an overall recovery in the Asian economy, and the absolute commitment and hard work of our people, DPI is a key catalyst of that growth."

ED GRONDEL, CEO
FNB HOMELOANS
JOHANNESBURG,
SOUTH AFRICA

Years ago things were not going at all well at First National Bank (FNB) HomeLoans. The company was running a loss of about US$33 million, and in the words of current CEO Ed Grondel, "FNB HomeLoans wasn't really even considered a player" in its market. Yet in the financial year 2002–2003, the company cleared a *profit* of about $40 million, and transformed itself into a significant force in the South African residential home loan market, more than doubling its market share.

In between, FNB HomeLoans' management team, with the help of DPI's Strategic Thinking Process, devised a strategy that clearly changed the game in their market and resulted in this dramatic change of fortune.

When Ed Grondel joined the business in 1999 he found a company bereft of any clear direction and a workforce resigned to poor performance.

"There was really a losing culture," says Ed Grondel. "People were bureaucratic. There was no desire to *win*. Nobody knew how much business we'd written that month, including top management. There was no sales culture. The modus operandi was 'keep on doing the processing. Do it like we've always done it. Don't rock the boat. The industry's bad, the market is bad, and it will get worse. Maybe one day it will get better.' That was the kind of thinking that went on around here. We needed to get a new winning culture in the business, and we needed a business model that would give us a competitive advantage. However the foundation for change had been laid by bringing in DPI.

FNB HomeLoans is a major division within First National Bank that was acquired and integrated into FirstRand, one of South Africa's largest financial services companies. FNB HomeLoans was formed through FirstRand's famous "chunking" approach to business, a philosophy that has been credited with making FirstRand the phenomenal success it is today.

"The FirstRand Group was formed several years ago from four different companies—two insurance companies (Momentum Group and Southern Life) and two banks, a retail bank (First National Bank) and a merchant bank (Rand Merchant Bank). FirstRand has the philosophy of 'chunking off' individual business units. One of those was home loans. Home loans had been treated simply as a product at the various branches of the retail bank. So, home loans were identified as an opportunity to establish a separate business unit," says Ed Grondel.

But merely splitting the business would not automatically lead to success.

"We were a business which was quite unwieldy in terms of cost. We operated a huge branch network. We had a one-size-fits-all product pricing approach and lots of inefficiencies and very low staff morale. Our approach to sourcing business was that if a customer wanted a home loan at a branch, we would provide it. But we had no clear strategy for going out and getting business," says Ed Grondel.

The result was a home loan, or mortgage, company with declining market share and a "book" made up largely of the least desirable loans—small, high-risk loans.

"At the time there were about seven players in the residential home loan market, with the bulk being held by four players, us being one. We had about an 8 or 9 percent share, but our share of *new* business was only about 6 or 7 percent, so our book was running off fast. We also had a high number of properties in possession, which was a huge factor contributing to our losses. We were pretty competitive in the small, high-risk category, but in the juicy market—low-risk, bigger mortgages—we were very uncompetitive. We applied the same sort of price across the market, so we were turning away a tremendous amount of good business."

It was clear to Michael Jordaan, chairman of FNB HomeLoans, that incremental changes wouldn't be enough to refloat the sinking ship and get it on a course toward growth. The company was in dire need of an innovative strategy and a means of quickly lining its people up behind it.

"We knew we could fix our cost problems, our properties in possession, and so on. But what we really needed to do was to find a new model that would take us into the future. We wanted to look at what was taking place worldwide in the industry, what was happening in our market, and how to position ourselves uniquely in that market—to offer something different than all the other me-too competitors."

Adds Jordaan: "We also needed a tool that would help us surface and filter out the most significant issues and also to help us evaluate whether or not our existing management team was the right one to implement the kinds of changes we knew we would have to make. The DPI process is very useful, particularly for a new CEO, for evaluating not only the business and key issues but also the skills and abilities of the people involved."

The decision to use DPI's Strategic Thinking Process was strongly influenced by the fact that this approach had been used very successfully by FirstRand to gain alignment behind the overall corporate strategy throughout its management team. Said FirstRand CEO Laurie Dippenaar at the time: "We went through this process to get a common understanding and buy-in into our business philosophy. And it definitely achieved that objective."

Said Ed Grondel of FNB HomeLoans' choice to use DPI's process: "One of the key factors was that the DPI process takes you along a very disciplined approach. At that time in our business, we needed a fairly rigid thinking process to get to where we wanted to be."

Facilitated by a DPI team that included South African DPI partners Rex Glanville and Greg Carolin, a management group representing a cross-section of departments became participants in the Strategic Thinking Process. Based on information supplied by the participants themselves, they proceeded to systematically analyze all relevant aspects of the business. The objective was to develop a complete picture of the business as it *was* in order to create a *new* strategy which would drastically alter their approach to the market.

During the sessions, it became clear that a change of Driving Force would enable them to make the shift from a me-too player to a game-changing competitor, breaking through the pack.

"Changing the game, for us, is the only way to do it," says Ed Grondel. "Our market's too concentrated to be just another player. If the market can't see a clear difference, they'll stay with the conventional tried and true. You can't build new business that way. You have to woo them away from their existing relationship. You *have* to change the rules. After a heated debate, we saw the need to make a major change if we were going to make a difference in the industry. Through the process that Rex and his team took us through, we saw it so clearly."

With all the players in the market pursuing what could be called Product-driven strategies, all products appeared to be the same. The key to the future lay in the recognition, through the process, of an emerging source of home loans—the mortgage originator.

"We spent a huge chunk of the day on that," Grondel says, "concluding that everyone's got the same old product, and the product can be copied.

So we determined our Driving Force to be Market type—mortgage origi-nators and estate agents who we have since come to recognize as partners in our business, as opposed to merely suppliers."

Furthermore, the First National Bank Branch Network was also rec-ognized as our internal mortgage origination channel. The mechanism was put in place to serve them as the very important business partners they would become.

This change would provide a new way to source business and enable FNB HomeLoans to structure unique products, services, and pricing that would meet the needs of the segment. That led to an extensive reorienta-tion of the corporate mindset.

"We had to completely change our thinking around, 'Who is the cus-tomer?' So in every decision we take today, we ask the question, 'How will it affect our relationship with the mortgage originator, the estate agent and the First National Bank Branch Network?' If it has a negative effect, we go back to the drawing board."

To effect such a major transition, fundamental changes were needed in the structure of the business itself. The shift in Driving Force also cre-ated the need to cultivate new Areas of Excellence. In building a Market-type Driving Force, the Areas of Excellence are related to understanding the needs of that market through Market Research, and delivering on those needs to build Customer Loyalty. To support those Areas of Excellence, new skills were needed. More importantly, perhaps, was the realization by both Ed Grondel and Michael Jordaan that several key managers would not be suited to the new modus operandi.

"We made a huge change in the structure of our business, and in the processing of our business, to facilitate dealing with our intermediary part-ners. We approached all the originators and estate agent groups on a national basis, gained an understanding of their needs, and came to an agreement on levels of commissions, and levels of service and so on. We then began to source all of our business through a centralized channel, as opposed to the decentralized channels of the bank branches. We also concentrated on min-imizing the costs in each channel by tracing the whole process from origi-nation. We're the *only* ones in the business to align ourselves with the intermediaries to the extent that we have. We've made it very clear that they're our reason for being. Our competitors are bleeding about the fact that the originators are very expensive to deal with, and indeed they are if you don't structure the business to maximize the benefit of the originator market. We've cut our costs tremendously in that market, and our competi-tors haven't. And we've taken that market, through our alliances with the originators, to the next level. Some of our team just couldn't accept the change and left," Ed Grondel says.

Throughout the organization, an ongoing program of training and recruiting at both the line and management levels has altered the skill sets of the company's staff, and the new strategy has been extensively communicated.

The company has aggressively resolved a clear set of Critical Issues to assure that the strategy is implemented effectively and efficiently. In addition, periodic reviews keep the strategy fresh, enabling adjustments to environmental changes and new opportunities.

Says Ed Grondel: "Throughout the year we have four strategic breakaways to review the strategy and address any new strategic issues. In the last session I told Greg Carolin we wanted to do a quick review of where we are and then focus on the future. So we started to do a quick review, but soon realized that we had a lot of new members on our team, and some of them didn't really understand the strategy. They hadn't been through the process. So we went through the full process again. On the way home, one of the participants said to me, 'This has really enabled us to understand where we're going. Without it, we would not have been onboard with where this business is going with the strategy.'

"Today everybody in the business knows and grasps, down to the most junior staff, that the intermediary is the key to our lives and understands the strategic importance of that. The culture is completely different now. We've invested a huge amount in our people. We've taken them from *zero to hero*. Before, they didn't believe they could do anything. We really have a winning culture now."

The improvements in financial performance have been equally dramatic, right from the start. "We've taken the business from the point of writing 200 million Rand a month in new loans to writing in excess of a billion Rand every month. Next, we've set a target of 1.5 billion Rand," Ed Grondel states.

To continue to accelerate growth, FNB HomeLoans has also acquired the "book," or loan assets, of two of its competitors and are in the process of integrating those.

"Our strategic focus over the past year was growth—both organic and acquisitive growth—and we're achieving both of them. Our organic net growth was over a billion Rand this past year, and our acquisitive growth was 19 billion Rand. Our book size is now at about 38 billion Rand, or about $4 billion U.S. Our market share has gone from 6 or 7 percent to about 18 percent, and we will need to get our share of new business, which has grown to 18 percent, up to 20 percent a year. Our business is very much one of scale. It's no use running a 10-ton truck with a five-pound load. You've got to maximize it, to get a full load on that truck. We've got a long way to go but we're on our way.

"All the changes we've made have brought growth to the business. Growth costs, but we're building huge value now, securing future profits with the business we're putting on the books right now. We're excited about the potential that still exists out there, in terms of getting our organic growth, getting closer to the originators, and forming alliances with them," Ed Grondel states.

CHAPTER 26

Benjamin Salzmann, CEO ACUITY Sheboygan, Wisconsin

The year 2001 one was a big one for ACUITY. It was the year they broke into the A.M. Best 100 Largest Insurance Companies list, and Ward named them one of the Top 50 Best Run Companies. Other, perhaps even more significant awards, followed. All this in one of the most difficult insurance environments in recent memory. To understand why these honors are so remarkable, one only needs to look back a few years to when the company, then called Heritage, was one of the industry's most chaotic and inconsistent performers.

"In 1995," says CEO Ben Salzmann, "our combined ratio was 116— 10 points higher than the industry."

The combined ratio is a key measure of an insurance company's profitability—percentage of premiums paid back in losses, plus agent commissions plus expenses. The break-even point before investment income is 100. The higher the number, the less profitable the business.

"Prior management grew the company over 30 years," Salzmann says. "I'll give them credit for that, but it happened in a very tumultuous way. It was always zigzagging from profit to loss. There would be great growth with horrible losses, then a period of raising prices to get profitability back, but at the cost of huge chunks of market share. Market share dropped a full one third in 1997. Think of the turmoil a company goes through when it loses a third of its sales. And we had become infamous with our agents for this pronounced inconsistent behavior. One effect was that we were severing relations with some of our best agents—our distribution channel. And to make matters worse, product development consisted solely of creating products suggested by a few agents, even if none of the other agents were interested in it or it wasn't profitable for the company."

Partly because of all this tumult, and partly because of work rules, morale at Heritage was at an all-time low. As Salzmann says: "If you told people you worked at Heritage, the reaction was always 'Why?' It was so bad, we even had bells that went off to tell you when you could take a break."

Clearly things had to change. And they did. When management transitioned in 1997, Ben Salzmann's charge was to create a focus on "profitable growth, where the word *profit* came through," as Salzmann puts it. This called for very fundamental changes in the way business was done, relationships with agents, product offerings, the very culture of the company. To help develop a clear direction among the management team, they decided to bring in an outside firm to help them create a new strategy.

"We brought in about a half dozen planning companies at least twice on site. We did reference checks. We went through their methodologies. If they wrote books, we bought the books, read them, critiqued them. We created, I would say, a 500-page three-ring binder comparing content planning versus process and then critiquing the various consultants. What we liked about DPI was that, while they had an academically justifiable process, they didn't get lost in academia. In all of their books and materials they immediately took the theory and made it very pragmatic, constantly tying their methodology into case studies with real results. We had the full professors with Ph.D.s from the various big business schools in here talking about content planning, with their incredible rhetoric. But we kept saying, 'Show us your clients and what you actually did for them. And show us how it made a difference within their industries.' Whereas every piece of material from DPI said, '*This* is our client in *this* industry. This is how our process helped them find another way to conduct their business. And this is how it benefited them.' DPI kept tying the theory and processes back into real cases of clients in the practical business environment and the end results they achieved.

"We also learned the difference between content and process strategy consultants. With DPI, *we* do the thinking using *their* process. Content planners arrive with the most recent graduates and one semiseasoned planner who is billed at a horrific rate. They come in and do 'meatball surgery.' They leave you to figure out what to do next. With DPI, *we* created the strategy and there's a clear timetable and responsibilities for implementation. It just made more sense to us. With DPI we also knew we would be working with an experienced veteran, Mark Thompson. He commands your attention, and our officers respected him. A lot of strategic planners don't get that kind of respect because their methodologies don't work and their strategies never get implemented."

ACUITY's management assembled a team from across the company to go through the process.

"Mark told us we needed to have representation from throughout the company to get the maximum buy-in. We had been building a culture that involves people in decision making so that immediately dovetailed with who we are. He also said, 'Look for rising stars, such as an underwriter who you see growing with the company. They bring frontline exposure. Take advantage of that.' Those things matched our culture. It was a natural fit."

As the process progressed in the first three-day session, a major revelation emerged that would lead to significant shifts in how the company did business. After extensive debate over the company's Driving Force, the team realized that they had been Distribution-driven *by default*. In other words, the distribution system—its agents, and actually only a portion of them—were dictating everything from product development to commission structure to geographic reach.

As Salzmann recalls, "We had a very strong debate over whether we should be Distribution-driven—where it is the agent that drives us—or whether we should be Product/Service-driven. We were defaulting under previous management to giving away the selection of future products and marketing and sales to our *agents*. That doesn't mean we don't value our agents; we do. They are our lifeblood, a vital link to our customers. We listen to them very carefully. But *we* should be developing the products because that's our expertise, *and* we underwrite the risk.

"The agents' job is to bring us together with potential insureds. But we had been listening to anecdotal evidence from individual agents and developing products that the majority of agents didn't want. An agent might also say, 'I'm on the border of this particular state and I want to write business there,' and we'd go into a new state without ever looking to see if that would be profitable for us. We should have been doing the research across many agents, and across the marketplace to develop products that meet the needs of the majority of agents—and *us*. In the end, as a result of recognizing our Product/Service Driving Force, we decided to completely reorient the organization, taking back ownership of marketing, sales, product development, communications."

Out of the process came a list of eight Critical Issues that would begin to make this major change in their business.

Issues such as increasing the pace of e-commerce, taking ownership of marketing and sales, customer-direct service, data utilization—even a communications program that involved changing the company name to signify the depth of changes taking place—were created and assigned to individuals to manage to completion.

One the Critical Issues involved moving the responsibility for service from the agents back to ACUITY. This has accomplished two ends. It relieves agents of a complex task for which they are not compensated, and it also provides a means for ACUITY to create direct links to its customers, strengthening those relationships, developing brand loyalty. Most of all it enables ACUITY to leverage an Area of Excellence it now nurtures to support its Driving Force.

"Superior service in insurance isn't just getting the customer something faster," Salzmann explains. "Superior service means things like helping your customer with loss control. You could save 8 percent this year by going with Acme, and have more losses and wind up paying 30 percent more in premiums the following year. We now help commercial customers to *reduce* losses, which lowers their premiums. That's just one of the ways we can provide value-added service and really please the customer."

One of the most important Critical Issues was the creation of *new* products and services. These could range from new types of insurance to new services to the customer.

To catalyze this effort they decided to use DPI's Strategic Product Innovation Process (SPI). This process applies a systematic approach to flushing out new ideas. It then allows participants to filter them against a matrix of strategic fit, ease of implementation, risk/reward, and various other measures. The result is a short list of concepts that further the strategic goals outlined in the Strategic Thinking Process. Also, an integral output is a practical implementation plan with timelines to assure crisp development and rollout.

"The whole idea of using this process was to get fresh, new ideas from across the whole company," says Laura Conklin, ACUITY's Vice President of Business Consulting, who has headed up the product development effort. "We brought in a group of people from all levels and parts of the company, people who we identified as having a lot of drive and openness, to bring out ideas that might have been stifled in the past."

Out of the SPI sessions came a series of innovative services and products. Some are as simple as online availability of Certificates of Insurance for contractors. This helps the contractor to get the certificate quickly, relieves the agent of having to drop everything to deliver it, provides a link to the end-customer that helps strengthen the relationship and streamlines the process of being a customer.

Other products are actual insurance products, one of which is a major innovation designed for the next time a "soft market" occurs.

Understandably reluctant to provide details, Salzmann explains: "We came up with an outstanding new product. We're timing its release for the next period when commercial rates start to fall again—a soft market. This product will be tremendous in counterbalancing the commercial insurance market when we go from the present hard market, where rates are at a premium, to a soft market, where we can't get enough for the risks we're assuming. That's the most important time to have a strategy, and the DPI processes have helped us to get to products like this that are crucial to our 'profitable growth' objective."

The development of such profit-making products and services has become part of ACUITY's modus operandi. Says Conklin: "The DPI process got us thinking this way all the time now. We don't even think of new product development as a Critical Issue anymore. It's become part of our culture. It's how we work."

The results of the new strategy have been steady and impressive. "Remember," says Salzmann, "the challenge was to grow premiums and remain profitable, and to have our agents respect us again, to be able to say to them, 'We will be profitable and grow and not disappear on you.' Now, at the end of 2001 we were wonderfully profitable. Here's an example. The whole industry's combined ratios (remember, lower is better) have risen from 105.6 in '98 to 117 in 2001; ours have gone from 99.9 to 101.8 in the same period—15.2 points more profitable than the industry. Add in our investment income, and we made $7 million. That's really incredible. And what about premiums! In '97 it was $225 million. At the end of 2001 it was $425 million, so we grew by $200 million. Our anticipated premium at the end of 2002 is $500 million. We've cleaned up the way the company was doing business, become consistently profitable and stopped the zigzagging."

As to the awards ACUITY has received, Salzmann is justifiably pleased. "The one I'm most proud of is making the *Fortune* 100 Best Places to Work, considering what our reputation was just four years ago," he says.

"Second, remember I said that we were formerly running as a Distribution-driven organization, where Distribution means our agents, and then changed to Product/Service-driven. Ironically, since we've made that change to Product-driven, we're doing a better job for our agents. The National Professional Independent Agents voted ACUITY the Best Insurance Company in the nation—the singular *best*. That means we're rated above all the big-name insurance companies whose names you know! I think that's just amazing. Because we recognized our true Driving Force and did it better, our distribution channel named us *the* top insurance company in the nation.

"On top of that, Ward, which rates all 3,000 insurance companies doing business in the United States, named us to the 50 Best Run Companies in 2001 and 2002. And as if all that's not enough, ACORD, which rates technology use, named us Technology Champion.

"But the real rewards come from customers. The numbers speak for themselves."

CHAPTER 27

Rak Kumar, CEO
Raster Graphics
Palo Alto, California

Judo experts have always known that size doesn't matter. In fact with the right strategy, small size can be used as an advantage as competitors vie for supremacy. In business, a smaller combatant may be able to use its agility and its focus as strategic weapons so powerful that it can topple and defeat larger competitors by simply using the right leverage in the right place.

An undaunted commitment to this principle enabled a small, specialized printer manufacturer to leverage its Driving Force and Areas of Excellence so effectively that it not only defeated two much larger competitors but also ran them completely out of business. Says Rak Kumar, CEO of Raster Graphics: "The only way you can beat the bigger players at their game is by clearly understanding the sandbox you're playing in and developing a way to dominate that sandbox. You need to understand the whole concept of your Driving Force and the one or two areas you must excel at—your Areas of Excellence. You have limited resources and you need to understand where to use those resources to strengthen those Areas of Excellence. That's the only way to win."

And win they have, as dedication to this simple credo has enabled Kumar's company to grow from $25 million in sales in 1996 to over $200 million today, with 30 percent annual growth predicted going forward. This despite the fact that they were playing in a sandbox dominated by much larger companies—divisions of Xerox and Lockheed (not to mention Hewlett-Packard)—that dwarfed them in size.

Here's how it happened, as Kumar recounts this David-and-Goliath (actually David and Goliath and Goliath's bigger brother) tale.

"Back in 1996 we were a small company growing at about 25 percent a year. We make what we call printers for wide format imaging. That means we make printers for displays on the side of a bus or a Macy's window or a billboard," Kumar explains. But when you are only about $25 million in revenue, you have limited resources, and we had very large companies as competitors. We were competing with Calcomp, a $400 million Lockheed division, and a division of Xerox that was at about $200 million at that time. Our big challenge was, as a small business with a good growth rate and good technology, what should we focus on? What should be our strategy or main focus over the next three to five years to continue to build the business at that rate and not get killed by these big giants like the Xeroxes and the Lockheeds?"

To assist the management team in making these crucial decisions, they enlisted the help of DPI and its Strategic Thinking Process, which they went through in mid-1996. The DPI approach appealed to them because of its participatory nature.

"We looked at all the traditional BCG type models, and we felt that there are two approaches to developing strategy. One approach is you get outside people to *tell* you what to do. At the root of the *other* approach, as Mike Robert always says, is the concept that the people who know your business best are the people *on your own team* and that they should create their own strategy. So, working with DPI was really an attempt on our part to get some help, and get the whole team to sit down together and come up with a game plan that made sense with the size of the company and the environment we're living in.

"We felt that the DPI Process was excellent in the sense that it was really a process that forced us to answer our own questions. And since *we* know the industry and *we* know the issues and *we* know the challenges, we felt this was the best way for us to define our strategy, one that is our peoples' own strategy. And when it's your peoples' own strategy, execution becomes that much easier because they developed it, it's their belief in it and ownership in it. And it's been the same strategy since '96. We have not changed it in the slightest, even when we went through a very bad hiccup in 1998 because of some technology failures. Some technology provided to us by one of our partners failed in the field. We went through a disaster, but we never took our eyes off the ball. And you know, the whole management team still feels that what kept us going was this *incredible focus* on that single sentence that DPI helped us develop through this process called the Business Concept—to be a leader in wide-format imaging systems and only that. And we continue to live by that every day."

The process provided the forum that the company's management needed to get agreement on that concise Business Concept. In the course of the sessions it quickly became clear that the selection of a Driving Force and its related Areas of Excellence would be the platform from which their future would spring. As in most companies, there were, at the beginning of the sessions, a variety of opinions among the key players as to the right Driving Force.

Says Kumar: "Some people said we should be Customer Class–driven, a solutions provider. We should offer everything a customer needs—the printer, the software, the ink, the paper. Some said, let's just stay focused on one area we know well and be Technology-driven. Others said, let's just build printers—a Product-driven strategy.

"We had always talked about those three things without knowing that there is a way to look at them in the form of what DPI calls the Driving Force. Before we went through the process and began to sort out these things," says Kumar, "we had people who would say, 'Look we sell to this customer, why don't we develop some complementary products and just sell them at the same time?' And the issue with those kinds of things is that when you're small, with only $25 million in business, your marketing people can focus on only so many things. They really only have the resources to focus on your own products. And we began to realize, through the reasoning of the process, that when they go out and say to the customer, let me show you some paper, or let me show you some laminators or let me show you some PCs, we really don't get any value from these additional activities. They don't make us stronger in our own competitive arena that we are playing in. In fact they make us weaker because they dilute our limited resources. Also, we had to look at our technology, which is very good. Were we successful because we were a technology company? Were we successful because we understood the market the best?"

In order to fully envision the implications of each choice, the process enabled the work teams to create a picture of what had been successful in the past and where each Driving Force might take the company in the future.

"So we played out all three scenarios: Product, Technology, and User Class. But it was very clear the moment we began having these discussions about what a Customer Class Driving Force is, that as a $25 million company trying to fulfill the needs of a commercial printer in every aspect of his needs, there was no way we could be anywhere near that. And the same thing with Technology. We had a technology that had been successful only in a very small niche area, and we couldn't see how we could expand it into other applications. But the thing that really convinced us more than anything else was that over the previous six years in the history of the company—the company was six years old at that time—every time we launched a new wide format printer product we saw tremendous growth. Then we'd get to a certain stage and for about six months we'd have a dry spell. And then we'd have the next product and we'd go through another dramatic surge. Everybody kind of looked at each other and said, boy, this is so simple isn't it? We are so well-known as a wide format printer *product* company. If we just focus on this one Area of Excellence called Product Development, and everybody, the whole team, makes sure that the product doesn't slip, that we do everything possible to nurture, support, and help the R&D Team ... and make them part of the strategy process, and they appreciate how critical they are for our business if we expect to compete with the Xeroxes and the Lockheeds, then we can be the *best* at Product Development. We can beat the other guys at *their* game since they move slowly, because they're bigger companies that have other products and different Driving Forces than ours. And they don't have our focus. So it became clear to everyone that we should be Product-driven. We make a specific category of wide format printers and that's it.

"The Business Concept we developed, in simple terms, was that we were going to be a leading provider of wide format imaging systems. And we have never deviated from that. We defined our Driving Force to be Product. We defined our Areas of Excellence as Product Development and Sales and Service. And that focus through all the difficult years allowed the team to say, if we can just get the next printer out and the sales force can sell it, we'll be successful. And believe it or not, it was that simple concept that has set us on the path to supremacy in our sandbox."

Like the judo expert, they proceeded to use their R&D expertise and agility to move faster than their larger competitors. They began to work their Critical Issues, nurturing those Areas of Excellence, developing a stream of innovative new products and supporting them with the most knowledgeable sales and marketing force in their niche.

Gradually, this absolute dedication to refining and enhancing these Areas of Excellence took its toll on their competitors. Incredibly, a couple of years later, both Xerox's and Lockheed's wide format printer divisions were *out of business* in spite of healthy growth in demand for this particular class of printer.

"I believe these competitors, because they were so much bigger first of all, couldn't focus on any one thing. As in any other business today, without as clear a concept as we created through the DPI process, we could all approach the business by saying we have to be ISO 9000 in manufacturing. We have to have the best balance sheet with the best inventory terms and the best receivables. We have to have the best of every function that you could think of. But the point is you really cannot be *excellent* at everything. You have to decide which one or two things will make the most difference. And we could spend management's focus on trying to get the best factory and be ISO 9000 certified and have the best GMP in the world. I'm not suggesting we ignore those issues, but the question is the amount of focus, the level of energy you put into a certain function. We could say we will be very good in manufacturing but we are really going to stretch ourselves in the areas of Product Development and Sales and Service. I think that was the key difference between our thinking process and what I believe our competitors were doing, because the competitors would come out with a product, and the next product would be basically the same product three years later. So we never saw a competitive product that we couldn't beat. And by understanding that we could beat them *at their game* by being superior in Product Development, I think that was the key. In the end they just gave up.

"One of them, Calcomp in this case, I think really wasn't clear on whether they were a product company or a technology company. They got into developing some futuristic technology, a printer technology. They used $100 million on R&D but never commercialized it. Instead of staying focused on developing printers, they got into developing something like an integrated circuit, a chip that goes *into* the printer. And it was just that lack of focus, in my mind anyway, that finally just destroyed their business.

"Xerox actually pulled out of the business completely," Kumar continues. "A $200 million division is gone. And Calcomp Lockheed no longer exists; it went bankrupt. So it is really very fulfilling to see that these huge corporations with all their incredible resources and market presence, but not a very focused, well-defined, articulated strategy—could fumble and just disappear. And I think it really had to do with our absolute focus on Product and Product Development."

The wide format group continues to operate autonomously and is on a rapid growth curve. But the world doesn't stand still and let a successful company like this own a profitable, growing segment unchallenged.

"We don't try to look 10 years out. If you are a natural-resource company, like Exxon for example, I think you have to look at 10 years. Being a technology-based company, we tend to look at three years and five years. And I would say that in three years we have been absolutely right on, and that in five years I would say that we have been at least 60 to 80 percent right on. So the process really forces you to go through and identify all those risks and opportunities. Without the process, you have a *feel* for this, you have a *feel* for that, but you don't put it down on a piece of paper so that the whole management team then says this is really an issue.

"We went through the process again in 1998. And it was interesting that even though we had gone through the process about two years prior, we found a few changes in the landscape, especially as the result of Xerox and Calcomp Lockheed pulling out of the business. Some other players that we had anticipated had become a lot stronger during those two years. And based on some of the moves they were making, we, as a team, said we need to do something about this. And we were able to define some actions with minimal, *minimal* changes to our strategy to prevent them from infringing on our sandbox."

Through the last few years Raster Graphics took several proactive and preemptive actions to defend the borders of their turf, as other companies appeared to be moving in their direction. And each time, they have been able to fend off the attackers without being yanked off their strategic course.

As Kumar says: "Within our segment we have been further able to define the strategy by, as DPI says, deciding who we're going to invite into the sandbox, and deciding whose turf we're going to play on. The other big player in the industry who had given us a tough time in the past was HP. And it had become very clear to us that we simply were not going to play in HP's sandbox by HP's rules. And HP, without going into too much detail, has a technology which is optimized for building a $200 printer on the desk. And because HP is optimized to build a $200 printer, it does a pretty good job at building a big printer. But there are limitations on what type of big printers they can make. Fundamentally, they can make big printers that are at a certain price point and a certain performance point with a certain amount of robustness to them. To say it in simple terms, they can make Chevrolet cars but they cannot make Mack trucks. Our strategy at that point was—let's get away from HP, and let's keep defining our own sandbox—which is a sandbox in which we're making Mack trucks and not Chevys. And we will absolutely make sure that we will never get anywhere near what looks like a Chevy.

"We can look back to about seven or eight years ago when, for about a year, we had a very difficult time because we had a product that was close to what HP was doing and HP came up with a new product which almost put us out of business. So we need to constantly watch what's going on and what sandbox we're playing in and who else is in there. And we have proven that with our technology—by applying it to the Product Driving Force, and being the best at getting those products off to market—we can beat them.

"I think the best result is that DPI gave us a process we still use. Every couple of years we go back and we review the whole process and we go through the main steps. And we see what has changed. And the other point I'd like to make, which is really interesting, is that when we go back and look at what we said four years ago in terms of what the world would look like five years later—who our number one competitor is, who our number two competitor is, who our potential competitors might be—we were 90 percent accurate! It is absolutely amazing that if you take the time to go through the process and you identify the issues and you identify the competitors, if you take the time to do that, the future is not a surprise when it gets here. It's as Mike says, you can pretty well predict the way the competition will behave if you take the time to understand it. What it has given us is a way to, every couple of years, go back and make sure everybody in the management team understands why we are pursuing this strategy, what it gives us. Then at the end of that we come out with a chart. It's a one-page chart which has the Driving Force, the things we should excel at, and about six key critical success factors for that year. Out of that, we drive our operational plan every year. And everybody stays focused."

Raster Graphics' strategy was so successful that it attracted the attention of Océ, based in Holland. Océ bought Raster Graphics in 2002 at a hefty premium.

INDEX

About the Author

Michel (Mike) Robert is one of the most in-demand consultants in the field of strategy. Over the last 20 years, he has personally worked with the CEOs and management teams of over 300 corporations in 15 countries. These include major companies such as Caterpillar, 3M, Newmont Mining, Bekaert, Pulte, Castrol, GATX, Dow Corning, Hartford Insurance, Outokumpu, LandAmerica, Giant Foods, Phelps Dodge, Overwaitea Food Group, Cancer Treatment Centers of America, and emerging ones such as Kirkhill Aircraft, FLEXcon, and Allied Motion Technologies.

Back in 1980, he coined the phrase "Strategic Thinking," which is now the rage among business strategy gurus and magazine writers. His concepts of strategic thinking, strategic heartbeat, and areas of excellence, and his views on strategic alliances and how to manage a competitor's strategy are the most contrarian and provocative developed in the field today. Moreover, they are being adopted by many of his clients on their way to success. His concepts are unique and pragmatic because they were developed while being present in the "war rooms" of major corporations when their executives were debating strategy.

He has had many articles published in a wide array of business magazines and journals, and he is the author of several books, all of which are best-sellers.

Mike is also the founding partner of Decision Processes International, a worldwide consulting firm with 30 partners in 15 countries.

Considered the best-kept secret in the field of strategy and critical thinking, Mike is a very dynamic and provocative speaker who will cause any member of corporate management to think twice about the strategy and directions of his or her organization by debunking fashionable concepts of strategy and exposing them as being conceptually flawed. His company has been engaged by clients in several instances in competition with, and instead of, better-known consultants such as Michael Porter, McKinsey, A. D. Little, Boston Consulting Group, Booz Allen, and Bain & Co.